Anti-dumping in the WTO, the EU and China

EUROPEAN MONOGRAPHS

Editor-in-chief Professor David O'Keeffe

In this series *European Monographs* this book *Anti-dumping in the WTO, the EU and China* is the sixty-ninth title. *The titles published in this series are listed at the end of this volume.*

Kluwer Law International

Anti-dumping in the WTO, the EU and China

The Rise of Legalization in the Trade Regime and its Consequences

Yan Luo

Wolters Kluwer
Law & Business

AUSTIN BOSTON CHICAGO NEW YORK THE NETHERLANDS

Published by:
Kluwer Law International
PO Box 316
2400 AH Alphen aan den Rijn
The Netherlands
Website: www.kluwerlaw.com

Sold and distributed in North, Central and South America by:
Aspen Publishers, Inc.
7201 McKinney Circle
Frederick, MD 21704
United States of America
Email: customer.service@aspenpublishers.com

Sold and distributed in all other countries by:
Turpin Distribution Services Ltd.
Stratton Business Park
Pegasus Drive, Biggleswade
Bedfordshire SG18 8TQ
United Kingdom
Email: kluwerlaw@turpin-distribution.com

Printed on acid-free paper.

ISBN 978-90-411-3207-9

Printed in Great Britain.

Table of Contents

List of Abbreviations

AD	Anti-dumping
ADA	WTO Agreement on Implementation of Article VI of the GATT 1994 (WTO Anti-dumping Agreement)
ADC	Anti-dumping Advisory Committee
ASCM	WTO Agreement on Subsidies and Countervailing Measures (WTO SCM Agreement)
CCP	Common Commercial Policy
CIF	Cost, Insurance and Freight
CNY	Constructed Normal Value
CVD	Contervailing Duty
DSB	Dispute Settlement Body
DSM	Dispute Settlement Mechanism
DSU	WTO Understanding on Rules and Procedures Governing the Settlement of Disputes (Dispute Settlement Understanding)
EU	European Union
GATT	General Agreement on Tariffs and Trade
MET	Market Economy Treatment
NME	Non-market Economy
OJ	Official Journal of European Union
SG&A	Selling, general and administrative cost
UNDP	United Nations Development Program
US	United States
TPRB	Trade Policy Review Body
TPRM	Trade Policy Review Mechanism
VCLT	Vienna Convention on the Law of Treaties
WTO	World Trade Organization

Foreword

This book traces the evolution of the multilateral trading system from a left-over chapter of the ill-fated ITO (and the Havana Charter) – through a long period of essentially political and diplomacy-driven management, based upon trading power – to the present day where a fully constituted International Organisation (the WTO) has been created along with a distinctive legal order and jurisprudence.

The title of the book highlights 'Anti-dumping' as a policy area to trace this evolution, starting from a specific rule which is clear in its principle but 'soft' as regards its application (GATT Article VI), and which through various transformations and additions has become the full international Agreement agreed during the Uruguay Round.[1] Its application by the EU and by China is explored to illustrate that such an agreement is dynamic in nature and seems to have led to some 'additional rules' to meet particular circumstances when applied at the national level.

In effect the book is divided into two distinct parts.[2] After an Introduction, two chapters set out the conceptual framework, defining the process of 'legalisation' and how it was applied in the trading system; then tracing its steady progress through the different functions of the system and relating it to theory drawn from International Relations studies. Then there are three chapters which examine the same evolution in detail as it affected anti-dumping rules at the international level; followed by how this was adapted within the EU legal framework and how it has impacted on China.

../..

1. Formally the 'Agreement on Implementation of Article VI of the GATT 1994'.
2. The introduction already sets the scene, drawing on academic studies of international organisations and International Relations literature – how they grow their institutional elements and acquire a constitutional character as well as greater legal authority.

I am a practitioner in the trade policy world, with many years within the system at the EU and in the GATT and later the WTO. The evolution described in this book is most easily experienced by such an observer (as opposed to an economist or a lawyer) in the way that disputes are dealt with and ultimately resolved within the system. This is ably traced in the book, starting from relatively informal consultations among the parties involved, developing to the concept of a panel (peer review?), and then to a pragmatic set of rules and procedures, codified in the Tokyo Round; and finally transformed into a self-standing legal system designed to address complaints, to investigate facts and the applicable rules, to reach a judgment on the matter and to ensure compliance of a member with its obligations as necessary.

From my personal vantage point the description of the system as it was in the 1960s and 1970s rings many bells. I was particularly struck by two phrases which for me epitomise much of the character of the GATT in those times: first, '...typical GATT obligations are rigorous on substance but...associated with broad exceptions'.[3] This captures so much of the essence of the compromise that the General Agreement was, the fact that Article I and Article XXIV and waiver provisions have to be read together as part of a whole flexible discipline, the fact that Article XI is accompanied by Articles XVIII and XIX and XX, all designed to permit certain exceptions and in certain circumstances.

Second: 'This contrast between rigid treaty language and flexible institutional arrangements generated uncertainty in the evolution of the GATT system.....'[4] Here again the first part of the phrase captures an essential feature of the system, which can be seen in operation in dispute settlements in the old GATT days and in the treatment of free trade areas.

While these descriptions are familiar, I have to admit that some of the structural analysis presented in the book appeared to be strange territory, although not a total surprise. The three components which form the core of the institution – obligation, precision and delegation – are recognisable and clearly relevant to the nature of the system – more political and diplomatic, or more judicial and legalised. Equally the three functions of the system – decision making, surveillance and dispute settlement – are an apt summary of what the GATT/WTO strives to do. It is perhaps the two features that emerge from the empirical evidence that are more troublesome: that the expansion of legalisation has been uneven and imbalanced across the whole system, and that it has led to complicated consequences when the new evolved principles are applied at national rather than international level.

I am not an anti-dumping specialist to comment in detail on the chapters tracing the evolution of this instrument. What I know is that the concept of being able to defend oneself against what was perceived in 1947 to be unfair competition was in the treaty from the start. All the evolution has been to add to and improve the application of GATT Article VI. But in these latter days economists will argue that there is no unfairness here, it is simply a matter of

3. See chapter 3, page 36, at the beginning of section 2.1.2.
4. See chapter 3, page 33, at the end of section 2.1.1.

making optimum use of comparative advantage – often in terms of much lower labour costs. It is perhaps when the economic concept faces a social concept – that of labour rights and minimum wages – that difficulties arise. Nonetheless what is clear to anyone is that the rules in this area have evolved steadily from the 1960s until today, and second that they continue to throw up complicated legal and economic issues. The obvious example of this is the current attention given to the practice of 'zeroing'.[5]

ADD

With the indulgence of the author and the reader, I would offer a further example of a policy area where similar evolution might be traced in the trading rules. This is to demonstrate my support for the basic thesis in the book and to set in comparison with the anti-dumping example that she has chosen.

My choice would be the rules applicable to Customs Unions and Free Trade Areas (GATT Article XXIV). These rules were written in order to be an exception to the basic rule of non-discrimination and MFN treatment in Article I, and met their first serious test with the formation of the European Community in 1957. As a customs union it performed well in the area of tariffs and other barriers to trade in industrial products; but the Common Agricultural Policy (set up later in the mid 1960s) presented a more complex picture, and the relationship between the EC and former colonies in Africa, designed to be a 'flexible' free trade area taking account of its development objectives was – in retrospect – moot.

During the 1960s and 1970s agreements flourished around the EC – EFTA for a start, then the EC agreements with Greece and Turkey, with the Maghreb and the Mashrak regions. Article XXIV had mutated into 'substantially all the trade outside the agricultural sector', and this perhaps mirrored the fact that the United States had obtained a waiver in the 1950s which permitted it to derogate from rules in that sector. In the 1990s the criteria gradually changed and second generation agreements were more complete – with NAFTA, the first free trade area in the Americas, leading the way – and extended into the area of services. Since 2003, with the Americans pursuing bilateral agreements_________ And EU WTO+_________ and the Asian region joining in with enthusiasm, the criteria have changed again and we now face a proliferation of preferential trade areas (PTAs). In this case, unfortunately, the evolution has been zig-zag fashion and 'legalisation' of the basic rules is currently in a backward-looking phase.

Roderick Abbott
Former Deputy Director General of the WTO

5. See chapter 4, page 87 . . . . This illustrates perfectly the flexibility of the system: a practice can be found to be illegal and a violation of rules while at the same time a chairman's draft in the negotiating context can include a change in those rules in contradiction to that jurisprudence. This is to accommodate one powerful member, and shows that the era of 'power politics' has not totally disappeared; but no one believes that in negotiation all parties carry equal clout.

Acknowledgements

I dedicate this book to my grandmother, Ms YANG Sixuan, who passed away on 21 March 2006, at the age of 88. In my heart, she was my beloved grandma – she gave me my name when I was born. But she was far more than just a beloved grandma – she was a great woman and inspired me to have an independent spirit to pursue whatever I want to achieve.

More than seventy years ago, she became the first woman from Guizhou Province to be offered a government scholarship to go to the college. When Japan invaded China in 1936, she was a junior in China Central University (now Nanjing University). During the World War II, she suffered as ordinary Chinese – losing family, living a difficult life. Yet, nothing changed her passion for knowledge. She graduated with honours and became a well-respected university lecturer and chemist. She has been the first role model for me, telling me how strong a woman can be and how much she can achieve with her education and intelligence.

I likewise own this thesis to my two 'doctoral mothers' – Professor Marise Cremona and Professor Janet Dine. As real experts in the field, they opened a door for me. Without their unconditional support, both personally and academically, it is impossible for me to complete this book.

Needless to say, I also own huge thank you to my parents, my other supervisors, my colleagues in Hammonds Brussels office and all of my friends around the world. For the past six years, it was their love gave me the courage to go through this sometimes painful yet always challenging and exciting process. I would like to thank all of them for their generosity.

Chapter 1
Introduction

When making his address before the European Society of International Law on 19 May 2006, Director General (DG) Pascal Lamy did not hesitate to express his view that 'the World Trade Organization (WTO) is a unique system within the international legal order'.[1] After more than sixty years of evolution, in DG Lamy's view, the WTO comprises a 'true legal order', which is 'integrated and distinctive' and produces 'a body of legal rules making up a system and governing a community'.[2]

Echoing his comments, it is widely observed that the proliferation of the General Agreement on Trade and Tariff (GATT)/WTO is associated with a phenomenal rise of legalization in the system, even though a consensus on the exact meaning of legalization is lacking. Numerous literature documents that despite the lack of an explicitly mentioned judicial organ to oversee the implementation and enforcement of Agreements and agreed Understandings, technocrats and experts of the GATT gradually developed a 'legal' system to operate the Agreements. This gradually 'legalized' system distinguished 'normal' legitimate trade policies from 'cheating' on the trade liberalization bargain and used the collective power of the system to punish the 'bad boys', regardless of their power.[3] After the establishment of the WTO, the WTO system has been frequently referred to as a 'true legal order' with 'two essential attributes', that is, the valid WTO rules and the enforcement mechanisms.[4]

---

1. P. Lamy, 'The Place and Role of the WTO (WTO Law) in the International Legal Order', address before the European Society of International Law (Sorbonne, Paris, 19 May 2006), <www.wto.org/english/news_e/sppl_e/sppl26_e.htm>, 14 Jun. 2006.
2. *Ibid.*
3. R. Howse, 'From Politics to Technocracy – And Back Again: The Fate of the Multilateral Trading Regime', *The American Journal of International Law* 96 (2002): 94, 98.
4. For a summary of academic developments, I Damme, 'Seventh Annual WTO Conference: An Overview', *Journal of International Economic Law* 11 (2008): 155, and M Raisch, 'Book Survey 2007', *Journal of International Economic Law* 11 (2008): 217.

Yet, this intensive institutionalization in the GATT/WTO system has rarely been examined in the broader context of legalization of international organizations.[5] Defined as a distinctive form of institutionalization, the process of legalization has arguably been observed in many international organizations, including the GATT/WTO.[6] The rise of legalization in the GATT/WTO has been widely discussed, but rarely systematically analyzed under a theoretical framework that is also used to analyze the similar experiences of other international organizations.

This monograph analyzes the phenomenal rise of legalization experienced by the GATT/WTO system in the past sixty years under a theoretical framework that is used by international relations scholars to analyze the phenomena of legalization in international organizations. It, on the one hand, focuses on exploring the unique path that the GATT/WTO followed to become a 'legalized' international organization with a treaty network and a dispute settlement mechanism (DSM). On the other hand, it recognizes the need to examine the GATT/WTO under a framework, which establishes a coherent set of attributes commonly identified among the process of legalization in international organizations that are experiencing a similar move to law. By examining the dynamic process of legalization in the GATT/WTO in a broader context, this monograph intends to offer a fresh perspective to analyze the developments of gradually 'legalized' trade institutions at the international level and the complicated, that is, both the intended and unintended, consequences of this process on domestic systems.

Since the early years of the GATT, trade 'legalists' engaged in extensive debates with trade 'pragmatists' over what role the law should play in the governance of the trade regime. The establishment of the WTO is generally considered to be a stunning victory for trade 'legalists' in this long-running debate.[7] To a large extent, the positive effect of legalization on the governance of the trade regime is commonly acknowledged.

Nevertheless, a closer look at the intensive institutionalization of the GATT/WTO, and its consequences, reveals another aspect of legalization that has rarely been discussed: contrary to the high expectation of trade 'legalists', empirical studies suggest that although the gradually 'legalized' system has been frequently used to advance the free trade agenda, the policy goal of trade liberalization cannot always be achieved by the functioning of the legal system.

There are many reasons that can potentially explain this phenomenon. This monograph focuses on two of them: the uneven and unbalanced expansion of legalization at the international level and the complicated consequences of legalization at the domestic level.

---

5. K. Abbott et al., 'The Concept of Legalization', *International Organization* 54 (2000): 401.
6. J. Goldstein et al., 'Introduction: Legalization and World Politics', *International Organization* 54 (2000): 385.
7. P. Sutherland et al., 'The Future of the WTO – Addressing Institutional Challenges in the New Millennium', Report by the Consultative Board to the former Director-General Supachai Panitchpakdi, 2005, <www.wto.org/english/thewto_e/10anniv_e/future_wto_e.htm>, 31 Jul. 2006, 10.

As will be demonstrated by this monograph, legalization has to be understood as a multi-faceted phenomenon and it has both intended and unintended impact on the trade regime.

The rise of legalization is not an isolated phenomenon happening only in a particular part of the GATT/WTO, but a systematic move to law in all parts of the GATT/WTO. In other words, if the development of legalization in a particular part of the GATT/WTO has fallen behind, there is a risk that the system cannot balance itself out and that this uneven and unbalanced expansion of legalization may undermine the function of the whole system.

The consequences of legalization are similarly complicated since legalization at the international level affects domestic systems in ways that are both intended and unintended.

All of these interrelated phenomena/factors have to be taken into account when depicting a full picture of the process of legalization in the trade regime.

The theme of this monograph is hence three-fold: First, it sketches the proliferation of legalization in the trade regime over the past sixty years. Second, it analyzes the uneven expansion of legalization with a view to providing a full picture of the legalization process in the GATT/WTO. Third, it investigates the complicated consequences of legalization by focusing on two aspects of the effects of legalization. It first examines the impact of legalization on formal legal institutions at the domestic level, by identifying the correlation between a higher degree of legalization in a particular subject area of GATT/WTO law and the corresponding changes in domestic policy-making, policy administration, and judicial review in that particular subject area. It then examines the impact of legalization on the utilization of the DSM to settle disputes in particular subject areas.

This monograph distinguishes itself from two types of existing studies: those focusing on analyzing fragments of the process of legalization, such as 'judicialization' of the DSM and those attempting to confer a normative stand on legalization. It may not be possible to understand this monograph in isolation from the broader debate of 'constitutionalization' in international economic law literature.[8]

8. In general legal theory, 'constitutionalism' refers to the principle that a legal system is based on and legitimated by a system of legal or law-like principles that stand outside the law-making system itself. It includes both the practical arrangements of political institutions within the system, and the idea of a system of supreme law that defines fundamental rights. See, H. Kritzer (eds), *Legal Systems of the World – A Political, Social, and Culture Encyclopaedia* (Santa Barbara: ABC-CLIO, 2002), 353. For the purpose of this introduction, the term 'consitutionalization' is used to refer to a collection of ongoing debates that discuss not only institutional arrangements of the GATT/WTO, but also the foundations of the trade regime. Two books significantly contribute to the 'constitutionalization' debate of the WTO: J. Jackson, *Sovereignty, the WTO and Changing Fundamentals of International Law* (Cambridge: Cambridge University Press, 2006) and D. Cass, *The Constitutionalization of the World Trade Organization: Legitimacy, Democracy, and Community in the International Trading System* (Oxford: Oxford University Press, 2005). The ongoing debates that may fall under the umbrella of 'constitutionalization' include, but are not limited to, good governance of the WTO, global regulatory legitimacy, the WTO and human rights, democracy and rules of law etc.

It may also relate to other works that examine the phenomenon of 'judicialization' in the GATT/WTO dispute settlement process. This monograph nevertheless differentiates itself from both types of works since it narrows its scope to explore the institutionalization of the GATT/WTO from a specific perspective, namely the rise of legalization in formal GATT/WTO institutions at the international level and the impacts of legalization on domestic systems. This monograph does not engage in discussions about whether legalization is normatively positive for the trade regime. It also does not take a normative stance to judge different views presented in the 'constitutionalization' debate. Instead, it observes the particular phenomenon of legalization and adopts a theoretical framework from international relations to analyze the phenomenon, its discourse, its dynamics and its effects on the trade regime.

An important feature of this monograph is therefore to illustrate the rise of legalization in the trade regime by taking the example of the development of anti-dumping (AD) regime. Given the pragmatic nature of the process of legalization, meaningful discussions on legalization have to include empirical examinations of how a 'legalized' trade rule functions in practice. Anti-dumping law is not only one of the most well-developed legal institutions in the GATT/WTO but also one of the most controversial 'trade defence' instruments. Hence, the development of the AD regime can best demonstrate the significant contribution that the process of legalization has made to trade liberalization, as well as the limitations of the 'legalized' GATT/WTO system. On the one hand, AD, an originally unilateral trade policy, has been successfully brought into the multilateral system and legalized over the past six decades. On the other hand, even after decades of legalization, the results of AD investigations at the domestic level do not always fulfil the expectation of those who consider that the more and more 'legalized' GATT/WTO system could guarantee that the international AD rules can be faithfully implemented in all AD investigations carried out by competent national authorities. Moreover, the results of those investigations that GATT/WTO rules are not faithfully applied are not always challengeable in the DSM. The impact of legalization at the international level is thus far more complicated than trade 'legalists' anticipated.

The rest of this monograph proceeds as follows: Serving as the theoretical framework, Chapter II introduces the definition of legalization developed by international relations scholars and adopts it to analyze the GATT/WTO system, focusing on three key points: elements of legalization, the uneven expansion of legalization and the consequences of legalization in the trade regime.

Chapter III describes the development of legalization in the GATT/WTO from a historical perspective. It demonstrates the evolution of the whole system from a 'diplomatic' treaty network to a 'legalized' framework, on the one hand, and the uneven and unbalanced expansion of legalization on the other.

Chapter IV, V and VI advances the research by examining the legalization process of GATT/WTO anti-dumping rules and the impacts of legalization at the international level on the European Union's (EU) AD regime and China's AD-related WTO activities. Chapter IV sketches the development of legalization in the multilateral AD framework by identifying increased obligation, greater precision and stronger delegation in the regime. Chapter V explores the impact of multilateral legalization on the EU anti-dumping regime. Chapter VI demonstrates the impact of the increasing legalization on the utilization of the DSM by WTO members, in particular in terms of the efforts China made to effectively utilize the DSM.

Chapter VII summarizes the key findings of this monograph.

Chapter 2
Conceptualizing Legalization in the WTO System

1 INTRODUCTION

The process of 'legalization' in many issue areas of international politics has particularly interested international lawyers and international relations scholars in recent years.[1] Many claimed that a growing number of international institutions are gradually legalized and the phenomenon of 'legalization' has been commonly observed.[2] Others, however, posed serious doubts, not only in relation to the empirical evidence of 'legalization', but also in relation to what it really means, whether it should be happening and whether it supports the trend predicted by international lawyers.[3] Instead of debating only the dichotomy between law or no law, or whether hard law is better than soft law, in international organizations, in-depth theoretical inquiries of legalization involve interlinked questions such as how to conceptualize 'legalization', what is the discourse of legalization in a particular subject area or region, and what are the effects of legalization.

Among the legal and international relations literature that analyzes the phenomenon of legalization, a special issue of *International Organization* in

1. K. Abbott et al., 'The Concept of Legalization', *International Organization* 54 (2000): 401. One special volume of International Organization was devoted to 'legalization and world politics' in 2000. Also, K. Abbott, 'The Many Faces of International Legalization', *American Society of International Law Proceedings* 92 (1998): 57; and the presentations in the Ninety-Sixth Annual Meeting of the American Society of International Law, 'The Legalization of International Relations', *American Society of International Law Proceeding* 96 (2002).
2. J. Goldstein et al., 'Introduction: Legalization and World Politics', *International Organization* 54 (2000): 385.
3. Presentation of Professor Friedrich Kratochwil and other speakers in the Ninety-Sixth Annual Meeting of the American Society of International Law, 'The Legalization of International Relations' (n. 1), 296.

2000 ('the special issue') presented a particularly interesting theoretical framework and several case studies of legalization.[4] The special issue developed an analytical framework to explain the common ground of the move towards law in various international/regional institutions and explore the consequences of legalization in various subject areas and regions. In order to analyze the highly diversified phenomenon of legalization in different subject areas and regions, authors of the special issue set forth and elaborated upon a definition of legalization, that forms 'a classificatory structure for comparative analysis' in case studies in the special issue.[5] Deploying this conceptual framework of legalization, contributors examined the status of legalization in different regional/international organizations and institutional arrangements in specific issue areas. Three articles examined the pattern of legalization and its effects on participants and policies in three regions: Europe,[6] North America[7] and Asia-Pacific,[8] whereas the remaining contributors focused on legalization in international monetary affairs,[9] trade,[10] and human rights.[11]

Despite the great efforts of the contributors to cover divergent phenomena of legalization in various regional/international institutions and issue areas, it is clearly stated that the purpose of the special issue is not to provide a coherent new theory to explain legalization in all institutions and issue areas. To the contrary, the principle interest of the special issue is to 'open some conceptual and analytical doors to a more sustained and explicitly theoretical analysis of the connections between law and politics in contemporary world politics'.[12] This monograph intends to follow the theoretical framework of the special issue and analyze empirically the process of legalization in the GATT/WTO in general and the AD regime in particular.

On three grounds, the theoretical framework established in the special issue provides a useful analytical tool to study the intensive institutionalization that took place in the trade regime. First, the definition of legalization provides a coherent set of identifiable attributes that can sufficiently characterize the evolution of the GATT/WTO, not only in terms of dispute resolution, but also in terms of the treaty

4. The whole summer 2000 issue of International Organization is devoted to 'Legalization', *International Organization* 54, no. 3 (2000).
5. Goldstein et al., 'Introduction', 385.
6. K. Alter, 'The European Union's Legal System and Domestic Policy: Spillover or Backlash?', *International Organization* 54 (2000): 489.
7. F. Abbott, 'NAFTA and the Legalization of World Politics: A Case Study', *International Organization* 54 (2000): 519.
8. M. Kahler, 'Legalization as Strategy: The Asia-Pacific Case', *International Organization* 54 (2000): 549.
9. B. Simmons, 'The Legalization of International Monetary Affairs', *International Organization* 54 (2000): 573.
10. J. Goldstein & L. Martin, 'Legalization, Trade Liberalization, and Domestic Politics: A Cautionary Note', *International Organization* 54 (2000): 603.
11. E. Lutz & K. Sikkink, 'International Human Rights Law and Practice in Latin America', *International Organization* 54 (2000): 633.
12. Goldstein et al., 'Introduction', 399.

network and the administration of the GATT/WTO as an international organization. The existing literature largely focuses on one or another function of the GATT/WTO, that is, as an institution of negotiation or surveillance or adjudication. The theoretical framework of the special issue, however, allows examinations of institutional arrangements of different parts of the GATT/WTO to be carried out under a uniform theoretical framework. Based on this theoretical framework, this monograph depicts the status of legalization of the GATT/WTO at a given point of time by describing three elements of legalization and demonstrates the trend by allowing meaningful comparisons of three elements of legalization at different points in time.

Secondly, the special issue laid the theoretical foundation to discuss the consequences of intensive institutional changes in the GATT/WTO. In the special issue, contributors addressed not only what 'legalization' is and what the variations of legalization are, but also the consequences of legalization, namely, how legalization, 'in creating a new institutional form, mobilizes different political actors and shapes their behaviour in particular ways'.[13] Although the particular angles presented in this monograph differ from the special issue, it benefits from the research works of the special issue. Three articles analyze the interaction between the increase of legalization in the trade regime and the trade-related interests of domestic actors,[14] the correlation between the degree of legalization in dispute resolution mechanisms and state behaviour in dispute resolution processes,[15] and the interaction between the process of legalization in international/regional organizations and domestic policies, are particularly helpful.[16]

Finally, the theoretical framework of the special issue provides the 'legalized' evolution of the GATT/WTO in a broader context. By using a uniform framework to analyze strongly variable institutions across issue areas and regions, the dynamic process of legalization of a particular institution such as the GATT/WTO could be better explained. Indeed, even though the GATT/WTO has developed in a rather unique manner, it shares common ground with the development of many other international organizations. When national governments negotiate trade agreements and make institutional choices for the GATT/WTO, they face similar constraints imposed by their political environments, as they do in many other issue areas. It is therefore helpful to analyze the GATT/WTO system within a framework that can explain the commonality among the processes of legalization in different international organizations as long as it also reflects the divergence between systems.

The limited scope and the distinctive approach of this monograph, however, have to be noted from the outset. Firstly, it does not intend to either compare or link

13. M. Kahler, 'Conclusion: The Causes and Consequences of Legalization', *International Organization* 54 (2000): 661.
14. Goldstein & Martin, 'Legalization, Trade Liberalization and Domestic Politics', 603.
15. R. Keohane, A. Moravcsik & A. Slaughter, 'Legalized Dispute Resolution: Interstate and Transnational', *International Organization* 54 (2000): 457.
16. Alter, 'The European Union's Legal System and Domestic Policy', 489.

the process of legalization in the GATT/WTO system with similar processes in other international/regional institutions discussed in the special issue. Although adopting the theoretical framework, this monograph treats the GATT/WTO system as a distinctive legal order and avoids engaging in discussions in connection to discrepancies among the processes of legalization in different international institutions.

Secondly, among the working hypotheses of the special issue, this monograph identifies the two hypotheses that are most relevant in analyzing the GATT/WTO system, namely the uneven expansion of legalization and the complicated consequences of legalization and structures its discussions on the basis of these two hypotheses. In particular, this study has no intention of seeking to explain why a particular institutional form appears in a given international organization at a given time, although it was a key research question intensively discussed in the special issue. Instead, this monograph describes the status of legalization in the trade regime as it was at a given point of time, and by assuming that over a particular period of time, the 'legalized' institutional settings of the trade regime are 'frozen' until the next institutional change occurs, and tries to demonstrate the trend by linking these points together. The discussions in the following chapters have therefore been put in specific time frames. Any coincidences of time between changes of status of legalization at the international level, and changes of institutions and legislation at the domestic level, are identified to the extent possible.

The rest of this chapter proceeds as follows. Section 2 outlines the definition of legalization and indicators for each element of legalization. It summarizes two features of legalization, namely the uneven expansion of legalization and the complicated consequences of legalization in the special issue. It also discusses criticisms of the theoretical framework with the intention of determining whether these criticisms can undermine the analysis of the GATT/WTO system to be carried out in this monograph. Section 3 adopts the theoretical framework to examine the current status of legalization in the WTO system, the uneven expansion of legalization in the WTO system and the consequences of legalization at domestic level. Section 4 concludes the chapter.

2 DEFINING LEGALIZATION IN INTERNATIONAL RELATIONS

2.1 Elements of Legalization

In the first article of the special issue, 'The Concept of Legalization', legalization is posited as a particular form of institutionalization characterized by three components, obligation, precision, and delegation.[17] Obligation refers to a rule/commitment or a set of rules/commitments by which states or other actors

17. Abbott et al., 'The Concept of Legalization', 401.

are legally bound, that is, their behaviour becomes 'subject to scrutiny under the general rules, procedures, and discourse of international law'.[18] Precision means that 'rules or commitments unambiguously define the conduct they require, authorize or proscribe', that is, the certainty of legal rules and their elaborations.[19] Delegation is defined as whether third parties have been granted authority 'to implement, interpret, and apply the rules; to resolve disputes and (possibly) to make future rules'.[20] Put differently, delegation refers to the acceptance of third-party authorities for rule making, rule interpretation and dispute resolution.

In order to better explain the variations of legalization in different international institutions or in different portions of an international institution/instrument, this article also identifies several indictors of each element of legalization. It first formulates obligations as commitments ranging from 'coercion, comity to morality'.[21] Commitments made by states can vary widely from 'unconditional obligations with language and other indicia of intent to be legally bound' to 'instruments that explicitly negate any intent to create legal obligations'.[22] In between, there are obligations with implicit conditions, contingent obligations and escape clauses. This article argues that the contrasting legal forms of obligations have 'distinctive implications on their discourse' in the international legal system.[23] The breach of unconditional obligations may lead other states to 'assert legal claims, engage in legal discourse, invoke legal procedures and resort to legal remedies'.[24] The breach of obligations in non-binding instruments, however, can only result in normative claims, normative discourse and political resorts.

The indicator of precision is whether the scope of 'reasonable interpretations' can be narrowed.[25] The more precise a set of rules/commitments, the clearer and more unambiguous the expectation of states or other actors under particular circumstances will be. Precision implies not only that each rule/commitment in the package is clear and unambiguous, but also that the set of rules/commitments, as a whole, creates a framework within which 'coherent and non-contradictory interpretations can be carried out in each case'.[26] High precision is therefore represented by elaborated 'rules' with detailed conditions of application, required or proscribed behaviour and a narrow scope of interpretation. Rules that have lower precision range from rules with a substantial but limited scope of interpretation, rules contained broader areas of discretion, 'standards' that are 'meaningful only with reference to specific situations' to rules that are 'impossible to determine what conduct complies'.[27] It is possible that in a highly developed legal system,

18. *Ibid.*
19. *Ibid.*
20. Abbott et al., 'The Many Faces of Legalization', 60.
21. Abbott et al., 'The Concept of Legalization', 408.
22. *Ibid.*
23. *Ibid.*
24. *Ibid.*
25. *Ibid.*, 412.
26. *Ibid.*
27. *Ibid.*

'precise' rules can be formulated as relatively general 'standards' without detailed conditions and open to interpretation. However, the more 'standard-like' a rule, the more *ex post* interpretations by courts or tribunals are needed. To enable 'standard-like' rules to be operated as a precise rule, the institutional context has to be sufficiently thick to allow courts or tribunals to determine the acceptableness of a particular behaviour in a specific situation.[28]

Indicators of delegation describe the extent to which states and other actors delegate authority to designated third parties, such as courts, arbitrators or administrative organizations, to implement agreements.[29] The most characteristic forms of high delegation are mechanisms for the third-party dispute resolution, where 'third parties are authorized to interpret rules and apply them to a particular set of facts'.[30] Indicators of delegation in terms of dispute resolution constitute a spectrum from the most highly legalized dispute settlement mechanisms, where parties agree to binding third-party decisions, to the least legalized dispute settlement mechanisms that involve political bargaining between parties. Yet the delegation of legal authority is not confined to dispute settlement. It also includes the delegation to administrative institutions in elaborating imprecise legal norms, implementing agreed rules and facilitating enforcements. Indicators of delegation in this respect range from institutions that are authorized to elaborate agreed norms and implement them, to institutional arrangements purely for the purpose of negotiation and consultation.

In addition to the definition and indicators of each element of legalization, this article presents three central assumptions that form the theoretical foundation of the rest of the articles in the special issue. Firstly, each of the three elements is a reflective criterion of different types of legalization and can vary independently. For different international institutions, the form of legalization can be a continuum that ranges from the absence of law, where none of the three elements exists, through various forms of 'quasi' or 'soft' legal institutions, to 'hard' law, in which all three indicators are maximized.[31] Laws and regulations in a highly developed national legal system is taken as the prototype of hard legalization.[32] While generally speaking international institutions are less legalized than institutions in domestic rule-of-law systems, most international institutions, such as the WTO, can be located in the middle of this continuum. To precisely locate a particular international institution in the continuum requires a more detailed specification of obligation, precision and delegation. Secondly, three elements of legalization characterize the special form of institutionalization in terms of rules and procedures, but not in terms of effects. One example discussed in this article is that although the definition of legalization includes the delegation of legal authority to international courts or the equivalent agencies, the factor 'delegation' as described

28. *Ibid.*, 413.
29. *Ibid.*
30. *Ibid.*
31. *Ibid.*, 402.
32. *Ibid.*

in the definition does not include 'the degree to which rules are actually implemented or to which states comply with them'.[33]

Thirdly, the substantive content of the rules and the degree that rules have been legalized are distinct matters. This article argues that given that the process of legalization does not necessarily bear a normative stance, a higher degree of legalization of a particular legal instrument may not justify its content from a normative standpoint. For example, although a non-binding declaration could have 'exactly the same substantive content as a binding treaty', they are very different instruments in terms of legalization.[34]

Based on this definition of legalization, other articles in the special issue continue to discuss the two most prominent features of the legalization process in contemporary world politics, that is, the uneven expansion of legalization and the complicated consequences of legalization. The following two subsections summarize the discussion of these two features in the special issue and present the link between the discussion in the special issue and the analytical work in this monograph.

2.2 The Uneven Expansion of Legalization

The expansion of legalization into new domains, and the unevenness of that expansion, is one of the key themes of the special issue.[35] The discussion in the special issue focused on two aspects: first, the existence of variations of legalization across subject areas and regions and second, the reasons that among available institutional forms, particular forms of legalized institutions are preferred in some circumstances and not in the others. These two aspects are interrelated in the sense that the existence of variations of legalization is in fact a result of the choices governments made under different circumstances. Under the broadly defined functionalist approach promoted by the special issue, legalized institutional arrangements will be selected only if they provide 'superior net benefits' to governments, in comparison with non-legalized or less legalized institutional alternatives.[36]

These two aspects are, however, different because the first aspect examines what is the status of legalization, namely the combination of three factors of legalization, at a particular point of time in a particular institution, whilst the second aspect explores the rationale behind the choice of the institutional solutions at that time.

This monograph agrees that legalization is hardly a uniformed process, although it has no attempt to engage in the discussion of the second aspect. Moreover, it approaches the first aspect from a different angle. Instead of focusing on the

33. *Ibid.*
34. *Ibid.*
35. Goldstein et al., 'Introduction', 388.
36. Kahler, 'Conclusion', 663.

horizontal comparison of the degree of legalization among different international/regional institutions, this monograph focuses on the uneven expansion of legalization in different parts of the GATT/WTO at different points of time.

2.3 Consequences of Legalization

The special issue examines three frequently discussed consequences of legalization in international relations. As summarized in the 'Conclusion: The Course and Consequence of Legalization', these three consequences are effects of legalization on state behaviour, effects of legalization on the evolution of international norms, and the spread and retrenchment of legalization.[37] Although all three consequences are important in understanding legalization processes across issue areas and regions, this monograph narrows the focus to the effects of legalization on the institution changes of domestic regimes and dispute settlement activities of states and, therefore, particularly benefits from three articles in the special issue that conduct in-depth investigations on the impact of legalization on international dispute resolution,[38] mobilization of domestic actors[39] and the change of national policies by a legalized region institution.[40]

In the article 'Legalized Dispute Resolution: Interstate and Transnational', Keohane, Moravcsik and Slaughter analyze the dynamics of international dispute resolution process by constructing two ideal types of legalized dispute resolution, namely interstate and transnational dispute resolution. They examine these two types of dispute resolution along the dimensions of independence, access, and embeddedness, and use the International Court of Justice (ICJ), the European Court of Justice (ECJ) and the GATT/WTO Dispute Settlement Mechanism (DSM) as examples.[41] According to them, although the contrasting experiences of the ICJ and the ECJ suggest that 'the distinction between the two ideal types appears to be associated with variation in the size of dockets and levels of compliance with decisions', the experience of the GATT/WTO DSM does not reflect the two ideal types of legalized dispute resolution faithfully.[42] Since the caseload of the GATT/WTO DSM and the effectiveness of their decisions 'increased without higher formal levels of access or embeddedness', the GATT/WTO DSM exemplifies that 'legal form does not necessarily determine political process'.[43]

The article 'Legalization, Trade Liberalization, and Domestic Politics: A Cautionary Note' examines another aspect of the consequence of legalization, that is, 'how increases in the legalization of the international trade regime interact

37. *Ibid.*
38. Keohane et al., 'Legalized Dispute Resolution', 457–488.
39. Goldstein & Martin, 'Trade Liberalization and Domestic Politics', 603–632.
40. Alter, 'European Union's Legal System and Domestic Policy', 489.
41. Keohane et. al., 'Legalized Dispute Resolution', 487.
42. *Ibid.*
43. *Ibid.*

with the trade-related interests of domestic actors'.[44] This article argues that although it is generally true that increased legalization has a positive impact on trade liberalization by 'reducing incentives for an individual nation to behave opportunistically and renege on trade agreements', certain unintended effects of legalization on the activities of domestic actors could interfere with the pursuit of trade liberalization at the international level.[45] Three issues that are affected by legalization at the international level are particularly examined: whether 'greater precision at the time of negotiating treaties changes the incentives of antitrade groups to mobilize',[46] whether greater legalization provides incentives to exporters to mobilize in order to maintain agreements already in force, and finally to what extent a system of highly deterministic penalties impact the activities of domestic actors. The authors argue that 'the prediction about the effects of changes in the information environment varies, depending upon whether we are considering the expansion of trade liberalization or compliance with enacted treaties'.[47] The conclusion is that there is a need to 'carefully examine the trend toward increasing legalization, weighting both its benefits and its costs'.[48] Although the authors cannot demonstrate that legalization in the trade regime has already gone so far to be a threat to trade liberalization, they do, however, wish to make a cautionary note on the potential impact of legalization on the mobilization of domestic protectionist groups.

Finally, Alter's work 'The European Union's Legal System and Domestic Policy: Spillover or Backlash?' examines how domestic actors utilize the legal system of the European Union (EU) to influence national policies of Member States (MS).[49] She argues that by offering the preliminary reference, a powerful legal tool, to private litigants, EU laws can be used to force changes in national policies once certain thresholds are met. The availability of this European law tool shapes behaviour and expectation of domestic groups.[50] Consequently, 'the pursuit of self-interest leads litigants and national courts to challenge national policies and advance European integration'.[51] In this context, Alter investigates 'the factors shaping each step of litigation process' and reveals many factors that 'keep private litigants and national courts from facilitating the expansion of European law'.[52] She observed that 'the very factors that have led to the success of the EU legal process in expanding and penetrating the national order have provoked national courts and European governments to create limits on the legal process and to repatriate powers back to the national level'.[53] As a result, 'the dynamic expansion

44. Goldstein & Martin, 'Trade Liberalization and Domestic Politics', 603.
45. *Ibid.*
46. *Ibid.*, 630.
47. *Ibid.*, 631.
48. *Ibid.*
49. Alter, 'European Union's Legal System and Domestic Policy', 489–518.
50. *Ibid.*, 490.
51. *Ibid.*
52. *Ibid.*
53. *Ibid.*

created by the ECJ may well have provoked a backlash that contributed to disintegration'.[54]

These three articles are closely related to the analytical work of this monograph in different ways. The first article provides useful insights into how the institutional differences between international courts and tribunals significantly impact the dispute settlement process and, more generally, the process of legalization. This monograph, however, examines the effects of legalization on state behaviour in trade disputes from a different perspective. In the WTO system, the DSM is institutionalized by the Dispute Settlement Understanding (DSU), an agreement that is part of the single undertaking of the Uruguay Round.[55] Once a WTO member chooses to use the WTO DSM to settle a trade dispute, the variable of institution is fixed. Hence, other variables, such as obligation and precision of the covered agreement(s) to be applied in the dispute settlement process, determine state behaviour in a trade dispute. This monograph, in particular, explores how a WTO member balances the incentives provided by the 'legalized' DSM and the limitations imposed by the uneven expansion of legalization that cause a large number of trade barriers to become legally unchallengeable.

The discussion of the consequences of legalization in this monograph also benefits from the analysis of the second and the third article. The second article argues 'when exporters know that they are likely targets of retaliation, they are more motivated to organize in support of the trade regime than those subject to an imprecise threat of retaliation'.[56] This monograph agrees with this comment and exemplifies it by examining the mobilization of Chinese export-dependent industries in the AD cases targeting China. The moves of Chinese industries in those AD cases, including to push their government to more effectively utilize the WTO DSM, epitomize Goldstein and Martin's argument that the rise of legalization that results in 'greater precision, better transparency, stronger delegation of monitoring and dispute-resolution to centralized organizational agency and more certain penalties for rule violation', provides better information to domestic pro-trade industries and gives them stronger incentives to mobilize.[57] This monograph, however, does not particularly address two other issues discussed in the second article, namely the impact of increasing legalization on trade negotiations and whether the WTO laws should allow more flexibility.

In the context of the GATT/WTO system, this monograph also observes, as Alter does in the context of the EU, that the expansion of legalization heavily influenced the evolution of domestic systems. In the meantime, legalization at the international level provoked national governments and other stakeholders to create various domestic law vehicles to limit the impact of legalization on domestic systems and to retain power at their hands. The discussion here, however, does not

54. *Ibid.*
55. *Understanding on Rules and Procedures Governing the Settlement of Disputes*, (15 Apr. 1994) LT/UR/A-2/DS/U/1 <http://docsonline.wto.org>.
56. Goldstein & Martin, 'Trade Liberalization and Domestic Politics', 631.
57. *Ibid.*

limit the effects of a particular legal tool, but more broadly cover the impact of legalization on national trade legislation, the administration of national trade policies and the adjudication of trade politics at national courts.

2.4 A Richer View of Legalization?

One year after the publication of the special issue, International Organization published an article, 'Alternatives to 'Legalization': Richer Views of Law and Politics' by Finnemore and Toope. In this article, the authors criticize the theoretical framework promoted by the special issue. They consider, in particular, that the theoretical framework of legalization is neither adequate nor useful for two reasons. Firstly, 'the framers of the legalization concept are not explicit... about their limited view of law or about alternative views of law that might yield different understandings of their cases', and secondly, 'they have not adequately theorized their definition of legalization so as to provide clear help to the empirical researchers seeking to apply the concept'.[58] This subsection analyzes these criticisms and examines whether they undermine the theoretical foundation of the analytical work of this monograph.

On the first account, Finnemore and Toope argue that the view of law, as presented in the special issue, 'though important, is limited'.[59] They criticise that in the special issue, 'law is constructed primarily through cases and courts, or through formal treaty negotiation' and 'the processes of law are viewed overwhelmingly as processes of dispute resolution, mostly within formal institutionalized contexts'.[60] To further elaborate their arguments, Finnemore and Toope discuss 'three interrelated features of international law neglected in the volume', namely 'custom', 'defining' characteristics of law' and 'law as process'.[61] Finally, they criticise the way in which the special issue treated law, which 'equates legalization with three features of the form of an artefact' and claim that 'law, and by implication legalization, may be more about process than about form or product'.[62] They conclude that 'the concept of legalization provides little help to these researchers, not only because it contains a narrow notion of law but also because it is inadequately theorized'.[63]

Although this monograph agrees with Finnemore and Toope's general comment that the specific legalization phenomenon analyzed in the special issue is among law's many influences in politics and this formalized legalization 'interacts with other work law does in the world', it disagrees that by focusing on formal institutions, the theoretical framework in the special issue cannot be helpful to empirical researches.

58. M. Finnemore & S. Toope, 'Alternatives to "Legalization": Richer Views of Law and Politics', *International Organization* 55 (2001): 743, 756.
59. *Ibid.*, 744.
60. *Ibid.*, 745.
61. *Ibid.*, 746–751.
62. *Ibid.*
63. *Ibid.*, 751.

As a work with limited scope, namely that analyzing of the special form of institutionalization experienced by the GATT/WTO, focusing exclusively on the development of formal institutions in the trade regime, this monograph considers this special form of institutionalization is one of the most important features of the trade regime and worth an in-depth research. This is the reason that this monograph situates itself in the broader debate of 'constitutionalization' of the WTO, but at the same time distinguishes itself from other works in the debate.

With respect to the three interrelated features of international law analyzed by Finnemore and Toope, these are either irrelevant or have been properly addressed in this monograph. Firstly, given the special institutional setting of the GATT/WTO, customary international law does not formally play a role in the institutionalization of the trade regime. Secondly, precision and delegation are two of the most important characters of the GATT/WTO rule and it is justified to include them as indicative variables. The definition and indicators of obligation in the special issue properly capture the 'defining' characteristics of the GATT/WTO system, as to be demonstrated in the next section.

Finally, this monograph addresses the relationship among three factors of legalization as part of the discussion concerning the uneven expansion of legalization in the GATT/WTO. It disagrees with Finnemore and Toope that the theoretical framework of legalization in the special issue, by focusing on forms, is less useful in explaining changes.[64] To the contrary, in the context of the GATT/WTO, the theoretical framework is helpful since it provides an effective tool to describe process, by identifying the value of three factors of legalization at a particular point of time and enabling meaningful comparisons between the status of legalization over a period of time. An abstract description of the process is not sufficient if there is no theoretical framework to allocate values to variables and provide a reference system to cross-examine variables over a period of time. The theoretical framework therefore facilitates the empirical research of this monograph by providing such a reference system.

In summary, the criticisms raised by Finnemore and Toope indeed provide another perspective to explore the broader interaction between law and politics. Nevertheless, their particular arguments and criticisms are either irrelevant or have been properly addressed. These criticisms therefore do not have an impact on the theoretical foundation of this monograph.

3 APPLYING LEGALIZATION IN THE WTO SYSTEM

3.1 Elements of Legalization in the WTO

This section adopts the definition of legalization from the special issue and analyzes the status of three factors of legalization in the WTO system: obligation, precision and delegation.

64. *Ibid.*, 750.

Obligation

Obligation refers to norms set in all WTO agreements, agreed Understandings and other binding documents, such as the Ministerial Decisions and Declarations. The WTO treaty system is generally described as highly legalized and closely resembles a modern municipal legal system since it has 'a comprehensive collection of legally binding primary rules'.[65]

However, if considering the indicators of obligation in the previous section, wide variations between WTO obligations can be identified. Despite the fact that all WTO obligations are legally binding, the collection of WTO obligations constitutes a full continuum of obligations, ranging from specific and unconditional obligations that require or prohibit certain behaviour from national authorities to general principles that may tolerate divergent practices of WTO members. Thus, it is impossible, not only to characterize the features of obligations in different WTO agreements, but also to characterize the obligations with different natures in the same covered agreement. An analysis of obligations in the WTO therefore has to be not only sector specific, but also provision specific. For this reason, Chapter IV below identifies the nature of obligation in each provision of the Anti-dumping Agreement (ADA), instead of giving a general statement on the features of obligation in the ADA.

Precision

Precision in the context of the WTO system measures not only the clarity of the wording of covered agreements, but also to what extent the scope of reasonable interpretations is narrowed by requiring (or prohibiting) specific actions by WTO members. Many claim that the lack of precision of many WTO rules leaves a wide range of latitude enjoyed by national trade authorities in acquiescing to or, on the contrary, rejecting a specific WTO rule in both formal and informal means.[66]

One explanation provided by existing works is that the 'legislative branch' of the WTO is its members who make decisions on all matters and act by consensus. The nature of such a broad decision-making power of the plenary organ decides that 'rules made through it can only be the compromise between parties and lack of extensive certainty'.[67]

This monograph agrees with this observation as it is largely confirmed by the evolution of AD rules in the GATT/WTO. As elaborated in Chapter IV below, one of the key reasons that many provisions in the ADA lack precision, and are unable to cover sharp differences among national practices, is that the text of the ADA is a

65. *Ibid.*, 466. The author noted that by any means, the WTO is one of the most comprehensive collections of primary obligations existing in the field of public international law.
66. J. Gathii, 'Insulating Domestic Policy Through International Legal Minimalism: A Re-characterization of the Foreign Affairs Trade Doctrine', *University of Pennsylvania Journal of International Economic Law* 25 (2004): 1, 105.
67. P. Kuijper, 'Some Institutional Issues Presently Before the WTO', in *The Political Economy of International Trade Law – Essays in Honour of Robert E. Hudec*, ed. D. Kennedy & J. Southwick (Cambridge: Cambridge University Press, 2002), 82.

result of compromises. Trading partners with different agendas put together the text of ADA at the last minute as part of the Uruguay Round bargaining.[68] It is therefore not surprising that the text of the ADA, although fairly detailed, does not achieve high precision because a large number of provisions do not narrow the scope of reasonable interpretation.

Delegation

Delegation reflects the willingness of WTO members to delegate authority to designated WTO institutions to implement agreements and solve trade disputes. It first refers to the acceptance of the quasi-judicial DSM. It also refers to the acceptance of activities of other regulatory agencies and administrative bodies of the WTO, such as the WTO Secretariats and the Trade Policy Review Body (TPRB).[69]

WTO members treat delegation to the DSM with extreme caution and clearly distinguish rule interpretation from dispute resolution. In terms of dispute resolution, the DSM enjoys a high level of delegation as expressed in Article 1 of the DSU.[70] When it comes to the interpretation of WTO laws, the delegation conferred to the DSM is restricted to a specific dispute.[71]

Formal delegation of the interpretation of WTO laws to other WTO bodies is also restricted. For example, the TPRB is forbidden to amend or interpret WTO obligations during the process of trade policy review. On the other hand, it is observed that, although without explicit delegation, WTO bodies and trade diplomats are making their own contributions to the WTO rule interpretation through their day-to-day activities. The WTO Secretariat produced a large number of soft law-like publications to guide the interpretation and application of WTO rules, such as the WTO Analytical Index, which is influential to national trade policies, and later WTO dispute settlement cases.[72]

In addition to the limited delegation conferred to the DSM and administrative bodies of the WTO in terms of rule interpretation, it is also observed that there is no

68. For more details on GATT negotiations, see T. Stewart (ed.), *The GATT Uruguay Round: A Negotiation History 1986–1992, Volume II: Commentary* (Deventer: Kluwer Law and Taxation Publishing, 1992).
69. For the details of the role and activities of the WTO Secretariat, see H. Nordström, 'The World Trade Organization Secretariat in a Changing World', *Journal of World Trade* 39 (2005): 819.
70. *Understanding on Rules and Procedures Governing the Settlement of Disputes*, Art. 1, <http://docsonline.wto.org>.
71. For example, D. Blackmore, 'Eradicating the Long Standing Existence of a No-precedent Rule in International Trade Law – Looking Towards Stare Decisis in WTO Dispute Settlement', *North Carolina Journal of International and Comparative Law* 29 (2004): 487. More recently and from a different perspective, J Trachtman, 'Regulatory Jurisdiction and the WTO', *Journal of International Economic Law* 10 (2007): 631.
72. The WTO Analytical Index is regarded as the authoritative guide to the interpretation and application of findings and decisions of WTO panels, the WTO Appellate Body and other WTO bodies. See, WTO Website, <www.wto.org/english/res_e/booksp_e/analytic_index_e/analytic_index_e.htm>, accessed 15 Oct. 2004.

parallel delegation of rule interpretation to political organs of the WTO.[73] Examples can be found in the AD regime where significant controversies are caused by the tension between the DSM and the negotiation forum. Take 'zeroing' as an example. Despite having a series of Panel and Appellate Body (AB) reports that ruled that 'zeroing' is WTO-inconsistent in a number of specific investigations (both original investigations and reviews), Article 2.4.3.3 of the draft 'Consolidated Texts on Anti-dumping and Subsidies and Countervailing Measures circulated by the Chair of the Negotiating Group on Rules' (the Chair's text) allows the utilization of zeroing under certain circumstances.[74] The reactions of WTO members are mixed. On the one hand, the US, by criticizing the panels and the AB's interpretative approach in 'zeroing' cases, publicly expressed its view that zeroing is 'allowable under current global trade rules, penned in the 1994 Uruguay Round accord,' and any agreement emerging from the six-year-old Doha Round of talks must recognize its validity'.[75] On the other hand, officials from countries that are frequent targets of AD measures warned that the Chair's text that 'reinstate zeroing and reverse the earlier WTO rulings' poses a 'major challenge to the organization's dispute settlement system and could undermine its credibility'.[76] This example illustrates that delegation in terms of rule interpretation in the WTO is low, although by contrast, delegation in terms of dispute resolution is high.

3.2 Uneven Expansion of Legalization in the WTO

Although the GATT/WTO system originates from a single undertaking and commonly regarded as a uniform regulatory infrastructure, as the system expanded, a close look shows that three elements of legalization differentiate among different parts of the WTO. This section, by describing the current status of each factor of legalization in each part of the WTO, intends to demonstrate that although the rise of legalization is generally observed in all parts of the WTO, the expansion of legalization in different parts is uneven and unbalanced. The uneven expansion of legalization may explain the widely observed long-lasting tension between the diplomatic negotiation and the operation of legalized multilateral institutions,

73. C. Ehlermann & L. Ehring, 'Decision-making in the World Trade Organization – Is the Consensus Practice of the World Trade Organization Adequate for Making, Revising and Implementing Rules on International Trade?', *Journal of International Economic Law* (2005): 51.
74. *Draft Consolidated Chair Texts of the AD and SCM Agreements*, TN/RL/W/213, 30 Nov. 2007, available at: <www.wto.org/english/tratop_e/rulesneg_e/rules_chair_text_nov07_e.htm>, accessed 10 May 2008.
75. 'U.S. import penalties new problem for WTO pact', *Reuters*, 12 Dec. 2007, available at: <http://in.reuters.com/article/businessNews/idINIndia-30957720071212?pageNumber=1&virtualBrandChannel=0>, accessed 5 May 2008.
76. BNA International Trade Reporter 'WTO Members Discuss Services Conference; Doha Rules Chair Promises New Revised Text', 20 Mar. 2008, <http://pubs.bna.com/NWSSTND/IP/BNA/itr.nsf/SearchAllView/259E1C65883BD6B18525741100071B0E8?Open&highlight=ZEROING>, accessed 5 May 2008.

which, as correctly observed, has not disappeared even with a complicated legal system in place.[77]

Generally speaking, three parts are covered under the roof of the WTO, which function relatively independently. The WTO is at first a decision-making mechanism, where trade negotiators 'bargain in the procedural context to achieve certain kind of compromises'.[78] It is also a locus of surveillance activities, aiming to oversee the implementation and operation of the WTO agreements already on the book.[79] Finally, the WTO provides a quasi-judicial DSM to its members, which results in 'centrally authorized sanctions against recalcitrant violators of the multilateral trade agreements'.[80]

Based on the definition of legalization, a simple (if not overly simple) chart is constructed to demonstrate the status of legalization in different parts of the WTO. One of the two values, High or Low, is assigned to each factor, as shown in Chart 2.1. The value of 'High' or 'Low' refers to two extremes of the legalization spectrum. High value is typically represented in most advanced domestic legal systems, while low value can normally be found in a system with loose rules and institutions, such as the traditional international law system.

Chart 2.1 Different Factors of Legalization in Different Parts of the WTO

	Decision-making	*Surveillance*	*Adjudication*
Obligation	Low	Low	High
Precision	Low	High	High
Delegation	Low	Low	High

Decision-making

The first and foremost part of the WTO is its decision-making body that has a negotiation forum as its centrepiece. The negotiation forum is formally the resource of all WTO laws. As an institution of barter, it is analogized in the literature as a private market, a place where states 'trade' their regulator power

77. Many prominent observers in particular expressed their concerns about the tension between the (quasi-judicial) dispute settlement process and the diplomatic and treaty-making activities of the WTO. Legalization in this study, however, refers to a process that includes, but not limited on, the evolution of the dispute settlement process, as to be discussed in later chapters. For comments on the tension between the dispute settlement process and treaty-making, C. Ehlermann, 'Tensions Between the Dispute Settlement Process and the Diplomatic and Treaty-making Activities of the WTO', *World Trade Review* 1 (2002): 301.
78. R. Steinberg, 'In the Shadow of Law or Power? Consensus-Based Bargaining and Outcomes in the GATT/WTO', *International Organization* 56 (2002): 339.
79. Nordström, 'The WTO Secretariat', 819. The term 'surveillance' is used to in a different context of dispute settlement in some literatures. Here it refers to the professional activities conducted mainly by the WTO Secretariat.
80. W. Schwartz & A. Sykes, 'The Economic Structure of Renegotiation and Dispute Resolution in the World Trade Organization', *Journal of Legal Study* 31 (2002): S179, S179.

towards international trade.[81] In this multilateral 'market', low legalization is observed. With no tight obligation, no precise rule and no third-party delegation, it represents the lowest level of legalization of the spectrum.

The above observation, however, does not necessarily mean that there is no formal procedure in the WTO negotiations. Three provisions in the Marrakesh Agreement establishing the World Trade Organization (the WTO Agreement) formulate rules for this negotiation forum, namely Article IX on Decision-making, Article X on amendments and Article XII on accession.[82] The provisions stipulate that the principle of WTO decision-making is by consensus; if consensus cannot be reached, the issue can be decided by voting. Each member of the WTO has an equal vote in decision-making.

Voting is, however, never used in practice.[83] As is rightly observed, powerful parties simultaneously dominated bargaining outcomes and supported the consensus decision-making rule in the WTO.[84] In practice, the WTO largely inherited the paradoxical practice of the decision-making of GATT – the coexistence of 'Green Room' practice and the consensus principle.[85] Only when a deal has emerged between major developed countries and a representative set of developing countries, would it then be submitted to the whole WTO membership for discussion. Therefore, the assessment of obligation and precision of the decision-making mechanism cannot rely on the formal wording of the WTO Agreement. Rather, the practice of the WTO to date supports the 'low' mark of obligation and precision in this part.

The rule of delegation in the WTO decision-making mechanism is laid out in Article IX paragraph 2 of the WTO Agreement. This provision explicitly imposes the exclusive authority to adopt interpretations to intergovernmental institutions, namely the Ministerial Conference and the General Council.[86] In *Japan –Alcoholic Beverages II*, the AB emphasized that the exclusive authority of decision-making is conferred to the Ministerial Conference and the General Council. On this basis, the AB reversed the Panel's finding that panel reports adopted by the Dispute Settlement Body (DSB) constituted 'subsequent practice' within the meaning of Article 31 of the Vienna Convention on the Law of Treaties (VCLT).[87] Hence, it is confirmed by jurisprudence that no delegation to any third party exists in the WTO.

81. J. Dunoff & J. Trachtman, 'Economic Analysis of International Law', *The Yale Journal of International Law* 24 (1999): 1, 14.
82. WTO *Marrakesh Agreement Establishing the World Trade Organization*, LT/UR/A/2, 15 Apr. 1994.
83. B. Hoekman & M. Kostechi, *The Political Economy of the World Trading System – The WTO and Beyond*, 2nd edn (Oxford: Oxford University Press, 2001), 58. Also, Nordström, 'The World Trade Organization Secretariat in a Changing World', 821.
84. Steinberg, 'In the Shadow of Law or Power', 365.
85. Hoekman & Kostechi, 'The Political Economy of Trading System', 61. The 'Green Room' is originally a conference room adjacent to the Director-General's office. Later, Green Room meetings referred to a consultative process of a small group of diplomats from major countries and a representative set of developing countries, which tried to hammer out the outlines of acceptable proposals or negotiating agendas.
86. WTO Agreement, Art. IX, 15 Apr. 1994.
87. WTO *Japan – Taxes on Alcoholic Beverages*, WT/DS8/R, WT/DS10/R, WT/DS11/R, as modified by the AB report, WT/DS8/AB/R, WT/DS10/AB/R, WT/DS11/AB/R, para. 132.

Surveillance

The second part of the WTO system is its surveillance mechanisms, represented by Trade Policy Review Mechanism (TPRM). Labelled as 'low' in obligation and delegation but 'high' in precision, this part of the WTO abstains from creating new obligations or delegating legal authority. Trade technocrats, however, intend to employ these 'soft' mechanisms to improve the transparency of national trade policy and induce compliance with the GATT/WTO rules.

Annex 3 of the WTO Agreement sets the rule for the TPRM. It stipulates the mission of TPRM, the reporting obligation of governments and the procedure of reviews.[88] There is little doubt that precision of the TPRM can be marked as 'high' given the sufficient elaboration of the rules, yet its delegation and obligation can only be marked as 'low'. The TPRM, in the words of the TPRB, 'had been conceived as a policy exercise and it was therefore not intended to serve as a basis for the enforcement of specific WTO obligations or for dispute settlement procedures, or to impose new policy commitments of Members'.[89] The obligation of members under the TPRM is to report their trade policies, but the change of WTO inconsistent trade policies is only voluntary. It is not the mandate of the TPRB to either make or to enforce WTO rules. The TPRM is therefore in the intermediate zone along the spectrum: low obligation, low delegation but high precision.

Adjudication

The third part of the WTO system is its adjudicatory system. The WTO DSM is significantly different from other international tribunals and dispute settlement regimes since it is 'to a large extent similar with the court in domestic law with compulsory jurisdiction and clear procedural rules'.[90] It reaches the 'high' end of the spectrum in all three factors.

Obligation in the DSM was covered by the DSU, a comprehensive instrument dealing with all aspects of the process.[91] Not only is the DSU binding on WTO members, but the panel or the AB reports adopted by the DSB are also binding on parties to the dispute. The value of obligation of DSM is therefore 'high', even if the panel and/or the AB reports have no precedent status.

With twenty-seven articles, the DSU undoubtedly provides precise rules, for the DSM. Precision is also unquestionably 'high', particularly in terms of procedural rules.

The issue of delegation in the DSM is more complex as mentioned in the previous subsection. On the one hand, all WTO members accepted delegation to the DSB in terms of settling a particular dispute. On the other hand, the extent to

---

88. WTO *Annex 3 Trade Policy Review Mechanism*, LT/UR/A-3/TPR/1, 15 Apr. 1994. ('TPRM')
89. WTO *Report of TPRB to the Third Ministerial Conference*, WT/MIN (99) 2, 8 Oct. 1999, para. 3.
90. A. Schneider, 'Getting Along: The Evolution of Dispute Resolution Regimes in International Trade Organizations', *Michigan Journal of International Law* 20 (1999): 697, 719.
91. *Understanding on Rules and Procedures Governing the Settlement of Disputes*, <http://docsonline.wto.org>.

which the DSB is delegated to produce legally binding interpretations is a contested issue. WTO members showed a certain degree of reluctance to empower the DSB to produce binding interpretations in the process of dispute settlement. One piece of evidence is that there is no *stare decisis* in the WTO dispute settlement. Nevertheless, it is still fair to conclude that the DSM represents the highest level of legalization in the whole WTO system.

In conclusion, the above demonstrates that the level of legalization in different parts of the WTO is not uniform and the expansion of legalization has been uneven. This is an important feature of the legalization process in the WTO. It may explain why the emergence of a complicated system cannot wipe away the tension between different parts of the GATT/WTO.[92]

3.3 Consequences of Legalization in the WTO

3.3.1 'Legalizing' National Trade Policy in the GATT/WTO System

The first consequence of legalization examined in this study is the impact of legalization on national trade policies. When the GATT/WTO evolved away from its origin as a decentralized and relatively powerless institution and became a legal entity, the formalized interaction between the rise of legalization at the international level and domestic systems became apparent.[93] Considering the impact of legalization on national trade policy outcomes, a two-way process can be identified: first, there are more and more examples where national policy choices are constrained by the gradually 'legalized' multilateral system, and second, domestic actors are increasingly mobilized to utilize domestic laws or create domestic legal vehicles to limit the impact of legalization in order to protect their interests. The rise of legalization therefore has both intended and unintended effects due to the uncertain economic and political environment at the domestic level. Again, given the difficulty to generalize the intended and unintended effects of the rise of legalization in all subject areas, this subsection limits itself to provide certain general remarks, which have to be read together with the empirical study of the EU anti-dumping regime discussed below in Chapter V. It should also be noted that although the discussion in this subsection draws certain ideas from the special issue, it does not follow the line of argument in any particular article of the special issue.

As is well argued in the special issue, one noticeable consequence of legalization is increased obligation. The intended effect of this change is to 'expand the

92. P. Sutherland et al., 'The Future of the WTO – Addressing Institutional Challenges in the New Millennium', report by the Consultative Board to the former Director-General Supachai Panitchpakdi, 2005, <www.wto.org/english/thewto_e/10anniv_e/future_wto_e.htm>, accessed 31 Jul. 2006, 10.
93. Goldstein & Martin, 'Trade Liberalization and Domestic Politics', 603.

breadth of the trade regime' and to 'enhance compliance so as to increase the benefit of membership by using a discourse focusing on rules, their applicability and exceptions, rather than on interests'.[94] An illustrative example in the trade regime is that major trading partners, through different domestic legal vehicles, transposed the WTO agreements to their domestic systems.

Yet, increased obligation, frequently joined by greater precision and stronger delegation, has unintended effects on domestic trade policies. While a higher level of obligation puts pressure on domestic systems to be consistent with WTO rules and deters opportunism of a WTO member, there are strong incentives for individual WTO members to create certain vehicles that can be generally referred to as 'WTO-plus' to balance interests of different domestic groups and retain the power to deal with economic uncertainty at the hands of national authorities.

Similarly, increased precision has both intended and unintended effects. Greater predictability and transparency are typically associated with the improvement of precision. Nevertheless, a higher degree of predictability and transparency affects the behaviour of both pro-trade and domestic protectionist groups.[95] Hence, increasing precision can have two different, and competing, effects. On the one hand, increased precision, which in turn results in an increase in transparency, can undermine trade liberalization movements by activating import-competing groups in importing WTO members. On the other hand, precise rules also result in more trade liberalization by activating export-dependent industries in exporting countries to support their governments to utilize the legal tools offered by the system in order to ensure compliance with WTO rules.

The unintended effects of stronger delegation, namely 'a system of highly deterministic penalties', have the same logic with tight obligation: 'too little enforcement may encourage opportunism; but too much may backfire, undermining the ability of domestic actors to find support for an open policy', as argued by Goldstein and Martin.[96]

The above arguments are well illustrated in the evolution of the EU anti-dumping regime. It is a striking trend of the evolution of the EU Trade Defence Instruments (TDIs) that the TDI rules are essentially repeating basic principles of the GATT/WTO agreements and using similar vocabulary with the corresponding covered agreements in the majority of provisions. Nevertheless, a number of WTO-plus provisions, such as injury margin, the Union interest, anti-circumvention and Non-market Economy Treatment, institutionalizes the discretion of the EU institutions and allows them the flexibility to deal with economy uncertainties in the EU. An analysis of the WTO-plus provisions of the EU anti-dumping instruments suggests that there are two common features of these legal tools: first, they are developed in the areas where no precise WTO rule exists (or no rule at all); and second, these rules can result in different outcomes in specific investigations, even if other parts of the investigations are conducted in a manner

94. *Ibid.*, 605 and 619.
95. *Ibid.*, 606.
96. *Ibid.*, 631.

that is fully WTO-consistent. One example is that in cases where both injury and dumping have been found, the European Commission can still propose to terminate the investigation and not to impose the AD duty on the ground of the Union interest. Chapter V below analyzes both the WTO-transposed and WTO-plus provisions of the EU anti-dumping laws and provides more details of the practice of the EU institutions, with a view to demonstrating both the intended and unintended effects of legalization.

3.3.2 Building up Capacity to Utilize the DSM

In addition to formal institutionalized interactions between the process of legalization in the GATT/WTO and domestic systems, this monograph examines another consequence of 'legalizing' the trade regime, namely the impact of the rise of legalization on the utilization of the DSM by WTO members.[97]

The rise of legalization in the GATT/WTO makes the DSM an adjudication site that is 'generally able to enforce, in an economically and politically meaningful way, rulings sufficient to compel a violating party to reform its act or omission'.[98] Strong incentives provide for a WTO member to utilize this mechanism to strategically protect its trade rights or advance its trade interests. As well documented, more and more WTO members realized that 'the legal rules in the treaties and agreements overseen by the WTO can be turned into instruments of power and means of persuasion against others in a legitimate way'.[99] Given the growing interests at stake, scholars argue that WTO members, such as Japan and Korea, are embracing 'aggressive legalism', namely 'a conscious strategy where a substantive set of international legal rules can be made to serve as both 'shield' and 'sword' in trade disputes among sovereign states'.[100]

It is, however, not an easy task to effectively utilize the WTO DSM. WTO members must have a sufficient legal and institutional capacity to be able to make full use of the DSM. It is observed that '[W]ith more rigorous disciplines and a growing body of jurisprudence, the dispute settlement system has, however, become significantly more legalistic and consequently more arduous to

97. Legal capacity has been defined as a state's ability to identify violations of its right under the WTO. For recent literature, for example G. Shaffer, 'The Challenges of WTO Law: Strategies for Developing Country Adaptation', *World Trade Review* (2006): 177, 178; and T. Walsh, 'Dispute Settlement at the World Trade Organization: Do Municipal Laws Promoting Private Party Identification of Trade Disputes Affect State Participation?', *Journal of World Trade* 40 (2006): 889.
98. H. Nordström & G. Shaffer, 'Access to Justice in the World Trade Organization: The Case for a Small Claims Procedure – A Preliminary Analysis' ICTSD Issue Paper No. 2, June 2007, Forward.
99. S. Pekkanen, 'Aggressive Legalism: The Rules of the WTO and Japan's Emerging Trade Strategy', *The World Economy* 24 (2001): 707, 708.
100. *Ibid.*, For Korean experience, D. Ahn, 'Korea on the GATT/WTO Dispute Settlement. System: Legal Battles for Economic Development', *Journal of International Economic Law* 6 (2003): 598.

navigate'.[101] In order for a WTO member to use the DSM effectively, it must 'develop cost-effective mechanisms to perceive injuries to its trading prospects, identify who is responsible, and mobilize resources to bring a legal claim or negotiate a favourable settlement'.[102] In other words, even when a WTO member is aware that it has sufficient legal grounds to act in the DSM, this awareness will not be 'automatically transformed into the invocation of formal panel procedure'.[103] The decision to start the formal DSM procedure can only be made under the condition that a WTO member is confident that its claim is worth pursuing, taking into account a number of factors, such as the capacity to elaborate the law, litigation cost, possible remedies and associated political risks.

The progress of the legalization in the GATT/WTO system impacts upon both the institutional and legal capacity building of WTO members. This study, from two aspects, analyzes how the rise of legalization provides incentives for a WTO member to build up capacity to utilize the DSM, *inter alia* the institutional capability to mobilize domestic resources for WTO complaints, and the legal capacity to elaborate the law, which mainly involves the ability to advance trade claims in the circumstances where the degree of obligation and precision of the provisions in the corresponding covered agreements that are expected to be applied is low. The two factors are referred to in this study as 'engaging the private sector' and 'litigating the unlitigatable'.

The mobilization of domestic interest groups enters into the discussion since the process of legalization 'entails a process of increased precision of rules and transparency of agreements' and therefore it 'affects the behaviour of domestic groups by increasing the information available to actors about the distributional implications of trade agreements'.[104] Scholars therefore argue that well-placed private actors have more incentives, under a more legalized DSM, to actively engage in the WTO litigation process that has traditionally been dominated by public actors.[105] The emerging public-private network in trade disputes brought together private enterprises, their lawyers and public officials by structural changes at the international level, namely the move to a higher level of legalization in the GATT/WTO, and pressure at the domestic level, that is, 'firms more aggressively demanding the removal of foreign trade barriers in a globalising economy'.[106] As a result, one of the key reasons for major trading partners, such as the EU and the US, to be successful in the DSM is that they 'fostered the development of a reflex

101. Nordström & Shaffer, 'Access to Justice in the World Trade Organization', Forward.
102. Shaffer, 'The Challenges of WTO Law', 178.
103. *Ibid.*, 179.
104. Goldstein & Martin, 'Trade Liberalization and Domestic Politics', 606.
105. G. Shaffer, 'What's New in EU Trade Dispute Settlement? Judicialisation, Public-private Networks and the WTO Legal Order', *Journal of European Public Policy* 13 (2006): 832, 832.
106. G. Shaffer, 'Behind the Curtains of International Trade Dispute', for a book on Changing Patterns of Authority in the Global Political Economy, 6, <www.law.harvard.edu/students/orgs/hela/papers/pub-priv-teubingen-new.doc>, 6 Jul. 2008. For general discussion on national procedures engaging private actors to identify foreign trade barriers, See Walsh, 'Dispute Settlement at the World Trade Organization', 889.

within their export sectors to assist them in investigating claims and building factual and legal cases in order to enforce their trading rights through the DSM'.[107]

The ability to sufficiently elaborate WTO laws and bring claims in areas where the level of obligation or precision are low, that is, litigating the unlitigatable, is another important dimension that affects the utilization of the DSM by WTO members. This monograph argues that the frequent utilization of the DSM is not only due to a higher degree of delegation, as commonly understood, but also closely related to the higher level of obligation and precision in covered agreements. The reason that the level of obligation or precision in particular provisions of a covered agreement has an impact on state behaviour in trade disputes is as follows: WTO litigations involve a huge amount of resources and are associated with high political risks, therefore a WTO member has to accurately access the legal merits of a particular claim before taking any initiative to challenge foreign trade barriers. To a large extent, to be able to access what might be a winning claim in the WTO DSM and to focus on the winning claims instead of wasting time and resources on losing claims signals the maturity of a WTO member in terms of the utilization of the DSM.

With the development of legalization in the GATT/WTO, in particular with a higher level of obligation and precision in more and more covered agreements, the number of claims with 'good' textual bases is increasing. In the meantime, stronger delegation gives incentives to WTO members to make efforts to bring claims that used to lack strong textual bases in the covered agreements. It is not uncommon for the panel and the AB to evaluate the WTO-consistency of long-existing trade barriers when the level of obligation or precision of relevant provisions in the covered agreement has changed.

A typical example is the series of 'zeroing' cases. Before India challenged 'zeroing' methodology in *EC – Bed Linen*,[108] zeroing had already been challenged by Japan in *EC – Audio Cassette*,[109] albert unsuccessfully. In *EC – Audio Cassette*, although the panel did not preclude that the EC methodology might in certain cases be inconsistent with the 1979 Code, it nevertheless concluded that the EC's practice, namely not to take negative dumping into account, was not inconsistent with the 1979 Code in that case.[110]

India, under the WTO ADA, successfully challenged the EC's zeroing methodology in *EC – Bed Linen* case. Part of India's success can be attributed to its effective advocacy strategy, namely in constructing its zeroing arguments, India did not simply assert that all aspects of 'zeroing' practice are against 'fair comparison' and therefore WTO inconsistent. For example, India did not challenge the

107. Shaffer, 'The Challenges of WTO Law', 185.

108. WTO, *European Communities – Anti-Dumping Duties on Imports of Cotton-Type Bed Linen from India*, Report of the Panel (Part 1, 2 and 3) (30 Oct. 2000) WT/DS141/R and WTO *European Communities – Anti-Dumping Duties on Imports of Cotton-Type Bed Linen from India*, AB-2000-13 – Report of the Appellate Body (1 Mar. 2001) WT/DS141/AB/R.

109. GATT, *European Community-Anti-dumping Duties on Audio Tapes in Cassettes Originating in Japan*, Report of the Panel (28 Apr. 1995) ADP/136 (unadopted).

110. *Ibid.*, para. 366.

EC's determination of different models of the like product, and acknowledged that comparisons for individual product types within a single like product are appropriate in the context of an AD investigation.[111] However, India clearly described the zeroing practice of the Commission and sufficiently elaborated upon why this practice is WTO-inconsistent.

India's successful challenge of zeroing, however, also benefits in part from the improvement of precision of Article 2.4.2 of the ADA. The wording of Article 2.4.2 of the ADA is more precise than the equivalent provision in the 1979 Code, which was the legal basis of Japan's challenge in *EC – Audio Cassette*. It is still controversial whether Article 2.4.2 of the ADA disallows all forms of zeroing in AD investigations; it is nevertheless clear that the panels and the AB considered that the Article 2.4.2 is precise enough to serve as the legal basis to challenge the zeroing practice in *EC – Bed Linen* and the following cases.

This monograph chooses China as the subject of its empirical study to exemplify the effects of legalization on the utilization of the DSM on two grounds: firstly, as the most frequent target of AD investigations worldwide by far, China's utilization of the WTO DSM to advance its AD agenda is an important dimension of the consequence of legalization in this subject area. Second, AD investigations against Chinese products are governed by special rules of Non-market Economy (NME) in China's Accession Protocol, which were vaguely drafted and have a low level of legalization. China's efforts to litigate NME therefore illustrate the strong incentives provided by the legalization process, whilst indicating the limitations of legalization.

3.4 Conclusion

This chapter provides a theoretical description of the rise of legalization in the trade regime and the complicated consequences of legalization. It serves as a theoretical foundation for the discussion in the chapters below. It first sketches the concept of legalization in international relations and summarizes the discussions in the special issue, in particular those concerning the uneven expansion of legalization, and its complicated consequences. It then applies the theory of legalization to analyze the GATT/WTO by providing a general account of the status of three factors of legalization in the WTO system, and discusses the uneven expansion of legalization in the GATT/WTO. It also discusses two consequences of legalization, namely 'legalizing' national trade policies in the GATT/WTO system and the legal capacity building to utilize the DSM.

---

111. WTO, *European Communities*, WT/DS141/AB/R.; see also, Goldstein & Martin, 'Trade Liberalization, and Domestic Politics', 603.

Chapter 3

Rise of Legalization in the Multilateral Framework

1 INTRODUCTION

To better understand the dynamic process of legalization in the trade regime, it is necessary to trace back how the GATT/WTO system has evolved from a loose, short-sighted 'diplomatic' treaty network, to a 'legalized' multilateral framework in terms of both formal rules and daily operations.

From a historical perspective, significant events or institutional changes in the GATT/WTO system mark turning points in the development of legalization. This chapter picks up those events and links them together to demonstrate the trend of legalization in the trade regime. As a general remark, this monograph considers different parts of the GATT/WTO have been significantly legalized and there was a certain degree of correlation between the processes. However, the 'legalizing' processes of each of them were sometimes disparate. The original GATT institutional framework was chosen as a consequence of the particular political constellation in which trade negotiators were operating. After four decades' development, by the time of the Uruguay Round, the evolution of both the institutional framework and the substantive treaty network required a new WTO package to re-strike the balance. Yet, the new WTO system is not perfectly balanced and the expansion of legalization is still uneven.

The discussion of the rise of legalization at the international level starts with an assessment of the development of legalization in the GATT. The first section summarizes the most noticeable features and changes that have occurred in the development of the GATT system in line with the three-factor framework of legalization established in the previous chapter. The next section elaborates on institutional changes of the WTO system that significantly improved the value of three elements of legalization. The third section surveys theoretical debates relating to 'juridicialization' of the WTO, which are closely related to the analytical work of this monograph. The fourth section concludes the chapter.

2 RISE OF LEGALIZATION IN THE MULTILATERAL FRAMEWORK

2.1 From Politics to 'Diplomat's Jurisprudence': The Evaluation of the GATT

As the prototype of the WTO, the GATT system shares a great number of similarities with the WTO system. Among them, the most distinct one is the unique 'legal' system developed by GATT diplomats to manage the trade regime. This unique type of legalization was referred to as 'diplomat's jurisprudence' by late Professor Hudec, meaning that the diplomats conducted power-based bargaining in a 'legal', mostly procedural, context.[1] This section analyzes the general institutional development of the GATT and the development of legalization in each part of the GATT system, demonstrating how 'diplomat's jurisprudence' gradually developed to a unique type of legal system and how increased legalization exerted its influence on the overall development of the trade regime.

2.1.1 Elements of Legalization in the GATT

The most widely acknowledged institutional feature of the GATT system is that it has a 'constitutionally flawed' origin, yet it managed to develop an institutional structure to run the multilateral trading system.[2] Being only a chapter of the International Treaty Organization (ITO) Charter, the original GATT text provided no sufficient 'decision-making apparatus and dispute machinery'.[3] However, when it reached the point of the completion of the Uruguay Round, the GATT had already become a de facto institution 'with fairly elaborated procedures for conducting its business through trial and error'.[4] The three functions, that is, decision-making, surveillance and dispute settlement, which are currently carried out by the WTO, all have their origins in the GATT system.

The institutionalization of the GATT started from the establishment of the GATT Council. Originally, the Contracting Parties comprised the only

1. R. Hudec, 'GATT or GABB? The Future Design of the General Agreement on Tariffs and Trade', in *Essays on the Nature of International Trade Law* (London: Cameron May, 1999), 77. This essay was original part of a larger article published in the *Yale Law Journal* 80 (1971): 1299–1368; and J. Jackson *The World Trading System – Law and Policy of International Economic Relations*, 2nd edn (Massachusetts: The MIT Press, 1997), 35.
2. For the comprehensive discussion of the history of GATT, J. Jackson, *World Trade and The Law of GATT* (New York: Bobbs-Merrill, 1999), 35–37.
3. Hudec, 'GATT or GABB?', 37–38.
4. J. Jackson, *Sovereignty, the WTO and Changing Fundamentals of International Law* (Cambridge: Cambridge University Press, 2006), 97.

administrative organ mentioned in the treaty.[5] To prepare the GATT to play a better role as the central international institution for trade, the Contracting Parties took a decision in 1960 to establish a council without any explicit treaty language as the legal basis.[6] The Council is 'a self-selected body composed of a group of countries interested in GATT', numbering about half of the total membership.[7] It was set up to conduct 'intersessional' business, that is, the day-to-day running of the GATT, in particular when the Contracting Parties were not sitting in their full-scale session.[8] Over time, the Council became the 'principal permanent institution for the GATT' and 'increasingly shouldered the burden of directing it'.[9] Numerous specialized committees and working parties that have a limited membership were set up to assist the Council, especially after the Tokyo Round.[10]

This 'organic' process of institutionalization was highly successful, as many believed. However, when the system expanded and became more complicated, it was confronted with 'the rigidity of the underlying treaty'.[11] The flexibility of institutions that was based mainly on the voluntary tolerance and respect of Contracting Parties was not supported by an equally flexible treaty system. This contrast between rigid treaty languages and flexible institutional arrangements generated uncertainty in the evolution of the GATT system and made the expansion of legalization uneven and unbalanced in many aspects.

2.1.1.1 Decision-making

As a negotiation forum, the GATT successfully hosted eight rounds of multilateral trade negotiations, expanding its disciplines from tariff to non-tariff restrictions and adding the development provisions, such as the Enabling Clause in the 1970s. Yet, the uncertainty created by the tension between the treaty languages and the operation of institutions kept the development of legalization in this forum at a bare minimum. The GATT decision-making remained a combination of the 'legal' process, 'one member one vote' where rule applies, and the 'political' invisible weighting process, where 'powerful parties have exercised their invisible weight to dominate agenda setting and outcomes of the multilateral talks'.[12]

---

5. V. Price, 'New Institutional Developments in GATT', *Minnesota Journal of Global Trade* 1 (1992): 87.
6. Jackson, *Sovereignty, the WTO and Changing Fundamentals of International Law*, 97.
7. GATT, *Rules of Procedures for Sessions of the Contracting Parties – Other Procedures*, BISD 9th Supp. 7, 7 (1961).
8. Price, 'New Institutional Developments in GATT', 87–88.
9. Jackson, *Sovereignty, the WTO and Changing Fundamentals of International Law*, 97.
10. Price, 'New Institutional Developments in GATT', 88. As a result of the Tokyo Round 'side agreements', nice permanent committees were established in the following areas: anti-dumping practice, customs valuation, government procurement, import licensing, subsidies and countervailing measures, technical barriers to trade, trade in civil aircraft, diary products and meat.
11. *Ibid.*
12. *Ibid.*, 365.

As analyzed by Steinberg, trade rounds can be divided into three overlapping stages: launching, informal agenda setting and closing.[13] Typically, a trade round is launched while a vague mandate for negotiation has attained consensus. A consensus on the drafting negotiating mandate will be blocked until 'virtually all topics of interest to members have been included and until the language has been sufficiently vague so as not to prejudice the outcome of negotiations'.[14] After being launched, important works took place on an informal agenda-setting process, which 'largely rested with the coordinated action of major trading powers and a secretariat that is strongly influenced by them'.[15] Most initiatives that broadly conceptualize a new area or a new form of regulation have been developed 'first in Brussels and Washington DC, discussed informally by the transatlantic powers, then in increasingly larger caucuses such as Organization for Economic Cooperation and Development (OECD), and ultimately in the "Green Room"'.[16] The draft that emerged from the Green Room was then 'presented to a formal plenary meeting of GATT Contracting Parties and is usually accepted by consensus'.[17]

During the negotiation process, there is no tight obligation, no precise rule and no third-party delegation. The fact that the decision-making was set in a procedural context has little impact on the level of legalization. It is important to make a distinction between the status of legalization of the rules that were produced by the decision-making body of the GATT and the development of legalization in the body itself. While the level of legalization of GATT rules has greatly improved over time, the decision-making practice of GATT has evolved in a modest manner, and remained in the low end of the spectrum of legalization.

2.1.1.2 Surveillance

The idea of keeping national trade policies under surveillance in the GATT can be traced back to the Tokyo Round.[18] In 1979, the 'Understanding Regarding Notification, Consultation, Dispute Settlement and Surveillance' provided, among others, special GATT Council meetings to review general developments in the trading system.[19] The GATT secretariat prepared documents for these meetings, on the basis of a combination of 'official trade policy notifications' and on what it was

13. R. Steinberg, 'In the Shadow of Law or Power? Consensus-Based Bargaining and Outcomes in the GATT/WTO', *International Organization* 56 (2002): 339, 350.
14. *Ibid.*
15. *Ibid.*, 354.
16. *Ibid.*, 355. Green Room caucuses normally consist of twenty to thirty-five countries that are interested in the particular text being discussed and include the most senior members of the secretariat, diplomats from the most powerful members of the organization, and diplomats from a roughly representative subset of the GATT membership.
17. *Ibid.*
18. Price, 'New Institutional Developments in GATT', 97.
19. GATT, *Understanding Regarding Notification, Consultation, Dispute Settlement and Surveillance*, BISD 26th Supp. 210 (1980).

able to glean from 'the press and unofficial sources'.[20] In April 1989, built on previous experiences, GATT technocrats established, on a provisional basis, the Trade Policy Review Mechanism (TPRM), as the first fruits of the Uruguay Round. The TPRM differs from previous Special Council meetings as 'it provided a mechanism to periodically review trade policies of all member countries at fixed intervals on a country-by-country basis'.[21] As a 'soft' legal device, the TPRM provides a continually updated and comprehensive inventory of trade policy measures. The question remains whether the peer pressure and increased transparency supposedly generated by the TPRM have more than a marginal effect on the development of legalization, since it locates in the middle of the specturm of legalization with low obligation and low delegation, but high precision.

2.1.1.3 Adjudication

The most controversial part of the GATT system – its Dispute Settlement Mechanism (DSM) – is the part that has been 'legalized' most. It is commonly observed that the GATT DSM largely overcame most of the deficiencies it shared with other public international law organizations, such as lack of autonomous judicial rules and a strong enforcement mechanism, to become a 'legalized' organ.[22] At the beginning of GATT, disputes were generally taken up by 'the diplomatic procedures', firstly at semi-annual meetings of the Contracting Parties and then through a working party that was set up for the purpose of dispute settlements.[23] Around 1955, a major shift in the procedure occurred, when the Contracting Parties decided that rather than use a 'working party' composed of nations, a dispute would be referred to a 'panel' of experts. This development, as commonly acknowledged, 'represented a major shift from primarily a "negotiating" atmosphere of multilateral diplomacy, to a more judicial procedure of dispute settlement'.[24] During the Tokyo Round, the Contracting Parties took the initiative to improve the procedure and produced the 'Understanding Regarding Notification, Consultation, Dispute Settlement and Surveillance', which became a landmark document in the history of the GATT.[25] This Understanding, along with its annex, consisted of a detailed description of dispute settlement processes of the GATT and 'formed a sort of "constitutional framework" for these processes in GATT after 1947 and prior to the WTO'.[26]

---

20. *Ibid.*
21. D. Keesing, *Improving Trade Policy Reviews in the World Trade Organization* (Washington DC: Institute for International Economics, 1998), 5.
22. D. Palmeter, 'The WTO as a Legal System', *Fordham Journal of International Law* 24 (2000): 444.
23. Jackson, *Sovereignty, the WTO and Changing Fundamentals of International Law*, 139.
24. *Ibid.*
25. GATT, *Understanding Regarding Notification, Consultation, Dispute Settlement and Surveillance*, BISD 26th Supp. 210 (1980).
26. Jackson, *Sovereignty, the WTO and Changing Fundamentals of International Law*, 140–141.

Although the sole dispute settlement procedure incorporated in the original GATT text was Article XXIII, 'nullification and impairment', the GATT DSM evolved over four decades and became a rather 'legalistic' institution. At the commencement of it, with vague treaty languages, obligation and precision were considerably low and since the DSM was based on the consensus principle, that is, parties to a dispute can block either the initiation or the completion of the process, delegation was also very limited.[27] Yet the shifts in its working procedure after the 1960s made the GATT DSM a more rule-oriented institution. By the time of the Uruguay Round, the DSM has significantly improved along the legalization spectrum and became the most 'legalized' part in the GATT.

2.1.2 Uneven Expansion of Legalization in the GATT

The genuine rise of legalization in the GATT was, however, largely restricted by two distinct characters of GATT obligations, which imposed fundamental restrains on the development of legalization of the GATT and largely offset the efforts in various trade rounds to enhance the level of precision and obligation of GATT rules.

Firstly, typical GATT obligations are rigorous on substance, but in the meantime associated with broad exceptions. On the one hand, drafters of the GATT, through bargaining in the negotiation forum, tried to set out detailed rules that would 'leave no doubt about the expected good trade practices'.[28] On the other hand, the operation of the system in practice rested more on 'less well-defined elements out of the rule-making process – the wide-ranging exceptions to the formal rules'. These exceptions may, to a large extent, justify the preference of national trade authorities under a particular circumstance. In other words, the diplomats acted in a more 'pragmatic' way to apply their 'law', which 'included the considerations of not only the legally binding obligation, but also the domestic preference of solutions, the fact of prior deliberation and commitment and the community consensus underlying substantive norms'.[29]

It is argued that the broad exceptions of GATT rules have developed in a particular historical context to facilitate the process of ratification so that the GATT could be put into force immediately. The drafters intended to show the public a clear picture of the restricted rights and obligations in this trade agreement and hoped it could be ratified easily. However, as observed by late Professor Hudec, 'as governments started to implement the GATT, the effectiveness of detailed substantive rules began to be seriously undermined by the wide exceptions after the first successful decade of GATT', namely late 1960s.[30] When the practice of formally deviating from the GATT became less fashionable, the Contracting Parties sought to justify their increasing non-compliance or negative compliance

27. B. Hoekman & M. Kostechi, *The Political Economy of the World Trading System – The WTO and Beyond*, 2nd edn (Oxford: Oxford University Press, 2001), 75.
28. *Ibid.*
29. Hudec, 'GATT or GABB?', 35.
30. *Ibid.*, 82.

by referring to the exception of GATT rules. A typical example is that Article XIX, the 'escape clause', served as the legal basis of the widely used quantitative restriction – 'voluntary export restrains' in late 1970s and to early 1980s.[31] The GATT rules hence obtained 'an equivocal status': it is generally considered as 'a source of binding obligations on trading partners'; yet 'under particular circumstances, it can be deviated by invoking the relatively broad exceptions'.[32]

Scholars consider that, to its credit, the wide exceptions in the treaty language enable the GATT to achieve institutional innovations and play a 'vacuum-filling' role even without explicit treaty text authority.[33] However, relatively imprecise texts significantly lowered the level of legalization, in particular the level of obligation and delegation of the whole system. This had a significant impact on the development of the system.

Another distinct feature of the GATT obligations is its 'grandfather' clause, namely the GATT norms were accepted only 'provisionally' and to the extent that obligations were 'not inconsistent with' existing national legislations.[34] This clause allowed the Contracting Parties' inconsistent legislations to be in effect until they expired. It expressed both the Contracting Parties' reservation to the system, namely 'no removal of existing trade barriers or restrictions', and their exceptions – instead of harmonizing national trade policies, the main function of the detailed GATT rules was to help 'prevent bad things from happening'.[35] Closely linked to it, the GATT developed a distinction between mandatory and discretionary legislations.[36] Only legislations, which 'mandated actions that would be inconsistent with the GATT', could be challenged as such, whereas legislation that merely 'gave the discretion to the executive authority to act inconsistently' with the GATT could not be challenged.[37] Under the historical background, it is understandable that the drafters hoped to make it easy for the GATT to be ratified, by leaving the existing trade barriers untouched. Nevertheless, this clause significantly weakened the capability of the GATT to touch the cornerstone of domestic protectionism and justified a considerable number of 'illegal' measures for a long time.

At the time of the Uruguay Round, it became apparent that it is difficult for the GATT to adequately address the complex new generation of trade barriers, such as anti-dumping measures, voluntary restraints, service regulatory measures and

---

31. For the details of the normative analysis of 'escape clause', A. Sykes, 'Protectionism as a "Safeguard": A Positive Analysis of the GATT "Escape Clause" with Normative Speculations', *University of Chicago Law Review* 58 (1991): 255.
32. O. Perez, 'Ecological Sensitivity and Global Legal Pluralism: Rethinking the Trade and Environment Debate', PhD Thesis, London School of Economics and Political Science (2001).
33. Jackson, *Sovereignty, the WTO and Changing Fundamentals of International Law*, 98.
34. Hudec, 'GATT or GABB?', 35–36.
35. *Ibid.*, 91
36. WTO, *United States – Anti-Dumping Act of 1916 – Complaint by the European Communities*, Report of the Panel (31 Mar. 2000) WT/DS136/R, para. 3.26.
37. WTO, *Canada – Measures Affecting the Export of Civilian Aircraft*, Report of the Panel (20 Aug. 1999) WT/DS70/R, para. 9.124.

intellectual property norms.[38] Hence, although the GATT has been significantly legalized, the Contracting Parties realized that a new form of 'legalized' institutions is in urgent need. Breakthroughs culminated with the conclusion of the Uruguay Round in 1994 and a new WTO system was established.

2.2 A New Hope of Legalization: The Establishment of the WTO

The establishment of the WTO on 1 January 1995 was a significant event in the development of legalization in the trade regime. The new WTO treaty system integrated the fruits of all previous multilateral negotiation rounds – about sixty agreements, understandings and decisions – into a comprehensive treaty network, supported by a constitution-like agreement: the Marrakesh Agreement Establishing the WTO (the WTO Agreement).[39] The WTO also established an international organization that is manifestly less 'diplomatic' and more 'legalistic' than the GATT.[40] Unlike the ambiguous and informal institutional build-up of the GATT, each function operated by the WTO has its explicit legal basis in the WTO agreements. This section details the institutional changes brought by the Uruguay Round for each part of the WTO system.

2.2.1 Decision-making

After the establishment of the WTO, the multilateral trade talking has been formally moved to the permanent negotiation forum of the WTO. Largely inheriting the GATT practice, the WTO negotiation forum hosts 'political' bargaining a procedural contest.

Consensus remains as the principle of decision-making of the WTO, with the exception to decide issues by voting when the decision cannot be reached by consensus.[41] In theory, this 'one country one vote' provision makes the WTO a more legitimate institution, and possibly, 'the most democratic one among international organizations'.[42] However, as discussed in Chapter II above, the

---

38. F. Abbott, 'NAFTA and the Legalization of World Politics: A Case Study', *International Organization* 54 (2000): 519, 520. ('NAFTA and the Legalization') The author notes that there are second- and third- generation of trade barriers. Second-generation trade barriers refer to non-tariff governmental measures directed towards trade, such as quotas, export subsidies and voluntary restraints. Third-generation trade barriers refer to internal government regulatory measures not specifically directed toward trade, but which may distort international competition, such as competition policies (over- or under- regulatory).
39. WTO, *Marrakesh Agreement Establishing the World Trade Organization,* LT/UR/A/2, 15 Apr. 1994.
40. Hoekman & Kostechi, *The Political Economy of the World Trading System*, 74.
41. WTO, *Marrakesh Agreement*, Art. IX, 15 Apr. 1994.
42. F. Weiss, 'WTO Decision-making: Is It Reformable?', in *The Political Economy of International Trade Law*, ed. D. Kennedy & J. Southwick – Essays in Honour of Robert E. Hudec (Cambridge: Cambridge University Press, 2002), 75.

consensus rule does not improve the status of legalization in the WTO decision-making. Even in cases where 'the rules called for a formal vote', negotiations and consultations, 'in particular between the larger trading partners, would usually be held to arrive at a consensus text before the formal vote was held'.[43] The tension between the informal oligarchy and the formal democracy led to, in part, the failure of the Doha Round, when negotiating objectives pursued by the developing partners and by the developed ones could not be reconciled.

In addition to the general decision-making procedure, several provisions of the WTO Agreement provide some special decision-making procedures, including Article X for amendment, Article XII for accession, etc. In theory, these rules, especially the rule of amendment, may improve the degree of precision and delegation in the WTO decision-making. For instance, Article X authorizes not only the member of the WTO, but also the Councils listed in paragraph 5 of Article IV, to initiate an amendment proposal.[44] Consequently, those Councils, by sharing the right of initiative with members, may become autonomous actors to some extent and push the progress beyond the expectation of some members. Nevertheless, it never happened in practice, largely due to the strict requirements of Article X. This provision requires to approve an amendment proposal a two-thirds majority, if WTO members cannot reach consensus within ninety days.[45]

In short, although the WTO added more 'constitutional' rules, such as various voting procedures, into its negotiation forum, the decision-making of the WTO largely followed the GATT practice and stays at the 'low' end of legalization spectrum with low obligation, low precision and no third-party delegation.

2.2.2 Surveillance

The previous chapter locates the TPRM in the intermediate zone of the spectrum of legalization, namely low obligation, low delegation but high precision. This feature of the TPRM partly relates to its creation time. The TPRM is a GATT product, with the common character of other GATT bodies, namely low obligation and low delegation. But it was the first fruit of the Uruguay Round, created at a time when the Contracting Parties had strong wishes to reform the GATT system. The TPRM enjoys a high level of precision and represents a 'soft' legalization formula.

Based on Annex 3 of the WTO Agreement, the Trade Policy Review Body (TPRB), a newly created organ responsible for conducting the reviews within the WTO secretariat, begins the review 'by selecting a set of countries each year, according to the intervals laid down in the WTO Agreement'.[46] The countries under review are required to complete and return a questionnaire prepared by the TPRB promptly and to submit its own report, referred to as a 'policy statement',

43. Jackson, *The World Trading System*, 97.
44. WTO, *Marrakesh Agreement*, Art. X, para. 1 and Art. IV, para. 5, 15 Apr. 1994.
45. *Ibid.*
46. WTO, *Annex 3: Trade Policy Review Mechanism*, LT/UR/A-3/TPR/1, 15 Apr. 1994.

on its trade policies and practices. TPRB staff draft a 'secretariat's report' based on sources such as the country's official publications, the country's notification of trade policy changes to the WTO, and information from a visit to the capital of the country under review. After the completion and distribution of the secretariat report, a review meeting is held by the TPRB. Representatives of members are invited to participate in the meeting and submit questions and comments for the reports. The representatives of the country under review then present their responses. TPRB staff complete the review 'by releasing the final report, which consolidates the secretariat's report, the chairperson's conclusion remarks, self-report of the country and the minutes of TPRB meeting'.[47]

The purpose of the TPRM is twofold: 'to improve adherence by all WTO Members to rules, disciplines and commitments', and 'to the smooth functioning of the multilateral trading system by achieving greater transparency'.[48] It is clear that, firstly, the TPRM is not a formal assessment of compliance and cannot impose new obligations on the WTO members under review. Secondly, the TPRM has formally distanced itself from the WTO DSM and emphasized that it only intends to 'provide a forum to discuss trade policies and practices of a Member by the whole membership'.[49] WTO members and the WTO secretariat were convinced that initiatives to increase transparency such as the TPRM is beneficial to the system.[50]

In practice, however, critics raise serious doubts concerning the effectiveness of this mechanism. Apart from comments about the substance of the review, an important criticism is that trade policy reviews (TPRs) were biased in general towards optimism – 'toward saying what the country under review would like them to say'.[51] Although occasionally WTO members offer sharp criticisms to trade policies of the member under review, it is often blunted by a 'glass house' effect: WTO members reach the understanding that their turn on the firing line will come soon, so that they tend to be more gentle when criticizing others. A well-discussed example is that, from mid-1990, the US and EU had entered into a sort of 'unholy alliance' not to criticize each other's AD actions in public. Therefore, even if AD has been considered as 'the most serious US and EU protective device after voluntary export restrictions, there has been no thorough treatment of this topic in TPRs'.[52] Moreover, due to the low level of delegation in the process, TPRB staffs often either are pressured by the country under review to give favourable remarks or without sufficient resources or authority to conduct a deeper and more comprehensive analysis.

To sum up, the TPRM, as a 'soft' legalization device chosen by the GATT Contracting Parties at the time of the Uruguay Round, represents a higher level of legalization in comparison with other GATT institutions, especially in terms of

47. Keesing, *Improving Trade Policy Reviews in the World Trade Organization*, 12.
48. *Ibid.*
49. *Ibid.*, Appendix B – A WTO Description of the Trade Policy Review Mechanism.
50. G. Marceau & P. Pedersen, 'Is the WTO Open and Transparent?', in *International Economic Regulation*, ed. J. Kelsey (England: Dartmouth/Ashgate, 2002), 7.
51. Keesing, *Improving Trade Policy Reviews in the World Trade Organization*, 30.
52. *Ibid.*, 45.

precision. Yet the deep-seated reluctance of trading partners to delegate power to international bureaucrats, resulted in the limited mandate of TPRM, which in turn limited the impact of TPRM on the legalization process of the WTO

2.2.3 Adjudication

It is commonly recognized that the WTO DSM is the greatest achievement of the Uruguay Round and is the core 'lynchpin' of the trade regime.[53] It is the first time that a unified and comprehensive dispute settlement system was established in this regime. The new DSM has the highest level of legalization in the WTO, with high obligation, high precision and high delegation, as characterized in the previous chapter. This subsection describes the institutional innovations introduced in and after the Uruguay Round, including the introduction of 'reverse consensus' and the rise of the Appellate Body (AB) as the centrepiece of the DSM, and demonstrates how these institutional changes profoundly improved the level of legalization of the DSM.

The most significant institutional innovation took place in the new DSM is the introduction of the 'reverse consensus' requirement for the adoption of panel reports.[54] This institutional development significantly promoted the level of obligation and delegation in the DSM. Since a panel report is automatically binding on the parties, the panels enjoy greater authority to apply the rules in resolving disputes, which in turn 'resolved the problem of blockage and paralysis which existed in the GATT DSM'.[55]

However, it raised WTO members' concern of losing control over the adoption of 'bad' or undesirable panel reports. The introduction of 'reverse consensus' also unintentionally justified the establishment of a standing AB to review panel reports.

The ambition of negotiators was modest when they established a standing AB to allow parties to appeal from panel reports. It is argued that they did not intend to 'create a strong international trade court at the apex of the new DSM'.[56] Instead, their intention was to ensure that the biggest innovation, namely the quasi-automatic adoption of panel reports by the DSB, would not have 'the undesirable side-effect of having no protection from occasional bad panel reports.[57]

Despite the limited ambition of Uruguay Round negotiators, the AB, however, 'has risen as the centrepiece of the WTO DSM'.[58] Several developments in the procedural and substantive rules of appellate review have contributed to this rise to prominence. These developments include the compositions of the AB, the

53. Jackson, *The World Trading System*, 124.
54. P. Van den Bossche, 'From Afterthought to Centrepiece: The WTO Appellate Body and its Rise to Prominence in the World Trading System' Maastricht Faculty of Law Working Paper 2005/1, 5–6.
55. *Ibid.*
56. *Ibid.*, 7.
57. *Ibid.*
58. *Ibid.*, 13.

Working Procedures for Appellate Review, the early embracement and consistent application of the rules of interpretation of the VCLT, the AB's authority in the appellate review and the development of jurisprudence.[59]

The first two developments, especially the Working Procedures for Appellate Review adopted in February 1996, reassure, from a procedural perspective, 'the judicial nature of the appellate review proceedings and the quality and authority of the decisions of the AB'.[60] They advanced the level of precision and delegation of the DSM by providing precise rules for judicial-type proceedings and court-like appeals. The three developments concerning the rules of interpretation, the authority of appellate review and the development of jurisprudence enable the panels and the AB to improve the level of obligation and precision in the covered agreements, by offering precise interpretations to the obligations in these agreements and filling the gaps of the agreements.

To sum up, the institutional innovation of 'reverse consensus' has been the most important change in the WTO DSM in terms of legalization. Reverse consensus not only resulted in direct improvements of obligation and delegation in the DSM, but also pushed the establishment of a standing AB. The rise to prominence of the AB is another important development of legalization, which extended its influence to the whole system and profoundly advanced the level of legalization on all aspects and dimensions of the WTO.

3 THEORETICAL DEBATES RELATED TO JUDICIALIZATION

While previous sections sketch the rise of legalization in the multilateral framework, theoretical debates surveyed in this section provide a more detailed account of the most important manifestations of legalization in the trade scholarship, namely 'judicialization' of the GATT/WTO. Although, as discussed above, this monograph considers legalization as a special form of institutionalization that happens not only in the DSM but also in other parts of the GATT/WTO, the literature concerning judicialization of the GATT/WTO is the most relevant in the field.

Based on the mark of legalization of the DSM in the previous chapter, this section reviews various schools of scholarly comments on three interrelated contentious issues: the role of the DSM, the standard of review, and remedy and compliance of dispute settlement reports. These three issues cross-refer to the discussion of three elements of legalization in this study.

The first issue, the role of the DSM, relates to the value of obligation of the DSM. The second one, the standard of review, relates to obligation and precision of the DSM, since it decides to what extent the DSM can interpret the WTO covered agreements by deferring or rejecting the decision of national trade authorities.

59. *Ibid.*, 13–14.
60. *Ibid.*, 15–17.

The third issue, namely remedy and compliance of dispute settlement reports, closely relates to delegation of the DSM from a different perspective. The purpose of this section is therefore two-fold: it is a brief survey of the contemporary literature in the field; it also provides further insights into the relationship between three elements of legalization and the ongoing debates surrounding them.

3.1 The Role of the DSM

To answer the question what is the role of the DSM, a distinction must be made at first between the formal role of the DSM in the WTO legal text and the normative role claimed by scholars. In the words of the DSU, the preliminary role of the DSM is to effectively and peacefully 'solve the trade dispute between WTO Members'.[61] The institutional change engendered by the DSU over the old GATT dispute resolution system is widely viewed as a great development that enables the DSM to better serve its purpose.[62] However, over time, some argued that the practice of the panels and the AB in fact developed a body of jurisprudence that may exceed their authority, that is, the alleged goals in the WTO legal text.[63] Due to the controversy surrounding some of the panel or AB reports, the DSM, as argued, may even 'undermine the governmental support for the multilateral trading system'.[64] Another group of scholars, on the other hand, by referring to the DSB as a 'world court for trade', expressed their expectation that the DSM should become 'a legal institution more than just a diplomatic club'.[65] They insisted that the DSM should play a more important normative role in the WTO system –to become the engine of constitutional norm-generation or judicial law-making.[66] The WTO DSM should be a 'court' system to 'provide "justice" not some of the time, or most of the time, but all the time, and judicially fill in the gaps of treaty language'.[67]

The key questions of this debate are, first, whether the DSM has done a good job and second, whether the DSM is or should be a 'court'. Based on different normative preferences, there are three main lines of discussion in the trade law commentary.

---

61. WTO *Understanding on Rules and Procedures Governing the Settlement of Disputes* (15 Apr. 1994) LT/UR/A-2/DS/U/1, Art. 3.2.
62. J. Ragosta, 'Unmasking the WTO – Access to the DSB System: Can the WTO DSB Live Up to the Moniker "World Trade Court"?', *Law and Policy of International Business* 31 (2000): 739.
63. W. Davey, 'Has the WTO Dispute Settlement System Exceeded its Authority? – A Consideration of Deference Shown by the System to Member Government Decisions and Its Use of Issue-avoidance Techniques', *Journal of International Economic Law* 4 (2001): 79.
64. *Ibid.*, 80.
65. S. Wilson, 'Can the WTO Dispute Settlement Body be a Judicial Tribunal Rather than a Diplomatic Club?', *Law and Policy of International Business* 31 (2000): 779.
66. For example, D. Cass, 'The "Constitutionalization" of International Trade Law: Judicial Norm-Generation as the Engine of Constitutional Development in International Trade', *European Journal of International Law* 39 (2001): 31.
67. Ragosta, 'Unmasking the WTO', 768.

The first group, including the majority of legal practitioners, academics, and even members of the AB, takes the view that the WTO DSM was and is functioning well.[68] The role of the DSM has been clearly defined in the DSU, that is to settle disputes and to clarify WTO members' rights and obligations by interpreting the relevant covered agreements.[69] Despite the fact that some institutional changes are still in the process, the DSM presented 'a very satisfactory result to both the diplomats and academics'.[70] The DSB in general, and the AB in particular, were 'responsible' and 'well-functioning' institutions that 'have secured, in practice, the authority it was given on paper in the Uruguay Round'.[71] What the DSM needs is not to consider the possibility to reintroduce elements of the original diplomatic model of the dispute settlement, but to go ahead along the road 'which has been taken, and which has proved so far to be a notable success'.[72]

On the other side, the voice of critics is also very strong. Among them, there are two subgroups holding opposite arguments on almost two extremes. The first subgroup takes the view that WTO panels and the AB have been too active and 'overly instructive' with respect to policy-making of sovereignty WTO members.[73] Especially in trade remedy cases, the panels and the AB were accused of 'selling their policy preferences rather than reading the language of the WTO agreements neutrally'.[74] For instance, this group of observers argued that the AB's ruling has 'essentially disregarded' the Article 17.6 (ii) standard of review in the WTO ADA.[75] Although the gaps or ambiguity of WTO treaties have been commonly recognized, the cons still claimed that the panels and the AB are 'not the authorized institutions to fill the gaps by promoting their favored policy', and it may create 'differential obligations' to the members.[76]

Another subgroup consists of ambitious reformers. In their view, the DSM, in particular the AB, is 'a dynamic force behind constitutional-building by virtue of its capability to generate constitutional norms and structures during dispute

---

68. For example, C. Ehlermann, 'Six Years on the Bench of the "World Trade Court" – Some personal Experiences as Member of the Appellate Body of the World Trade Organization', *Journal of World Trade* 36 (2002): 605; and J. Greenwald, 'WTO Dispute Settlement: An Exercise in Trade Law Legalization?', *Journal of International Economic Law* 6 (2003): 113.
69. WTO *Understanding on Rules and Procedures Governing the Settlement of Disputes*, Art. 1.
70. D. Steger, 'The Appellate Body and its Contribution to WTO Dispute', in *The Political Economy of International Trade Law*, ed. D. Kennedy & J. Southwick – Essays in Honour of Robert E. Hudec (Cambridge: Cambridge University Press, 2002), 493.
71. R. Hudec, 'The New WTO Dispute Settlement Procedure: An Overview of the First Three Years', *Minnesota Journal of Global Trade* 8 (1998): 1, 28 and 31.
72. C. Ehlermann, 'Reflections on the Appellate Body of the WTO', *Journal of International Economic Law* 6 (2003): 695, 706 and 708.
73. Davey, 'Has the WTO Dispute Settlement System Exceeded its Authority?', 80.
74. Greenwald, 'WTO Dispute Settlement', 115; also, D. Tarullo, 'Hidden Costs of International Dispute Settlement: WTO Review of Domestic Anti-dumping Decisions', *Law and Policy of International Business* 34 (2002): 109.
75. WTO *Agreement on Implementation of Article VI of the General Agreement on Tariffs and Trade 1994* (15 Apr. 1994) LT/UR/A-1A/3.
76. Greenwald, 'WTO Dispute Settlement', 114.

resolution'.[77] The DSM is assumed, or at least encouraged, to take a constitutional policing role, which may 'invalidate activities of national governments that are inconsistent with the world trade constitutions', modelling the activism of the European Court of Justice (ECJ).[78] The practice of the panels and the AB is by nature 'judicial supervision' but not 'dispute settlement', because of 'the compulsory jurisdiction of the panels and the AB over any cases brought by WTO members, and their ability to adopt reports which are not only binding to the parties of this dispute but also to be considered as valuable as precedent in the future practice'.[79] More importantly, as argued, there is a tendency of WTO members to bring complaints even if they have 'suffered no injury in a concrete and material sense'.[80] Therefore, the panels and the AB are not only doing the job of settling disputes, but also of securing WTO rules. As a matter of fact, 'what the growing jurisprudence of DSM provides is far more than the neutral interpretation of treaties'.[81]

In addition to the normative arguments above, the research of law and economic scholars shows another interesting aspect of the DSM.[82] They characterized the dispute process before the DSM as 'bargaining in the shadow of the law', and pointed out that 'the decision of Members to move from the negotiation phrase to the panel stage is linked directly to the consideration of transaction cost'.[83] When the subject matter of the dispute has an 'all-or-nothing' character and leaves little room for compromise, such as health and safety regulations, the parties' ability to reach an agreement is restricted and they are willing to bring the case before the DSB. In contrast, 'if the subject matter permits greater flexibility to be determined by the trade authority in domestic level, such as tariff rates and trade remedy cases, the parties can more easily structure appropriate transfer payments and settle their dispute out of the "court"'.[84] They argue that the DSM served as a legal framework in the WTO system, which, to a large extent, is neutral. The existence of this framework may influence the future actions of WTO members, but not because it promotes the ideology of trade liberalization. Instead, the members decide to empanel for the reason of saving transaction costs. The DSM is 'not a symbol of the free trade, but a legal framework, which can reduce the transaction cost of

77. Cass, 'Judicial Norm-generation', 42.
78. *Ibid.*
79. Y. Iwasava, 'WTO Dispute Settlement as Judicial Supervision', *Journal of International Economic Law* 5 (2002): 287. The definition of 'judicial supervision' is that a mechanism to control and secure compliance of international obligation undertaken by state by judicial means. There is opposite opinion about the WTO dispute settlement. Also, J. Pauwelyn, 'A Typology of Multilateral Treaty Obligations: Are WTO Obligations Bilateral or Collective in Nature?', *European Journal of International Law* 14 (2003): 907.
80. Iwasava, WTO Dispute Settlement as Judicial Supervision', 287.
81. *Ibid.*
82. M. Busch & E. Reinhardt, 'Bargaining in the Shadow of the Law: Early Settlement in GATT/WTO Disputes', *Fordham Journal of International Law* 24 (2000): 158; also, A. Guzman & B. Simmons, 'To Settle or Empanel? An Empirical Analysis of Litigation and Settlement at the World Trade Organization', *Journal of Legal Study* 31 (2002): S205.
83. Busch & Reinhardt, 'Bargaining in the Shadow of the Law', 158.
84. *Ibid.*, S222.

parties'.[85] Once the parties of a dispute are well aware of the fact that the cost of litigation may exceed the potential benefits of 'winning', they may choose to settle the dispute even if the final compromise may not in the line with the ideology of a 'rule-based' system.

Depending on normative preferences and perspectives, scholars offer different opinions on the role of the DSM. It is not the intention of this monograph to support a particular argument. Instead, this subsection focuses on demonstrating that the asymmetry of delegation to the DSM in terms of dispute resolution and rule interpretation is widely recognized, echoing the discussion in the previous chapter.

3.2 Standard of Review

With the development of the DSM, more precise rules are called on for the 'legalized' dispute settlement process. To respond to this need, the panels and the AB addressed a substantial number of procedural issues in their rulings.[86] An unexhausted list of those issues includes terms of reference, representation by private attorney, the relevance of general international law, burden of proof, the standard of review and so on. Most of those issues were addressed in a precise and less controversial way, which was recognized as 'within the authority of the panels and the AB'.[87] However, some lead to great controversies, such as the standard of review.[88]

By definition, the standard of review refers to 'the nature and intensity of a court scrutiny of the legal validity of a legislative or administrative decision', that is, 'the degree of deference judges should accord legislators and regulators'.[89] In the WTO, the standard of review refers to the 'margin of appreciation' that 'panels and the AB grant national authorities in enacting and enforcing their obligations under the WTO agreements'.[90] In other words, the standard of review defines to what extent panels or the AB, when providing international scrutiny of the contested national measures, should respect 'the prerogatives that the WTO agreements leave to individual members'.[91] The answer to this question not only shapes the jurisdictional competence of the WTO adjudicating body, but also influences the division of power between the judiciary and other bodies of the WTO. In the legalization analysis, the standard of review first related to the value

85. *Ibid.*
86. For example, D. McRac, 'What is the Future of WTO Dispute Settlement?', *Journal of International Economic Law* 7 (2004): 3, 5.
87. Davey, 'Has the WTO Dispute Settlement System Exceeded its Authority?', 110.
88. D. Palmeter & P. Mavroidis, *Dispute Settlement in the WTO: Practice and Procedure*, 2nd edn (Cambridge: Cambridge University Press, 2004), 85. ('Dispute Settlement in the WTO')
89. C. Ehlermann & N. Lockhart, 'Standard of Review in WTO Law', *Journal of International Economic Law* 7 (2004): 491, 493.
90. M. Oesch, *Standards of Review in the WTO Dispute Resolution* (Oxford: Oxford University Press, 2003), 14–15.
91. Ehlermann & Lockhart, 'Standard of Review in WTO Law', 494.

of obligation and delegation of the DSM since it establishes 'no go' areas for the panels and the AB, requiring them to respect the choice made by national trade authorities. It then related to precision because it restricts the scope of the AB or panels to interpret the WTO agreements. The standard-of-review question has thus become 'a touchstone regarding the relationship of sovereignty concepts to the GATT/WTO rule system'.[92]

In legal terms, the standards of review applied by the panels and the AB determine 'the appropriate level of deference in reviewing a member's measure in both finding of fact and legal interpretation'.[93] With respect to factual issues, in *EC – Hormones*, the panel and the AB rejected both the idea of 'total deference' and the suggestion to conduct a de novo review.[94] On the one hand, the AB made it clear that total deference to the findings of national authorities could not ensure an 'objective assessment' expected by Article 11 of the DSU. On the other hand, the panel's practice not to engage in a de novo review has been confirmed by the AB.[95] The AB gradually developed a doctrine that certain key elements need to be examined by a panel in assessing the factual evidence. These key elements include, for example, 'the objective assessments of whether the national authorities examined all relevant facts', and 'whether they provided adequate explanations of those facts supported the factual determination'.[96] In the meantime, the panels and the AB have shown great reluctance to define the precise standards of review of factual issues in general on the ground that the precise character of the review is 'not the same in each case'.[97]

With regard to the interpretation of law, the previous panels and the AB reports leave less doubt. It is clear that the WTO laws are a constant subject of the panels and the AB's de novo review. WTO provisions are consistantly interpreted pursuant to the VCLT and no deference should be made to legal interpretations set forth by the parties of a dispute.[98] Domestic laws are considered as a matter of fact rather than a matter of law. Hence there is no de novo review of domestic laws and the diverging national implementations of WTO laws are assumed legitimate. As the panel stated in *US Anti-dumping Act of 1916*, it was not the role of panels to 'develop our own independent interpretation of US law'.[99]

---

92. Jackson, *The World Trading System*, 6–8.
93. Oesch, *Standards of Review in the WTO Dispute Resolution*, 16.
94. WTO, *European Communities – Measures Concerning Meat and Meat Products (Hormones) –* Report of Appellate Body, (13 Feb. 1998) WT/DS26/AB/R, WT/DS48/AB/R, para. 45.
95. For example, *United States – Transitional Safeguard Measure on Combed Cotton Yarn from Pakistan* – Report of Appellate Body (5 Nov. 2001) WT/DS192/AB/R, para. 7.32; *Korea – Definitive Safeguard Measure on Imports of Certain Dairy Products* – Report of Appellate Body (12 Jan. 2000) WT/DS98/AB/R, para. 3.00; and *United States – Anti-Dumping Measures on Certain Hot-Rolled Steel Products from Japan*- Report of Appellate Body (23 Aug. 2001) WT/DS184/AB/R, para. 7.32.
96. Oesch, *Standards of Review in the WTO Dispute Resolution*, 106.
97. Ehlermann & Lockhart, 'Standard of Review in WTO Law', 497.
98. Oesch, *Standards of Review in the WTO Dispute Resolution*, 74.
99. WTO, *United States – Anti-Dumping Act of 1916*, para. 3.10.

The panel's job was to rule the conformity of the US law to the ADA, according to the interpretation of the US authority.

Except the general standard of review in the WTO system, the ADA is the only covered agreement with a specific standard of review clause.[100] It directs panels not to interfere with a member's interpretation of the ADA if the measure in question rests upon a 'permissible interpretation'.

Many argued that the AB regarded Article 17.6 as relatively 'insignificant in practice'.[101] Given the fact that exporting countries challenging the imposition of AD duties by other countries have frequently prevailed and national authorities' decisions have been frequently overturned, the AB was criticized for '"selling" its own normative preference and creating different obligations to the Members'.[102]

This bitter criticism of the AB's standard of review is rejected as 'exaggerated' by other scholars. As will be elaborated in the next chapter in the context of legalization of the AD regime, different answers to this question relate more to different understandings on the delegation to the DSM. If one agrees that the DSM has a high degree of delegation in terms of rule interpretation, it will be 'necessary for it to be able to conduct the de novo review of both fact and law since it can promote the uniform application of WTO laws'.[103] If this development is not welcomed, the panels and the AB will have to walk a stricter line in terms of standards of review. Arguably, the debate itself and the gradual development of standards of review in the WTO laws have evidenced that 'the WTO has started the journey from a functionalist and contractual framework towards a more constitutional structure'.[104]

3.3 Remedies and Compliance in the DSM

Once a panel or an AB report has been issued by the DSB, for most legal professionals, it is the end of the story. The panel or the AB has confirmed what is right and what is wrong, who is the winner and who is the loser, according to the WTO law. However, in reality, this is still far from a happy ending. In case of non-compliance, a few questions have to be asked: What are the remedies available for the breach of a WTO obligation? Are those remedies effective? What is the next step for this system to ensure greater compliance?

It is widely observed that the WTO system provides a bundle of legal options to be followed by the 'loser' of a dispute. Firstly, the most preferred solution indicated in the DSU is the wrongdoer to 'bring its measures into conformity' according to the recommendations of the panel or the AB.[105] Secondly, if the

100. Oesch, *Standards of Review in the WTO Dispute Resolution*, 88.
101. Tarullo, 'Hidden Costs of International Dispute Settlement', 114–120.
102. *Ibid.*, 123.
103. *Ibid.*, 519.
104. Oesch, *Standards of Review in the WTO Dispute Resolution*, 243.
105. WTO *Understanding on Rules and Procedures Governing the Settlement of Disputes*, Art. 19.

settlement or withdrawal of the WTO-inconsistent measure cannot be accomplished, the 'loser' can also choose to compensate its trading partners. Finally, if again the parties cannot decide on mutually acceptable compensation, the 'last resort' of the WTO system – retaliation – will be authorized. In principle, the 'winner' is authorized to suspend its concession in the same economic sector and at the same level of its injury. If this is not practical and effective, cross-sector suspension may be allowed.[106] Generally, the primary concern of the whole system of remedy is to 'induce compliance, rather than to repair the damage of injured party'.[107]

While there are general cheers for the successful experience of the DSM, some scholarly discussions highlight the structural tension within this enforcement mechanism.[108] Deep controversies persist over two main issues: the meaning of conformity and the effectiveness of sanction as the 'last resort'.

It is argued that a warning from a WTO panel, or the AB, that a member must bring itself 'into conformity' is 'sufficient directive, yet ambiguous enough'.[109] Ironically, even when a member lost the case in the DSM, the content of the obligation to 'bring into conformity' is left to be defined by the losing party. For disputes relating to those WTO rules with a high level of precision, it might be clear for the parties what conformity means. However, for those disputes regarding to WTO provisions with various interpretations and understandings, the term 'conformity' may indicate more than one outcome, that is, a series of possible outcomes across a spectrum. Many WTO members argue that conformity did not necessarily mean the withdrawal of the infringing measures.[110] For example, the EC in *EC – Hormone* argued that the losing member is free to do anything 'not inconsistent' with the recommendation of the panel. In addition, the DSM does not provide incentives for swift compliance of a panel or an AB report. Even after appeals are exhausted, the DSU still tolerates the delay of compliance for several months. Adding the fifteen months before the release of the report, the measure in question could last almost two years even if it has finally been declared as WTO-inconsistent.

It is unfair to say that there is no legal resort for a winning member. Article 21.5 of the DSU provides an arbitration mechanism for surveillance of implementation.[111] It has been proved as a useful system, since it has been 'frequently referred to by the parties of the disputes in case of

106. *Ibid.*, Art. 22.
107. C. Carmody, 'Remedies and Conformity under the WTO Agreement', *Journal of International Economic Law* 5 (2002): 307, 320.
108. For example, G. Horlick, 'Problems with the Compliance Structure of the WTO Dispute Settlement Resolution Process', in *New Directions in International Economic Law – Essays in Honour of John. H. Jackson*, ed. M. Bronckers & R. Quick (The Hague: Kluwer Law International, 2002), 636.
109. Carmody, 'Remedies and Conformity under the WTO Agreement', 321.
110. WTO *EC – Measures Concerning Meat and Meat Products (Hormones)*, para. 45.
111. WTO *Understanding on Rules and Procedures Governing the Settlement of Disputes*, Art. 21.5. Also, J. Kearns & S. Chornovitz, 'Adjudicating Compliance in the WTO: A Review of DSU Art 21.5', *Journal of International Economic Law* 5 (2002): 331.

non-compliance'.[112] However, due to the absence of retroactive remedies in the WTO, 'it is difficult for a government to refuse to pursue the entire range of delay tactics when pressured by domestic interest groups with a stake in maintaining protection'.[113] When domestic pressures are strong enough, the government may find that non-compliance is a better choice than to fully and timely comply with the report. For instance, in *EC – Hormone*, after utilizing all available legal tactics to delay the conformity, the EU 'finally chose non-compliance even facing the sanction from the US'.[114]

The results of this dispute raised another question: to what extent do the availability of sanctions promotes voluntary compliance? Numerous literature discusses the desirability of sanctions in the WTO DSM.[115] A popular view is that the retaliation itself has 'some undesirable economic features'.[116] It is particularly unattractive to smaller and poorer countries. Even if these countries have the authorization to retaliate against a member on whom they relied for imports, they can hardly benefit from the retaliation. Therefore, punitive remedies, such as collective retaliations and retrospective remedies, might be desirable to the WTO in the sense that they may improve the effectiveness of sanctions. Nevertheless, although some WTO members want the DSM to move away from a rebalancing approach, namely focusing on the rebalance of negotiated tariff, to a punitive approach, many others insisted that 'the basic assumption of the WTO DSM is to preserve further trading opportunities rather than redress past injury'.[117] When a WTO panel ruled that retrospective repayment of past subsidies was required, it was criticized as 'challenging the long-standing understanding of DSM and a one-time aberration of no precedential value'.[118]

The theoretical debate concerning remedy and compliance largely reflects the uneven expansion of legalization in the WTO system. It indicates that with a low level of legalization in the covered agreements, the functioning of the DSM, which itself has a relatively high level of legalization, is substantially constrained.

4 CONCLUSION

The past sixty years witnessed the phenomenal rise of legalization in the GATT/WTO as described in this chapter. Starting from the construction of a

112. *Ibid.*, 332.
113. *Ibid.*
114. B. O'Conner, 'Remedies in the WTO Dispute Settlement System – The Bananas and Hormones Cases', *Journal of World Trade* 38 (2004): 245, 249.
115. For example, P. Grane, 'Remedies under WTO Law', *Journal of International Economic Law* 4 (2001): 756, and K. Anderson, 'Peculiarities of Retaliation in WTO Dispute Settlement', *World Trade Review* 1 (2002): 123.
116. Anderson, 'Peculiarities of Retaliation in WTO Dispute Settlement', 123; and Horlick, 'Problems with the Compliance Structure of the WTO Dispute Settlement Resolution Process', 641.
117. G. Goh & A. Ziegler, 'Retrospective Remedies in the WTO after Automotive Leather', *Journal of International Economic Law* 6 (2003): 1.
118. *Ibid.*

'legalized' operational system of the GATT, institutional developments discussed in the first two sections illustrate the general pattern of the rise of legalization in the GATT/WTO. Key changes in decision-making, surveillance and dispute settlement parts of the GATT/WTO highlighted the dynamic process of legalization.

The literature review in the last part of this chapter reinforces the argument that the expansion of legalization in the trade regime is uneven. It identifies three highly controversial issues relating to the DSM: the role of the DSM, the issue of standards of review and remedy and compliance of the DSM reports. It concludes that despite the fact that the DSM has been significantly 'legalized' and has the highest level of legalization in the WTO, the uneven and unbalanced expansion of legalization in the whole system restrains the function of this highly 'legalized' mechanism.

Chapter 4

Legalization of Anti-dumping Rules at the International Level

1 INTRODUCTION

By conceptualizing legalization as a process of structurally manifesting law in the trade regime, the first three chapters conceptualize legalization as a special form of institutionalization and examine its discourse in the trade regime over the past sixty years. Although this monograph considers how the rise of legalization plays a positive role in the development of the trade regime, it also observes that the current process of legalization is uneven and unbalanced in many aspects.

Given the pragmatic nature of legalization, the analysis of legalization cannot be approached in an abstract or general way. This chapter, together with the proceeding two chapters, advances the research by examining the process of legalization in the international AD regime and the consequences of legalization at the domestic level. This chapter portrays how AD, an originally unilateral trade policy, has been multilateralized and legalized in the context of the development of legalization in the GATT/WTO as a whole. The proceeding two chapters focus on the effects of the rise of legalization at the international level on the development of domestic AD policy- and the AD-related dispute settlement activities.

There are two reasons to choose AD as the trade instrument to demonstrate the process of legalization: firstly, AD is one of the most well-developed legal instruments in the GATT/WTO arena; and secondly, it is one of the most controversial trade instruments. After more than a century's development, AD is a regime comprised of complex and intricate rules at both the international and domestic levels. However, all of these 'awfully technical' rules did not provide a sound solution rendering the AD regime any less controversial. Instead, AD has moved from 'being a little used unilateral trade policy to a major WTO-approved weapon in the protectionist arsenal', which provides the benefits of 'strategically harassing trading partners in the rough and tumble of trade policy'.[1] As such, the evolution of AD provides an illustrative example of both sides of the coin: the significant contribution that the process of legalization made to multilateral trade liberalization by restraining the potential abuse of AD instruments, and the uneven and unbalanced expansion of legalization in the AD regime, which makes the efforts by exporting countries to eliminate the abuse of the AD instrument difficult in many cases.

The development of legalization in the international AD regime echoes the general trend of legalization in the GATT/WTO. On one hand, the rise of legalization can be observed in all parts and dimensions of the AD regime. Multiple rounds of trade negotiations have generated tighter and more specific obligations in the AD regime over the past sixty years. Both the 'soft' surveillance mechanisms and the DSM enhance the precision of AD rules, whilst the AD regime, along with other areas of the WTO, benefits from the general improvement of delegation in the GATT/WTO DSM.

A closer analysis of the AD regime, on the other hand, demonstrates the uneven and unbalanced expansion of legalization. A large number of obligations in the ADA are unspecific or contingent in nature As a result, sharp differences between national practices are tolerated and national authorities have a substantial degree of freedom to decide how to run an AD investigation in practice. This feature of the ADA also influences the level of precision of the international AD rules and makes deference to national authorities a highly contentious issue. The development of the obligation beyond the ADA, mainly the judicial activities of the DSM and 'authoritative interpretation' of the Ministerial Conference and the General Council, has been forcefully criticized. In particular, irrespective of the significant contribution made by the DSM to the development of obligation and precision in the AD regime, considerable controversies surround the activities of the DSM.

This chapter proceeds as follows: The next section introduces the basic notion of dumping and the AD law, and provides a brief historical account of the evolution of the AD rules. Section 3 articulates the development of the AD laws in the GATT/WTO negotiation, surveillance and dispute settlement forums, demonstrating the process of legalizing AD rules at the international level. It also accesses the current status of three factors of legalization in the AD regime. Section 4 examines the uneven and unbalanced expansion of legalization in the AD. Section 5 concludes the chapter.

2 PHENOMENON OF DUMPING AND THE DEVELOPMENT OF AD LAWS

Originally, dumping is a trade practice defined as price differentiation or price discrimination among markets, namely 'selling the same product in different prices

1. W. Kerr & L. Loppacher, 'Anti-dumping in the Doha Negotiations – Fairy Tales at the WTO', *Journal of World Trade* 38 (2004): 211, 211.

at different markets'.[2] In classic economic literature, dumping has been classified in several groups according to different characters of dumping practices.[3] One of the chief classifications distinguishes between predatory and non-predatory dumping.[4] The former denotes the practice that the exporter sets low export prices, with the intention of eliminating more efficient competitors in the importing country and gaining, in the long term, a monopolistic position. After that, 'the exporter will be able to establish international monopolies which permit them to charge inflated prices without fear of competition and recoup its short-term loss'.[5]

Dumping may also appeal to an enterprise for a number of non-predatory reasons, such as different competitive processes and capitalization ratio in different countries.[6] Dumping that occurs for these non-predatory reasons is normally considered as harmless and 'fair' in competition policy terms, although it may also adversely affect the competitive structures of the importing country.[7]

According to economic literature, given the fact that dumping practices, in particular those with a predatory intention, may adversely affect the situation of a domestic industry, the importing country should react to dumping in two scenarios: 'if it causes or threatens to cause material injury to an established industry in the importing country; or if it materially retards the establishment of an industry in that country'.[8] This is the genesis of anti-dumping law. It provides the most often cited justification of AD legislation: 'the prevention of predatory pricing – an unfair trade practice and the perseverance of the level playing field in a liberal trading system'.[9]

Apart from economic efficiency, scholars and practitioners also put forward non-economic arguments in favour of AD laws, such as 'nationhood', 'communitarianism' or 'fairness'. For instance, Hutton and Trebilcock argued that 'the private non-pecuniary costs of the community and individual disruption would ensue when domestic production is displaced by low-priced foreign goods'.[10] In their view, since 'individuals are often left with comparatively few traditional attachments to institutions such as family and religion in a rapidly-changed

2. R. Bierwagen, *GATT Article VI and the Protectionist Bias in Anti-dumping Laws* (Deventer and Boston: Kluwer Law and Taxation Publishers, 1990), 1.
3. For example, J. Viner, *Dumping: A Problem in International Law* (Chicago: University of Chicago Press, 1923), 23–34.
4. *Ibid.*
5. J. Leclerc, 'Reforming Anti-dumping Law: Balancing the Interests of Consumers and Domestic Industries', *McGill Law Journal* 44 (1999): 111, 115.
6. Bierwagen, *GATT Article VI and the Protectionist Bias in Anti-dumping Laws*, 9.
7. G. Harpaz, ' "Dumping" the Anti-dumping Instruments in the Trade Relations Between the European Union and the State of Israel? – The European Union's Perspective', *Journal of World Trade* 39 (2005) 445, 451.
8. R. Bhala, 'Rethinking Anti-dumping Law', *George Washington Journal of International Law and Economics* 29 (1995): 1, 4.
9. For example, A. Lowenfeld, *International Economic Law* (Oxford: Oxford University Press, 2002), 245–248.
10. S. Hutton & M. Trebilcock, 'An Empirical Study of the Application of Canadian Anti-dumping Laws: A Search for Normative Rationales', *Journal of World Trade* 24 (1999): 123, 135.

society', job displacement caused by dumping practices may be 'particularly traumatic to the individuals and communities concerned'.[11]

The classical economic theories and non-efficiency rationales for AD laws, however, fail to convince many commentators.[12] Although not all criticisms are equally thorough, most critics focus on two arguments: first, dumping in most cases has positive welfare effects on the overall economy of the importing country and global economy; second, AD duties negate these effects and may be used 'as a surrogate tariff in protecting import-competing industry from cheaper imports'.[13] The combination of these two arguments then leads to the conclusion that AD duties normally have no justification on welfare analysis and are therefore merely protectionist of the local industry.[14]

Irrespective of the hotly debated normative and economic rationales of anti-dumping, AD rules are a well-established 'political construct' at both domestic and international arenas.[15] First enacted in 1904 by Canada, AD laws gradually acquired a worldwide status, 'with incredibly complex international rules and jurisprudence and a growing number of national laws'.[16]

Unlike some newly developed WTO norms, national AD laws have a much longer history than the GATT/WTO AD rules.[17] By mid-1920s, national AD legislation modelling the Canadian AD law, have been enacted by seven countries, namely, Australia, South Africa, United States, Japan, New Zealand, France and United Kingdom.[18] Although largely divergent in terms of administrative procedures, it is 'certain basic tests for determining normal value in anti-dumping actions had already been established'at that time.[19]

At around the same period of time, the first international deliberation on dumping and AD laws commenced.[20] When the preliminary ITO-GATT work began in 1945, AD rules found their way into the GATT 'as a counterbalance of the high tariffs on imports in several exporting countries'.[21] The US proposed to insert a standard into the GATT 1947, modeling roughly but not precisely on its

11. *Ibid.*
12. For detailed comments on the economic rationale of anti-dumping laws, T. Broude, 'An Anti-dumping "To Be or Not To Be" in Five Ads: A New Agenda for Research and Reform', *Journal of World Trade* 37 (2003): 305, 308–312.
13. *Ibid.*, 310.
14. *Ibid.*, See also, A. Sliberston, 'Anti-dumping Rules – Time for Change?', *Journal of World Trade* 37 (2003): 1063, 1078.
15. Sliberston, 'Anti-dumping Rules – Time for Change?', 1078.
16. M. Zanardi, 'Anti-dumping: What Are the Numbers to Discuss at Doha', *The World Economy* 27 (2004): 403, 407.
17. For a detailed on this history of national AD laws see, F. Snyder, 'The Origins of the "Non-market Economy": Ideas, Pluralism and Power in EC Anti-dumping Law about China', *European Law Journal* 7 (2001): 369, 375–378.
18. Zanardi, 'Anti-dumping', 408.
19. Snyder, 'The Origins of the Non-market Economy', 377.
20. Harpaz, 'Dumping', 453. Also, League of Nations, 'Final Report, the World Economic Conference of 1927', Geneva Final Report, C.E.I 44 L347, 33–34.
21. Sliberston, 'Anti-dumping Rules', 1078.

own Anti-dumping Act of 1921. This proposal was accepted by the Contracting Parties. After that, AD joined with other parts of the GATT/WTO in their journey to a higher level of legalization.

Worrying about the potential protectionism embodied in AD rules, the founding father of the GATT tried to 'design an instrument to balance the protectionist effects of the application of AD laws' at the same time.[22] From the very beginning, the GATT AD rule, GATT Article VI (Article VI), is a balance between 'the necessity of providing members with an international seal of approval for their use of AD laws' and 'the intention to regulate national AD practice to avoid its potential trade distorting effect'.[23]

Article VI established a framework for the AD law that has remained unchanged to this day. This provision first defines the term 'dumping' and commits the determination of dumping to authorities of the importing states.[24] It further states that the remedy against dumping is an AD duty, which is to be imposed 'only upon a finding of injury caused by the dumping imports'.[25] This provision arguably contained 'all the bare bones of international anti-dumping rules', but has 'left too much to interpretation by individual states'.[26]

Given the simplicity of Article VI, later efforts were made to reach agreements on more detailed and specific rules of AD. In the Kennedy Round, AD was placed on the agenda and the result of the negotiations turned out to be the first AD Code under the auspices of GATT – Agreement on Interpretation of Article VI (the 1968 Code). At the next round, the Tokyo Round, extensive negotiations were undertaken to establish a code on subsidies. When those negotiations on subsidies were completed, it was agreed that the 1968 Code should be revised to make it parallel (but not identical) to the Subsidies Code.[27] The new 1979 Code therefore conformed to their counterparts in the Subsidies Code. When the Uruguay Round was first launched in 1986, it was not expected that the 1979 Code would be a major subject of negotiations, as it had not been mentioned in the agenda set out in the Ministerial Declaration. As the negotiations unfolded, AD became a hotly contested subject. The outcome of negotiations, as set down in the 1994 Agreement on Implementation of Article VI (ADA),[28] was a package of compromises: procedural rules were tightened, while there were only few, rather minimal, tightening of substantive rules. For this reason, the new ADA, does not reflect 'so much a coherent philosophy' – some provisions favour imports, but others address the need of domestic producers.[29]

---

22. Lowenfeld, *International Economic Law*, 243.
23. Harpaz, 'Dumping', 453.
24. Article VI para. 1 of the GATT 1947.
25. Article VI paras 2 and 3 of the GATT 1947.
26. J. Jackson, W. Davey & A. Sykes, *Legal Problems of International Economic Relations – Cases, Materials and Texts*, 4th edn (St. Paul: West Group, 2002), 694.
27. *Ibid.*, 695.
28. WTO, *Agreement on Implementation of Article VI of the General Agreement on Tariffs and Trade 1994* (15 Apr. 1994) LT/UR/A-1A/3.
29. Lowenfeld, *International Economic Law*, 250.

Parallel with international efforts to establish a more legalized multilateral AD regime, significant progress was also made at the national level to introduce national AD rules. The spread of AD laws worldwide to a large extent illustrates the power of multilateralism. Pre-GATT, only the US, the UK, some members of the British Commonwealth, Japan and France had AD laws at their disposal.[30] As a consequence of the GATT Article VI, about twenty countries introduced their own AD laws in the 1950s and 1960s.[31] In the post-1979 Tokyo Code era, more than twenty-five countries adopted their national AD laws. After the WTO ADA, there was a surge of introducing national AD laws, which resulted the birth of more than thirty-five new AD laws during the past decade.[32] As of 31 December 2008, seventy-one members had notified the WTO AD Committee that they have national AD legislation, and sixteen members are in the process of legislating their own AD legislation.[33] Taking into account that twenty-eight WTO members have not made any notification of AD legislation and non-WTO trading partners have no obligation to notify its AD legislation, it is expected a total of around 120 countries have AD laws now.[34] The countries having national AD legislation cover almost all major trading partners in the world, including non-WTO members such as Russia.[35] It is therefore observed that 'more than 90% of worldwide imports are potentially subject to AD actions today'.[36]

Given the popularity of AD rules, not surprisingly, there are also a huge number of AD activities. Between 1 January 1995 and 31 December 2008, WTO members initiated 3,427 AD investigations and a total of 2,190 AD measures were in force worldwide as of 31 December 2008.[37]

Traditionally, there were four major users of AD rules – the US, the EU, Canada and Australia. Less developed or newly industrialized countries are the targets of their AD laws.[38] However, India reported fifty-four new initiations in

30. The eight countries are Canada, Australia, South Africa, United States, Japan, New Zealand, France and United Kingdom. Zanardi, 'Anti-dumping', 408.
31. *Ibid.* Those twenty countries include the industrial countries like Germany, Norway, Finland, Austria, and newly industrial and developing countries such as Zambia, Malaysia, Uganda and South Korea.
32. *Ibid.* In the last decade, most of the activities in introducing AD legislation have been in developing countries, as most of the industrialized world already had AD laws prior to 1990.
33. WTO, 'Report (2007) of the Committee on Anti-Dumping Practices', G/L/830, 26 Oct. 2007. The report stated: 'As of 23 October 2007, 98 Members had notified the Committee regarding their domestic anti-dumping legislation. Of these 98 Members, 27 notified the Committee that they had no anti-dumping legislation. . . . Twenty-eight Members had not, as of the end of the review period, made any notification of anti-dumping legislation and/or regulations'.
34. H. Vandenbussche & M. Zanardi, 'What Explains the Proliferation of Antidumping Laws?', *Economic Policy* 23 (2008): 93.
35. *Ibid.*, Russia adopted its AD law in 1998.
36. *Ibid.*, 407.
37. WTO, 'Statistics on Anti-dumping', available at: <www.wto.org/english/tratop_e/adp_e/adp_e.htm#statistics>, last visited 5 Jul. 2009.
38. R. Acharya & M. Daly, 'Selected Issues Concerning the Multilateral Trading System', (2004) WTO Discussion Paper No. 7, available at: <www.wto.int/english/res_e/booksp_e/discussion_papers7_e.pdf>, 5 Jan. 2006, 20; *Ibid.*

2008, the largest number in the world.[39] This indicates that the role of new users, most of which are developing countries, is more important than anticipated from past experiences.[40] Many observe that recent intensive uses of AD rules have a retaliatory motive, that is, 'countries started to use AD to offset the negative effect of unfair trade policies from another WTO Member'.[41] The increasing pace of the adoption of national AD laws thus has another possible explanation – countries have to equip themselves with national AD laws in order to 'not only defend, but also fight'.[42]

The brief account of the development of international and national AD rules suggests that there is an identifiable vicious circle in the AD regime, where all sorts of elements such as multilateralism, trade liberalization, retaliatory motives, protectionism etc., are part of the same circle. The original debate that whether dumping is an unfair trade practice is of only theoretical or historical interest now. Nor does the question whether a WTO member is a developing country or a developed one matter – 'the entire First World is not on one side or the other in terms of AD, nor is there a single Third World position'.[43] AD appears to be a popular legal game that 'no one can fortunately have a way out', although most of the time players are facing no-win situations.[44]

3 'LEGALIZING' AD RULES AT THE INTERNATIONAL LEVEL

3.1 Trade Negotiations and International AD Rules

3.1.1 AD Negotiations in Pre-Uruguay Trade Rounds

After the GATT's inception in 1947, six rounds of trade negotiations occurred before the commencement of the Uruguay Round in 1986. Although the first four rounds[45] were largely limited and focused on tariff reductions rather than other non-tariff barriers, the three decades from the 1950s to the 1980s, witnessed

39. WTO, 'Statistics on Anti-dumping',
40. Zanardi, 'Anti-dumping', 403, 405.
41. *Ibid.*, 411. The author argued that this is another crucial point that must be discussed in the Doha Round since the WTO ADA excludes the use of AD in a retaliation fashion, because it is a violation of non-discriminatory principle of the WTO.
42. C. Molyneux, *Domestic Structures and International Trade – The Unfair Trade Instruments of the US and the EU* (Oxford: Hart Publishing, 2001), 15.
43. R. Bhala, 'New WTO Anti-dumping Precedents (Part One: The Dumping Margin Determination)', *Singapore Journal of International and Comparative Law* 6 (2002): 335, 336.
44. As analysed by economists, the AD in general has negative global welfare effects, which is welfare reducing from both an international and a domestic point of view. For example, Broude, 'An Anti-dumping "To Be or Not To Be" in Five Ads, 307, and Zanardi, 'Anti-dumping', 404.
45. The four rounds are Annency Round in 1949, Torquay Round in 1950, Geneva Round in 1956 and Dillon Round in 1960–1961.

significant developments of legalization in the international AD regimes. During this period, four legal instruments highlight the evolutionary process of international AD rules: the GATT Article VI, the GATT Reports of Group of Experts, the 1968 Code (Kennedy Round) and the 1979 Code (Tokyo Round). The analysis of these four instruments along three indicators of legalization (obligation, precision and delegation), together with the negotiation background, offers insights into the 'legalizing' journey that international AD rules went through.

3.1.1.1 GATT Article VI

At the time of the ITO-GATT negotiation, the US insisted on 'addressing unfair trade in the form of dumping and subsidized exports' at the original ITO agreement and the GATT.[46] The US proposal was generally supported due to the conventional concerns on unfair trade practice. The Contracting Parties then agreed that 'the imposition of AD and countervailing duties would be allowed under the multilateral agreement, as long as such duties were imposed where conditions had been properly investigated'.[47] There were, however, two major areas of disagreement in the negotiations: the scope of the definition of dumping and the possible use of forms of retaliation other than AD duties against dumped imports.[48]

With respect to the scope of definition, the parties established four types of dumping early in the negotiations: price, service, exchange and social dumping.[49] It is documented that opinions on the definition of dumping was divided into two camps.[50] Developing countries argued that all forms of unfair trade practices should come under the dumping heading, while developed countries preferred a more limited definition with a special reference to price dumping. Since the parties worried that 'the broad definition favoured by the developing countries would have left open a wide range of retaliatory actions', a narrow definition of dumping was adopted in the GATT Article VI.[51]

The question of the use of retaliatory forms other than AD duties, centred on the use of quantitative restrictions against dumped imports. Due to 'the inconsistency of quantitative restrictions with the fundamental theme of the GATT negotiations', the possibility of utilizing quantitative restrictions against dumped imports was ruled out in of the text of Article VI.[52] Ultimately, the desire of

46. T. Stewart (ed.), *The GATT Uruguay Round: A Negotiation History 1986–1992, Volume II: Commentary* (Deventer: Kluwer Law and Taxation Publisher, 1992), 1405.
47. For example, *Draft Report of the Technical Subcommittee*, U.N. Econ. Social Council, GATT Doc No. E/PC/T/C.II/54 (16 Nov. 1946), at 11; and Tenth Meeting held on 19 Nov. 1946, U.N. Econ. Social. Council, GATT Doc No. E/PC/T/C.II/55 (20 Nov. 1946), at 2.
48. Stewart, *The GATT Uruguay Round*, 1046.
49. *Ibid.* Except price dumping, other types of dumping were either given less than cursory treatment or failed to produce a clear definition during negotiations.
50. *Ibid.*
51. *Ibid.*
52. *Ibid.*

the parties to avoid the use of quantitative restrictions in any circumstance limited the form of retaliation for dumping to AD duties.[53]

This GATT negotiation history on AD manifested the first multilateral efforts under the GATT to 'legalize' national AD rules under the GATT and led to the first multilateral rule in this area. Although fairly brief (with only seven paragraphs and just over two pages), Article VI laid out 'the multilaterally recognized definition of dumping and the conditions under which individual countries were justified in taking defensive measures'.[54] In an implicit way, Article VI established three basic obligations: the determination of dumping (paragraphs 1 and 2), the determination of injury (paragraph 1) and causality (paragraph 6 (a). These three obligations became the foundation for future developments of the AD regime. Regarding the obligation to determine dumping, the first paragraph of Article VI articulates a product will be considered as having been dumped. The second paragraph further requires that the amount of AD duty does not exceed the margin of dumping. Together they limit national trade authorities' ability to respond to alleged dumping practice, Only under certain circumstances is the imposition of an AD duty permissible and an AD duty cannot exceed the dumping margin.

With respect to the obligation to determine the injury suffered by the domestic industry, Article VI specified 'material injury' as the condition for the imposition of an AD duty, although the term itself was left undefined in Article IV. The absence of the definition of injury 'made this obligation at the time an area of contention, as different parties had different standards of injury in their domestic legislation'.[55] Nevertheless, Article VI prohibited a trade authority from imposing an AD duty without a statement of injury, despite the ambiguous meaning of 'injury'.

Finally, under paragraph 6(a) of Article VI, neither AD nor countervailing duties could be levied unless the effects of dumping or subsidization were 'to cause or threaten material injury to an established domestic industry, or such as to retard materially the establishment of a domestic industry'.[56] Again, it was clear that a trade authority is under the obligation to prove causality. The text, however, did not provide a functional framework to practically assess the casual link, in addition to the absence of a working definition of 'domestic industry'.

The lack of specificity and precision became 'a big concern' for many parties over years.[57] As a result of less precise wording of Article VI, countries implemented Article IV according to their own understandings. This led to enormous conflicts amongst the Contracting Parties. To reduce these conflicts, intensive

53. *Record of Work Performed*, UN Econ. Social Council, GATT Doc. No. E/PC/T/103 (19 Jun. 1947), 12. The Working Party on technical articles added an interpretative note as 'no measures other than anti-dumping and countervailing duties or charges shall be applied by any Member for the purpose of offsetting dumping or subsidization'.
54. *Ibid.*
55. Stewart, *The GATT Uruguay Round*, 1409.
56. Paragraph 6(a) of GATT Art. VI.
57. Stewart, *The GATT Uruguay Round*, 1409.

negotiations to expand rules to regulate national practices were held in later rounds of negotiations.

Delegation of settling AD disputes were not separately stressed in Article VI. All GATT disputes, including the AD disputes, were supposed to be settled under Article XXIII of GATT – the 'nullification and impairment' clause. As a DSM based on the consensus principle, the parties of a dispute could block either the initiation or the completion of the panel process. Also, the existences of pre-existing AD laws in contrast with Article VI were justified by the well-known 'grandfather clause' and not challengeable under the DSM. Under the 'grandfather clause', the parties were only required to comply with GATT provisions to the extent that it is not inconsistent with existing legislation. Consequently, in addition to individual conflicts with Article VI, the laws of the parties conflicted with each other.[58]

In short, at the time of Article VI, precision and delegation of the international AD rule are considerably low, despite that certain fundamental obligations have been established.

3.1.1.2 GATT Report of Group of Experts (1961)

From the birth of the GATT to the end of the 1950s, there was no major change to Article VI except the 1955 Interpretative Note that specified the rules of circumvention (Article 5) and state-monopoly (Article 6).[59] Also, during this period, only one formal challenge to an AD action was brought by Italy.[60] This however did not indicate that the multilateral efforts to modify and clarify international AD rules stopped. The Contracting Parties first asked the GATT secretariat to undertake a systematic comparative study of the AD laws of the Contracting Parties in 1956.[61] Then a Group of Experts was appointed to further research on a number of technical issues.[62] The Report of Group of Experts (the Report) was published in March 1961. This report was the first comprehensive consideration of the AD administration since the GATT's establishment. Although the Report itself was not a legally binding instrument, it had a critical influence on future developments of international AD rules and later emerged as 'the basis of a large part of the 1968 Code developed during the Kennedy Round negotiations'.[63]

The first effort made by the Group of Experts in the Report was to clarify a key substantive issue – 'price comparison' in the determination of dumping.

58. *Ibid.*
59. GATT, *Report of Review Working Party III on Barriers to Trade Other than Restriction on Tariffs*, L/334, 1 Mar. 1955.
60. Italy challenged a Swedish AD action against its nylon stockings in 1954. Swedish Anti-dumping Duties: Statement by the Government of Italy, GATT Doc. No. L.215 (29 Jul. 1954).
61. GATT, *Anti-dumping and Countervailing Duties*, GATT Sales No. GATT/1958–2.
62. GATT, *Anti-dumping and Countervailing Duties, Report of Group of Experts*, GATT Sales No. GATT/1961–2.
63. Stewart, *The GATT Uruguay Round*, 1417.

The Report stressed that the essential aim of paragraph 1 of Article VI was to 'make an effective comparison between the normal domestic price in the exporting country and the price at which the like product left that country'.[64] For the purposes of proper price comparison, three issues were addressed in depth, namely, normal value, like product and export price.

The Report first noted that an importing trade authority should aim at a comparison of normal value and export price 'at the same level in the trade and at the same date or dates as near as possible'.[65] It then considered the problem of the determination of domestic market price when more than one price on the domestic market occurred: 'direct price comparison of individual sales transactions' would be preferable and the use of weighted averages should be confined to cases where 'it was impossible to use a more direct method of establishing the normal domestic price'.[66] In addition, the Report set forth the opinion that two alternative methods of establishing normal value in paragraph 1(b) could only be used after 'the establishment of a normal market value under paragraph 1(a) of Article VI had failed'.[67] The ultimate goal of utilizing whatever method was to 'achieve a normal value which was genuinely comparable with the export price'.[68] It further noted the term 'production costs' under paragraph 1(b)(ii) should 'include all direct and indirect cost incurred in producing the product, such as the cost of materials and components, labour, general overheads and so on'.[69]

Next to normal value, the Report entered into the discussion of 'like product'.[70] The term was interpreted as a product 'which is identical in physical characteristics subject, however, to such variations in the presentation which are due to the need to adapt the product to special conditions in the market of the importing country (i.e., to accommodate different tastes or to meet special legal or statutory requirements)'.[71] The report noted that the term should not be allowed to be interpreted too broadly to cover products at a different price range. It also should not be interpreted 'too stringently so as to elude the application of paragraph 1(a) of Article VI'.[72]

Finally, the ideal 'export price' was stipulated as 'the ex-factory price on sales for export or the F.O.B. price, port of shipment'.[73] The ultimate aim was, again, 'in any event to arrive at a price which was genuinely comparable with the domestic price in the exporting country'.[74] If the importers sold imported products at a loss

64. GATT, *Anti-dumping and Countervailing Duties, Report of Group of Experts*, 7.
65. *Ibid.*, 8.
66. *Ibid.*, 16.
67. *Ibid.*, 9.
68. *Ibid.*, 10.
69. *Ibid.*
70. *Ibid.*, 11.
71. *Ibid.*
72. *Ibid.*
73. *Ibid.*, 7.
74. *Ibid.*

and were not recompensed by the exporters, they should 'not be considered guilty of dumping'.[75]

The next major achievement of the Report was to lay down certain rules on material injury and domestic industry.[76] The Group of Experts agreed that no precise definition of 'injury' could be given, but that 'a common standard ought to be adopted in applying this criterion and that decisions about injury should be taken by the authorities at a high level'.[77] National legislation that provided for 'injury' was suggested to be applied 'only as if the word material were stated therein'.[78] On the definition of 'industry', the Report noted that 'as a general guiding principle, judgements of material injury should be related to total national output of the like commodity concerned or a significant part thereof'.[79] The use of AD duties to 'offset injury to a single firm without proper justification' would be protectionist in nature.[80]

Apart from clarifying the substantive provisions of Article VI, the Report also revealed the opinion of the Group of Expert on a number of procedural issues, with a view to 'legalizing' the administrative process of AD investigation for the first time.[81] Under the heading of 'Application of Anti-dumping Duties', the Report considered those procedural issues that were unaddressed in Article VI but obviously divergent amongst national AD laws, such as hearings, provisional AD measures, the publication of AD measures and the duration of AD measures. In terms of hearing, no preference for a particular national practice was indicated.[82] The Report only emphasized that it would be desirable not to impose an AD duty unless interested parties had been afforded an opportunity to be heard by the competent authority.[83] Also, to increase the transparency of AD investigations, the Report suggested that 'decisions concerning the application of AD measures should be taken at a high administrative level and should be published'.[84] It further noted that AD duties should remain in force only for as long as necessary to counteract dumping. It is desirable for an importing country 'to review the AD measure from time to time and the exporters might request the competent authority to do so'.[85] On the issue of provisional AD measures, the Report states that while provisional AD measures might occasionally be justified for the purpose of limiting material injury, it 'should be used sparingly and for the shortest possible time in order to interfere as little as possible with normal trade and in order that they should not assume a protectionist character'.[86]

75. *Ibid.*, 11.
76. *Ibid.*, 10.
77. *Ibid.*
78. *Ibid.*
79. *Ibid.*
80. *Ibid.*
81. *Ibid.*, 15–19.
82. *Ibid.*, 17.
83. *Ibid.*
84. *Ibid.*, 18.
85. *Ibid.*, 19.
86. *Ibid.*, 18.

By the refining substantive terms of Article VI and clarifying certain procedural obligations of the competent trade authorities, the Report is a big step forward in the development of legalization. It established the framework for the determination of dumping that is still in use today, and it specified the 'material injury' criterion and certain procedural requirements in AD investigations. Many issues discussed in the Report, such as price comparison, provisional AD measures and the duration of AD measures, became the focuses of future trade negotiations. Because the Contracting Parties were under no obligation to take actions in order to comply with the Report, the Report was unable to add obligations to the GATT Contracting Parties. Nevertheless, the Report made a significant contribution towards increasing the precision of international AD rules. In terms of delegation, the Report did not address the issue of dispute resolution and therefore has had no impact on the level of delegation in the AD regime.

3.1.1.3 The Anti-dumping Code of Kennedy Round (the 1968 Code)

At the time that the Kennedy Round commenced in 1963, it is observed that 'non-tariff measures (NTMs) began to replace tariffs as the primary obstacle inhibiting the free flow of international trade'.[87] There were increased pressures for the GATT to set common parameters for the issues of NTMs in the multilateral agreements. In this context, the AD was placed on the agenda and the result of the negotiations turned out to be the first AD code under the auspices of the GATT, which was entered into force on 1 July 1968.[88]

The 1968 Code covered five main areas, namely the determination of dumping, the determination of material injury, investigation and administration procedures, AD duties and provisional measures, and AD actions on behalf of third countries.[89] Developed largely from the Report, the main purpose of the 1968 Code was to improve the level of precision, both in terms of procedural rules and substantive criteria for the determination of dumping and injury. While there was no obvious change for the determination of dumping on the 1968 Code in comparison with the Report, the 1968 Code substantially developed the discipline on injury. Article 3(a) of the 1968 Code provided:[90]

> A determination of injury shall be made only when the authorities concerned are satisfied that the dumped imports are demonstrably the **principal** cause of material injury or of threat of material injury or the **principal** cause of material retardation of the establishment of such an industry. In reaching their decision the authorities shall weigh, on one hand the effect of the dumping, and on the other hand, all other factors which may be adversely affecting the industry. (emphasis added)

87. Stewart, *The GATT Uruguay Round*, 1417.
88. GATT, *Agreement on Implementation of Article VI of the General Agreement on Tariffs and Trade (1968)*, reprinted in GATT, BISD 15th Supp., 26. (the 1968 Code)
89. Article 2–12 of the 1968 Code.
90. Article 3 (a) of the 1968 Code.

In addition to the determination of injury, the 1968 Code specified minimal procedural standards for AD investigations. For example, national authorities were required to conduct dumping and injury investigations simultaneously, and provisional measures could only be applied upon an affirmative finding for both dumping and injury.[91] The 1968 Code also established a permanent Committee on Anti-dumping Practices (the AD Committee), which is responsible for resolving disputes between contracting parties on the administration of national AD laws, considering and making recommendations on new AD laws or changes in existing legislation, and overseeing the efforts of the signatories to bring their legislation in line with the new Code.[92]

As the first separate multilateral agreement dealing with AD, the 1968 Code significantly promoted legalization in the AD regime. On the basis of the Report, the 1968 Code remarkably developed the obligation and precision of the GATT AD rules Although the 1968 Code was applied to those who signed it,[93] it converted most issues discussed in the Report into legally binding rules.[94] For example, it imposed more stringent obligations on importing trade authorities, in particular in the determination of injury.

The achievements of the 1968 Code are not limited to promote the level of obligation and precision, however. The establishment of the AD Committee to resolve disputes and superintend national AD laws was an important improvement of delegation in the AD regime.

Most significantly, a general article was inserted to oblige each signatory to ensure the conformity of its laws, regulations and administrative procedures with the provision of the 1968 Code.[95] The laws of, *inter alia* the US, the EU, Canada and Australia, were modified to reflect the 1968 Code, even though the US did not formally adopt the 1968 Code.[96] After the Kennedy Round, major trading partners' AD legislation were largely based upon the wording of the 1968 Code. For the first time, demonstrative convergence among national AD laws emerged as a result of the development of multilateral AD rules.

3.1.1.4 The Anti-dumping Code of Tokyo Round (the 1979 Code)

Launched in 1973, the Tokyo Round negotiations had 'an ambitious agenda', including 'significant tariff reduction' and 'a major focus on non-tariff measures'.[97] AD initially was not considered a priority because of the resistance of further legalization by major trading partners, in particular the US. It is argued

91. Article 5 and 10 of the 1968 Code.
92. Article 11 of the 1968 Code.
93. Article 14 of the 1968 Code. Due to the congress opposition, the US did not adopt the 1968 Code.
94. Article 14 of the 1968 Code. Due to the congress opposition, the US did not adopt the 1968 Code.
95. Lowenfeld, *International Economic Law*, 249.
96. Stewart, *The GATT Uruguay Round*, 1431.
97. *Ibid.*, 1435.

that the history of the US Congressional opposition to the 1968 Code 'made the US negotiators hesitate to undertake further AD negotiations'.[98] Given the political sensitivity of issue, trading partners were worried that 'a breakdown of negotiation in the AD regime could endanger the success of the entire Round'.[99] Until later in the Round under the auspices of the AD Committee, trading partners were starting to grapple with difficult issues that were in need of further clarification and tried to refine them through the negotiations.

The end result was the 1979 Code, which is officially titled 'Agreement on Implementation of Article VI of the General Agreement on Tariffs and Trade'.[100] The new 1979 Code continued the efforts of promoting a higher level of legalization in the AD regime. Despite its similarity with the 1968 Code, the new Code was intended to supersede the old one and signatories specially denounced the 1968 Code.[101]

With respect to obligation, although the 1979 Code did not change the language of the basic obligations concerning the determination of dumping and causality from the 1968 Code, several new obligations were added, and others were significantly modified or expanded. One area of significant reform was the determination of material injury.[102] On the one hand, the new Code revised the 1968 Code so that it was no longer necessary to show that dumping was 'the principal cause of injury' when other contributing factors existed.[103] Instead, a non-exhaustive list of all relevant economic factors and indices bearing on the state of injury was inserted into the text and the competent authority was expected to examine all of them.[104] On the other hand, the 1979 Code specified that a determination of injury should be based on positive evidence of: '(a) the volume of the dumped imports and their effect on prices in the domestic market for like products, and (b) the consequent impact of these imports on domestic producers of such products'.[105]

Other major obligations added or modified in the 1979 Code were the length of AD investigations (except in special circumstance, an investigation shall be concluded within one year);[106] the rule of evidence, especially those concerning confidential information (requiring the cause be shown as to why such data should be considered as confidential and the submission of public summaries of such data)[107] and the rule of price undertaking.[108] With the addition or modification of these

98. *Ibid.*
99. *Ibid.*
100. GATT, *Agreement on Implementation of Article VI of the General Agreement on Tariffs and Trade*, (1980) reprinted in GATT, BISD 26th Supp., 171. (the 1979 Code)
101. Article 16(5) of the 1979 Code.
102. Stewart, *The GATT Uruguay Round*, 1456.
103. Article 3.3 of the 1979 Code.
104. *Ibid.*
105. Article 3.1 of the 1979 Code.
106. Article 5.5 of the 1979 Code.
107. Article 6.3 and 4 of the 1979 Code.
108. Article 7 of the 1979 Code.

obligations, a comprehensive framework at the international level has been established to regulate the conduct of investigating authorities. The level of obligation and precision in the AD regime again has been significantly improved.

The last major area of change was the addition of a special dispute settlement provision: Article 15 'Consultation, Conciliation and Dispute Settlement'.[109] Article 15 stated that any Contracting Party that believed 'any benefit accruing to it under this Code is being nullified or impaired' could request consultations with the offending party and each party was to provide 'sympathetic consideration' to any request for consultation.[110] In case that parties fail to find a mutually agreed solution through consultation, the matter could be referred to the Committee for Conciliation.[111] The Committee should then 'meet within thirty days to review the matter' and 'encourage the Parties involved to develop a mutually acceptable solution'.[112] Finally, if these efforts were fruitless, the Committee, at the request of any Party involved, should 'establish a panel to examine the matter, based upon the written statement of the exporting country and the facts made available to the authorities of the importing country'.[113]

Procedures under Article 15 were governed by the provisions of 'Understanding regarding Notification, Consultation, Dispute Settlement and Surveillance'.[114] As the first dispute settlement provision inserted into an AD Code, this provision demonstrated the Contracting Parties' desire to strength the delegation to third-party adjudicators in the AD regime. Notwithstanding the imperfect general DSM in the GATT, this provision, by requesting the panel examination of both the statement of exporting country and facts available to the competent authorities, improved the level of delegation and pushed the process of legalization in the AD regime to a higher level.

In sum, the 1979 Code continued to improve the level of legalization in the AD regime. In particular in terms of obligation and precision, the 1979 Code carried forward the unfinished job of the 1968 Code, further clarifying both the substantive terms and the investigating procedures. The presence of a special dispute settlement provision illustrated the parties' concern regarding delegation in this particular regime. Although Article 15 of the 1979 Code did not necessarily make the AD regime special in the GATT in terms of dispute settlement, it makes dispute settlement in this regime more 'rule-oriented'. The impact of this movement of legalization was somehow mixed: on the one hand, it made AD rules one of the most comprehensive and sophisticated multilateral legal framework under the GATT; and on the other hand, it resulted in the distrust and hesitation of some trading partners, *inter alia* the US to further legalize the AD rules.

109. Article 15 of the 1979 Code.
110. Article 15.2 of the 1979 Code.
111. Article 15.3 of the 1979 Code.
112. *Ibid.*
113. Article 15.5 of the 1979 Code.
114. Article 15.7 of the 1979 Code.

3.1.2 The Uruguay Round and the WTO Anti-dumping Agreement (ADA)

3.1.2.1 The Uruguay Round Negotiation

Again, AD has not been expected as an area where intense negotiations would be conduced when the Uruguay Round was first launched in 1986. As the negotiations unfolded, serious contentions emerged in the AD area. As observed, on the one hand, 'the US and the EU determined to plug the "loopholes" of the 1979 Code, in particular regarding the use of certain devices to prevent the circumvention of AD duties'.[115] On the other hand, 'many of other countries commonly targeted by AD actions pressed for changes in both the basic concepts embodied in the 1967 and 1979 Code and the practices that seemed to tilt the required price comparison against imports, so as to make the AD rules less susceptible to use for the protectionist purpose'.[116] Due to lack of consensus on most of the major issues, drafting a text satisfactory to all parties appeared to be impossible at early negotiations. Finally, the parties managed to reach a set of compromises, which tightened the procedural rules, but left the majority of the substantive rules unchanged. In doing so, some of exporting countries concerns were addressed, but the interests of domestic producers in importing countries were also protected.[117]

At the early stage of difficult negotiations of the Uruguay Round, there were a number of 'open issues' raised in the AD regime.[118] These issues were first identified in the Ramsauer Draft Text, a draft text issued in 1991 to be the basis of negotiations[119] as follows:

(1) use of weighted averages in the calculation of export prices and normal value;
(2) sales below cost of production;
(3) constructed normal value: calculation of administrative, selling and other costs and profits;
(4) standing;
(5) de minimis margins of dumping and negative import volumes;
(6) cumulation of imports from multiple countries for the determination of injury;
(7) sampling;
(8) sunset review;
(9) anti-circumvention;
(10) dispute settlement;
(11) public interest.

---

115. Jackson, Davey & Sykes, *Legal Problems of International Economic Relations*, 695.
116. *Ibid.*
117. Lowenfeld, *International Economic Law*, 250.
118. Stewart, *The GATT Uruguay Round*, 1532.
119. GATT Draft Anti-dumping Code (26 Nov. 1991) (unpublished working documents), cited in Stewart *The GATT Uruguay Round*, 1533.

Given the divergent interests of negotiating parties, some issues enjoyed a fairly broad consensus, such as inserting a sunset review clause, strengthening transparency and procedural due process. Others, however, were 'characterized by a polarization of positions'.[120] The parties approached these contentious issues from very different perspective: some were of the view that international AD rules should be 'strengthened and improved so that relief from unfair trade practices would be more timely and effective'; others held that the 1979 Code should be revised 'to deal with implementation on the part of some countries that had led to arbitrary, burdensome and unfair results'.[121] As a result, the level of legalization in the final text of ADA has been significantly influenced by the competing positions of parties in the negotiation.

Despite substantial disagreements among parties regarding whether the changes contained in the final text were 'appropriate, necessary or sufficient', the 'clarifications, modifications and expansions' of the above mentioned key issues in the Uruguay Round demonstrated the latest major improvement of legalization in the AD regime, in particular in terms of obligation and precision.

3.1.2.2 Legal Status of the ADA

3.1.2.2.1 An Overview

In general, the new WTO ADA is 'a much more specific and detailed document than its predecessors'.[122] It particularly 'addressed some of the perceived shortcomings and abuses made possible by the vagaries of the old Codes and imposed more tight procedural obligations on trade authorities'.[123] However, before a close examination of the ADA starts, it has to be pointed out that the ADA, along with other covered agreements, is part of the political balancing between trade liberalization objectives of the GATT/WTO and WTO members' domestic concerns. The improvements on the level of legalization of the ADA did not successfully prevent AD from being the most important modern non-tariff barrier. As correctly observed, 'the concept of AD on paper might be disarmingly simple, whereas in practice, it is anything but that'.[124]

In total, there are eighteen provisions and two annexes in the ADA. Article 2 to Article 4 dealt three substantial issues, namely the determination of dumping, the determination of injury and the definition of domestic industry. By providing definitions to key words like *dumping, normal value, constructed normal value, sale below cost* and *fair comparison*, Article 2 sets forth detailed rules for determining the existence of dumping and the margin of dumping. To establish the existence of dumping, Article 2.1 requires 'a comparison of export price with the

120. *Ibid.*
121. *Ibid.*, 1537.
122. K. Steele (ed.), *Anti-dumping Under the WTO: A Comparative Review* (London: Kluwer Law International and International Bar Association, 1996), 3.
123. *Ibid.*
124. *Ibid.*, 6.

comparable price, in the ordinary course of trade, for like product when destined for consumption in the exporting country'.[125] If there are some situations, where no comparable price of domestic sale of the product in question exists, or domestic price cannot be relied on as the reference of comparison, Article 2.3 authorizes investigating authority to compare export price with constructed normal value of the product concerned, a price that does not actually exists, but is calculated by adding the cost of production, selling, general, and administrative (SG&A) costs, and profit.[126] Furthermore, Article 2.4 provides available methodologies available to investigating authorities in doing the comparison and calculating dumping margin.[127] Article 2.6 clarified the definition of 'like product' as either identical, or 'closely resembling' in case of absence of identical ones.[128]

Article 3 turns the focus to 'substantive obligations that a Member must fulfil in making an injury determination'.[129] Among them, Article 3.1 sets forth the fundamental obligation to determine the existence of material injury – a determination shall be based on both 'the quantity of dumped products and its effect on the price of like products and producers of such products'.[130] Although without a definition of either 'material injury' or 'threat of material injury', the succeeding paragraphs on Article 3 imposed more obligations to investigating authorities on the following issues: the determination of the volume of dumping imports and their effect on prices (Article 3.2), investigations of imports from more than one country (Article 3.3), the impact of dumped imports on the domestic industry (Article 3.4), causality between dumped imports and injury (Article 3.5), the assessment of the domestic production of the like product (Article 3.6) and the determination of the threat of material injury (Article 3.7 and 3.8).[131] This provision, similar to the 1979 Code, emphasized that injuries caused by factors other than dumping should not be attribute to dumping., However, it rejected the idea that 'dumping should be demonstrably the major cause of the injury' in the 1967 Code.[132]

Except for the first three substantive Articles, the majority of other provisions are dealing with procedural issues, investigation (Article 5), evidence (Article 6), provisional measures (Article 7), price undertaking (Article 8), imposition and collection of AD duty (Article 9), retroactivity (Article 10), duration and review

125. WTO, *United States – Anti-dumping Measures on Stainless Steel Plate in Coils and Stainless Steel Sheet and Strip from Korea* – Report of the Panel (Part 1 and Part 2) (22 Dec. 2000) WT/DS179/R, paras 6.90–6.91.
126. Article 2.3 of the ADA; also M. Matsushita, T. Schoenbaum & P. Mavroidis, *The World Trade Organization: Law, Practice and Policy* (Oxford: Oxford University Press, 2003), 316.
127. Article 2.4 of the ADA.
128. Article 2.6 of the ADA.
129. WTO, *Thailand – Anti-Dumping Duties on Angles, Shapes and Sections of Iron or Non-Alloy Steel and H-Beams from Poland*, AB-2000-12 – Report of the Appellate Body (12 Mar. 2001) WT/DS122/AB/R, para. 106.
130. Article 3.1 of the ADA.
131. WTO, *Thailand*, WT/DS122/AB/R, para. 106.
132. Matsushita, Schoenbaum & Mavroidis, *The World Trade Organization*, 326.

of AD duties and price undertakings (Article 11), public notice (Article 12) and independent judicial review at the national level (Article 13).

These procedural obligations are in general far more precise and less controversial than the substantive issues. The improvement of the level of precision of procedural standards offered great help to exporting countries when arguing their cases in front of the WTO panels or the AB. For instance, in United States – Hot-Rolled Steel, the US authority asked a Japanese exporter to submit evidence that was in the possession of its US joint venture. Since its request failed, the US authority decided to resort to a 'facts available' methodology because of the failure of the Japanese exporter to submit the required evidence, even though this was caused by the refusal of its joint venture to supply the information.[133] The AB ruled against the US, stating that the US was wrong in utilizing a fact-available approach because the Japanese exporter could not be considered to be uncooperative on the grounds of its joint venture's refusal to cooperate.[134] By refusing the US's interpretation of 'a cooperative producer', the AB required the trade authorities to act 'in a reasonable, objective and practical manner', which could mean closer adherence to the ADA's procedural standards.[135]

Part II of the ADA contains two important institutional provisions. Article 16 establishes a Committee on Anti-dumping Practice (APC), to which members are obliged to submit several types of notification, including Notifications of Anti-Dumping Legislation and/or Regulations, Notifications of Anti-Dumping Actions, Notifications of Preliminary and Final Actions and Notifications of Competent Authorities.[136] Article 17 concerning consultation and dispute settlement of AD disputes, is one of the most important, as well as controversial, provisions in the ADA.[137] In particular the sub-paragraph of Article 17 setting forth a special standard of review in the AD disputes brought 'serious criticism' towards not only the way that panels and the AB adjudicate AD disputes, but also the function of the DSM as a whole.[138] This provision, 'insisted upon by the US and accepted reluctantly by other parties as the Uruguay Round was coming to a make-or-break close' will be discussed extensively in the following section.

In short, the ADA continued the efforts of previous GATT codes to tighten and clarify the obligations imposed on investigating authorities in an effort to establish a fairly 'legalized' system.

---

133. WTO, *United States – Anti-Dumping Measures on Certain Hot-Rolled Steel Products from Japan*, AB-2001-2 – Report of the Appellate Body (24 Jul. 2001) WT/DS184/AB/R.
134. Matsushita, Schoenbaum & Mavroidis, *The World Trade Organization*, 311.
135. WTO, *Guatemala – Definitive Anti-dumping Measure on Grey Portland Cement from Mexico*, Report of the Panel (24 Oct. 2000) WT/DS156/R, para. 8.251.
136. WTO, Anti-dumping: Notifications under the agreement on implementation of Art. VI of GATT 1994, available at: <www.wto.org/english/tratop_e/adp_e/antidum3_e.htm>, last visited 4 Jan. 2005.
137. Matsushita, Schoenbaum & Mavroidis, *The World Trade Organization*, 331.
138. Lowenfeld, *International Economic Law*, 291.

3.1.2.2.2 Obligation

A central feature of the status of legalization of the ADA is the variety of its obligations. Although all obligations the ADA imposed on members are binding obligations,, the nature of these obligations differs, 'from resulting coercion, comity or even morality alone'.[139] Some obligations are specific and unconditional, which unambiguously require or prohibit certain behaviour of investigating authorities. Others, although worded to circumscribe their obligatory force, tolerate divergent practices of members. To a large extent, obligations in the ADA construct a continuum, from those that require specific implementations in national AD legislation, to those leaving great flexibility to national authorities in developing their own practice, as shown in Chart 4.1. Various degrees of conditionality and specificity of the ADA obligations influence not only the level of obligations of ADA, but also closely link to the level of precision of the ADA, as the following discussion demonstrates.

Chart 4.1 Degree of Conditionality and Specificity of ADA Obligations

Very Specific and Unconditional (for example, Article 6.1.1 – exporters or foreign producers receiving questionnaires shall be given at least 30 days for reply)	Detailed Rules but No Specific Implementation Required, Implicit Conditions (for example, Article 2.4 – fair comparison between export price and the normal value)	Contingent Obligations Subject to National Implementation (for example, Article 2.3 –'on such reasonable basis as the authorities may determine')	Very General Principles (for example, due process)

Chart 4.1 indicates that provisions in the ADA can be categorized as four types: unconditional and specific, specific with implicit conditions, contingent, and principle. The first group of provisions provides detailed rules that give national authorities direct instructions on how to conduct an AD investigations. The second and the third groups are fairly detailed. Nevertheless, in many situations it remains unclear from the wording of these provisions whether a particular decision or

139. K. Abbott et al.,'The Concept of Legalization'. *International Organization* 54 (2000). 401, 408.

action taken (or not taken) by an investigating authority during the course of an AD investigation is WTO-consistent.[140] The difference between the second and the third groups of provisions is instructive, rather than dichotomous – the third group of provisions may explicitly allow a competent authority to make decisions under special circumstances, whilst the second group implicitly tolerates divergent national practices. The last group of provisions contains general principles. The wording of this group of provisions makes normative claims instead of imposing specific obligations, such as 'sufficient', 'unbiased and objective manner' and 'due process'.

In general, the ADA articulates the substantive and procedural obligations in a different way. The majority of the substantive provisions of the ADA do not impose any specific obligations on the WTO members and thus do not require the WTO members to change their divergent practices.[141] It defines the key substantive terms in the first three provisions in a fairly detailed manner. Hence, most of the substantive provisions in the ADA can be grouped either into the second or third types. They play a baseline role in the AD regime: the ADA rules must be incorporated into domestic legislation, but those ADA transposed rules can be interpreted as the WTO members prefer. In other words, the substantive rules of the ADA do not instruct national authorities to act in any particular way.[142]

With respect to the procedural obligations, the ADA takes a different and tougher, stance. A number of the procedural provisions imposed specific obligations on national AD authorities, directly disciplining their behaviour. If those procedural requirements cannot be met, there is a real risk that the measures taken by the investigating authority can be easily challenged in the WTO DSM.[143] Most of the procedural provisions in the ADA are qualified as the first group. In the meantime, both the substantive and the procedural provisions can contain principle obligations, which 'inform' the rest of the provisions. Table 4.1 further illustrates the variety of obligations in the ADA.

140. M. Cetlan, 'WTO Dispute Settlement: Issues in Anti-dumping and Countervailing Duty Law', *Practising Law Institute/Corporate Law and Practice Course Handbook Series* 1075 (1998): 799, 828.

141. J. Kim, 'Fair Price Comparison in the WTO Anti-dumping Agreement – Recent WTO Panel Decisions against the "Zeroing" Method', *Journal of World Trade* 36, no. 1 (2002): 39.

142. The large degree of discretion of each WTO Member in AD regime has been widely discussed, in particular within the context of dispute settlement. For example, Cetlan, 'WTO Dispute Settlement', 804.

143. For example, if the investigation authority cannot conclude the investigation within the required time limit, it is very possible that, as a result, the measure might be challenged in the WTO. J. Czako, J. Human & J. Miranda, *A Handbook on Anti-dumping Investigation* (Cambridge: Cambridge University Press, 2003), 42.

*Table 4.1 Variety of Obligations in the ADA**

	Unconditional and specific	*Specific with implicit condition*	*Contingent*	*Principle*
Article 1	√			
Article 2.1		√		
Article 2.2		√		
Article 2.3			√	
Article 2.4		√		√ (fair)
Article 2.5	√			
Article 2.6		√		
Article 2.7	√			
Article 3.1		√		
Article 3.2	√			
Article 3.3	√			
Article 3.4			√	
Article 3.5		√		
Article 3.6		√		
Article 3.7			√	
Article 3.8				√ (special care)
Article 4.1		√		
Article 4.2	√			
Article 5.1	√			
Article 5.2	√			
Article 5.3	√			
Article 5.4	√			
Article 5.5	√			
Article 5.6			√	√ (sufficient evidence)
Article 5.7	√			
Article 5.8	√			√ (sufficient evidence)
Article 5.9	√			
Article 5.10	√			
Article 6.1	√			
Article 6.2		√		
Article 6.3		√		
Article 6.4		√		
Article 6.5		√		
Article 6.6		√		
Article 6.7	√			
Article 6.8		√		
Article 6.9	√			
Article 6.10			√	

Table 4.1 (Cont'd)

	Unconditional and specific	*Specific with implicit condition*	*Contingent*	*Principle*
Article 6.11	√			
Article 6.12	√			
Article 6.13		√		
Article 6.14		√		
Article 7.1	√			
Article 7.2	√			
Article 7.3	√			
Article 7.4	√			√ (as short as possible)
Article 7.5	√			
Article 8.1		√		
Article 8.2	√			
Article 8.3	√			
Article 8.4	√			
Article 8.5	√			
Article 8.6	√			
Article 9.1		√		
Article 9.2	√			
Article 9.3	√			
Article 9.4	√			
Article 9.5	√			
Article 10.1	√			
Article 10.2	√			
Article 10.3	√			
Article 10.4	√			
Article 10.5	√			
Article 10.6	√			
Article 10.7	√			
Article 10.8	√			
Article 11.1				√ (as long as and to the extent necessary)
Article 11.2		√		
Article 11.3	√			
Article 11.4	√			
Article 11.5	√			
Article 12.1	√			
Article 12.2	√			
Article 12.3	√			
Article 13			√	√ (independent)

Table 4.1 (Cont'd)

	Unconditional and specific	*Specific with implicit condition*	*Contingent*	*Principle*
Article 14.1	√			
Article 14.2		√		
Article 14.3		√		
Article 14.4			√	
Article 15.1				√ (constructive remedies)
Article 16.1	√			
Article 16.2	√			
Article 16.3	√			
Article 16.4	√			
Article 16.5	√			
Article 17.1	√			
Article 17.2		√		
Article 17.3	√			
Article 17.4	√			
Article 17.5	√			
Article 17.6	√			
Article 17.7	√			
Article 18.1	√			
Article 18.2	√			
Article 18.3	√			
Article 18.4	√			
Article 18.5	√			
Article 18.6	√			
Article 18.7	√			

* For the purpose of concise presentation, each provision is dissected to paragraphs and characterized as one of the four types of obligation. In exceptional circumstances, when an important principle obligation exists to inform the rest of the paragraph, a paragraph may be characterized under more than one type of obligation.

3.1.2.2.3 Precision

It is a popular argument that 'the current ADA is too vague or ambiguous on many key issues, leaving leeway to the authorities to interpret it in an unduly protectionist manner'.[144] This, in turn, causes 'inconsistency between different Members and

144. For example, K. Adamantopoulos & D. Notaris, 'The Future of the WTO and the Reform of the Anti-dumping Agreement: A Legal Perspective', *Fordham International Law Journal* 24 (2000): 30, 35.

consequent uncertainty for interested parties'.[145] In particular, the second and third types of provisions are accused of 'the main cause of the divergence of methods and modalities of national anti-dumping practices', which lead to 'greater difficulties in establishing a consistent and predictable AD regime' under the WTO.[146] A question then has to be asked: How do the ADA provisions create vagueness and uncertainty in practice, even if they have been articulated in such a detailed fashion?

In answering this question, an example – calculation of dumping margin in Article 2.4.2 – will be offered to illustrate how the 'precise' obligations on paper are interpreted by different investigating authorities in different ways, many of which can be hugely 'unfair' to exporters. In this context, the reason of lack in precision of this provision will also be explored.

According to Article 2.4, the existence and the degree of dumping are measured by the difference between the export price and the normal value, the so-called 'margin of dumping'. The scope of the final anti-dumping duty is based on the calculation of this dumping margin. The importance of dumping margin calculation in the administration of AD investigations lies in a simple fact: The AD duty cannot exceed the margin of dumping. If the dumping margin is inflated and 'spurious', exporters that are subject to the duty 'have to pay extra price for these fictitious differences between export price and normal value'.[147] Therefore, it is very important to have international rules unambiguously ensure fairness in dumping margin calculation, that is, to avoid that an investigating authority chooses among all available methods – the one that may result in the greatest dumping margin.

It is unfair to say that the ADA does not have detailed rules to address to this important issue. Article 2.4.2 is the provision that is devoted to this issue. It reads as follows:[148]

> Subject to the provisions governing fair comparison in paragraph 4, the existence of margins of dumping during the investigation phase shall normally be established on the basis of a comparison of a *weighted average* normal value with a *weighted average* of prices of all comparable export transactions or by a comparison of normal value and export prices on a *transaction-to-transaction basis*. A normal value established on a weighted average basis may be compared to prices of individual export transactions if the authorities find a pattern of export prices which differ significantly among different purchasers, regions or time periods, and if an explanation is provided as to why such differences cannot be taken into account appropriately by the use of a weighted average-to-weighted average or transaction-to-transaction comparison. (emphasis added)

145. J. Kempton & C. Stevenson, 'Agreement on the Implement of Article VI of the GATT 1994: Practical Problems and Possible Solutions', *International Trade Law and Regulation* 6 (2000): 6.
146. Cetlan, 'WTO Dispute Settlement', 804.
147. Kim, 'Fair Price Comparison in the WTO Anti-dumping Agreement', 39.
148. Article 2.4.2 of the ADA.

The wording of Article 2.4.2 is more precise than that of its predecessor. In the 1979 Code, Article 2.6 only required fair comparison 'at the same level of trade' and 'in respect of sales made at as nearly as possible the same time'.[149] In contrast, Article 2.4.2 specifies that normally, only weighted-average-to-weighted-average and transaction-to-transaction are allowed. The average-to-transaction comparison, a method accused as being 'inherently unfair', is banned except under circumstances of 'targeted dumping'.[150] Still, this provision is far from adequate to converge the difference between national rules and ensure a 'fair' comparison.

Some national laws allow the use of average – to – transaction method. For instance, the Czech Republic's AD law of contains a provision that 'allows the AD authority to use individual export prices in comparison with weighted average normal value'.[151] When the authority finds the weighted average-to-weighted average method is not applicable, they will have full discretion to make a choice among the other available methods, which may result in greater dumping margins.

Even where a weighted – average-to-weighted-average approach is adopted, there can be a practical issue for calculating the dumping margin where there is more than one type of the product concerned identified by the investigating authorities, as illustrated in *EC – Bed Linen.*[152] EC's practice before *EC – Bed Linen* was to identify a certain number of different 'models' or 'types' within the 'like product'. The weighted average-to-weighted average comparison was done on the type-by-type or model-by-model basis. If a particular type was not dumped, the negative dumping was zeroed and not able to offset the positive dumping of other types or models. So, 'when the EC added up the dumping margin of each type or model in order to determine the overall dumping margin for the product as a whole, the consequence of this zeroing was an increase in the resulting dumping margin'.[153] The EC argued that this was a practice perfectly utilizing weighted average-to-weighted average method, since Article 2.4.2 did not provide any guidance as to how the second stage of this method, that is, the combination of margins, should be put into practice. Nevertheless, this practice was found to be WTO-inconsistent by various WTO panels and the AB.

This example illustrates the problem of precision in the ADA: The complicated wording of the ADA did not narrow down the scope for 'reasonable' interpretations. Most substantive rules in the second or the third group were formulated as relatively general 'standard' rather than as relatively precise 'rules'.[154] Thus, although the ADA is highly elaborated, detailing a large number of conditions of application, spelling out required or proscribed behaviour in numerous situations,

149. Article 2.6 of the 1979 Code.
150. Kim, 'Fair Price Comparison in the WTO Anti-dumping Agreement', 41.
151. Kempton & Stevenson, 'Agreement on the Implement of Article VI of the GATT 1994', 12.
152. *Ibid.*
153. *Ibid.*
154. Abbott et al., 'The Concept of Legalization', 413.

an investigating authority can still make its determination *ex post* in relation to a specific set of facts.

Apart from the technical deficiencies of the ADA, the most important reason contributing to this problem was the fact that the ADA text is the result of a compromise between very different negotiating positions emerging during the Uruguay Round, which was put together at the last minute, as described in the previous subsection.[155] It is not surprising that the text of ADA lacks clear attitudes towards different practices between members. This is perfectly illustrated by the negotiation history of Article 2.4.2 of the ADA.

Before the Uruguay Round, the methods of comparing the average normal value to individual export prices were repeatedly challenged.[156] The GATT Panels in *US – Salmon* and *EC – Audio Cassettes*, however, did not take the view that Article 2.6 of the 1979 Code outlawed any particular method of comparing normal value and export price.[157] The exporting countries, including the Nordic countries, Japan, Korea and Hong Kong, therefore, made several proposals, intending to strengthen the requirement of fair comparison in the Uruguay Round.[158] They emphasized that the calculation should be conducted in a 'uniform and consistent', or 'symmetrical' manner.[159] They particularly argued that any differentiation in 'the method of calculation of normal value and export price without justifiable causes' should be disallowed.[160] On the other side, the US and the EC strongly resisted any changes in this provision in the direction of making it more restrictive to investigating authorities.[161]

In July 1990, a special Informal Group on AD headed by Charles Carlisle, then Deputy Direct-General of the GATT, released the so-called 'Carlisle draft', a draft 'temporarily hammered out the disagreement' between these two groups.[162] Regarding to dumping margin calculation, this draft advocated 'neutral methods'. The draft Article 2.4.3 provided that 'authorities shall in particular ensure that no margins of dumping are found when there are similar patterns of levels of

155. Adamantopoulos & Notaris, 'The Future of the WTO and the Reform of the Anti-dumping Agreement', 35.
156. Kim, 'Fair Price Comparison in the WTO Anti-dumping Agreement', 45.
157. GATT, *United States – Imposition of Anti-dumping Duties on Imports of Fresh and Chilled Atlantic Salmon from Norway*, Report of the Panel adopted by the Committee on Anti-dumping Practices on 27 Apr. 1994, GATT Document ADP87, November 1992, para. 474; and GATT, *European Community-Anti-dumping Duties on Audio Tapes in Cassettes Originating in Japan*, Report of the Panel (28 Apr. 1995) ADP/136 (unadopted).
158. Kim, 'Fair Price Comparison in the WTO Anti-dumping Agreement', 42.
159. The Nordic countries especially proposed that the normal value and export price should be calculated in a 'uniform and consistent' manner, while Japan argued that the Tokyo Code should be amended so that it could ensure symmetrical comparison of the normal value and the export price. GATT Submission by the Nordic Countries, MTN. GNG/NG8/W/64 (December 1989), 5 and Submission of Japan on the Amendments to the Anti-dumping Code, MTN. GNG./NG8/W/48 (August 1989), 5.
160. *Ibid.*, Japan's submission, 5.
161. G. Horlick & E. Shea, 'The World Trade Organization Anti-dumping Agreement', *Journal of World Trade* 29, no. 1 (1995): 1, 12.
162. Kim, 'Fair Price Comparison in the WTO Anti-dumping Agreement', 44.

movements of prices in the two markets'.[163] Unfortunately, when the final result of negotiation released in December 1991, as the so-called 'Dunkel text', the principle of 'fair comparison' was weakened therein. The Dunkel text dropped the expresses support for 'neutral methods', by which 'the price comparison would reflect the movement of prices in the domestic and export market'.[164] It also supported both weighted average-to-weighted average and transaction-to-transaction methods and explicitly departed from the Carlisle draft approach that 'normal value and export price shall, as a rule, be established on a weighted average basis'.[165]

To a large extent, the negotiation history of dumping margin calculation demonstrates the common situation of negotiations involving most provisions in the second and third groups of the ADA. Those negotiations almost always invoked debates between both sides. On the one hand, the exporting, or 'target', countries, advocated various changes that would reduce the investigating authority's discretion in administrating AD laws, mainly by codifying specific provisions and requirements for investigating authorities higher standard of fairness. On the other hand, the final outcomes of the negotiations were subject to repeated attempts by the EC and the US to legitimate their interpretations of AD rules and their established practices. Hence, the ADA has improved the precision of certain provisions, but overall, precision is hard to attain the level expected by exporting countries. There are always trade-offs in the negotiations and it is impossible to totally eliminate the discretion of national authorities. The imprecision of provisions in the second and third groups is thus not simply the result of a failure of legal draftsmanship, but rather a deliberate choice of the parties the Uruguay Round negotiation.

The imprecision of the ADA has, however, had mixed effects on the process of legalization in general and the development of the DSM in particular: on one hand, the imprecision of the ADA text affords the DSM an opportunity to push the level of legalization and to gain authority by clarifying the provisions. This, on the other hand, provokes heated debates about not only the interpretation of a specific ADA provision, but also the nature of the DSM and the desirability of the progress of legalization in the trade regime in general.

3.1.2.2.4 Delegation

The ADA in general has the most characteristic form of delegation in the WTO system. Article 17.1 sets the tone as 'the Dispute Settlement Understanding is applicable to consultations and the settlement of disputes under this Agreement'.[166] Although given the difference of language between Article 17 of the ADA and the DSU, especially in terms of standards of review, many, including

---

163. GATT, Report of the Acting Chairman of the Informal Group on Anti-dumping, MTN. GNG/NG8/W/83/Add5 (July 1990), 7.
164. GATT, *Draft Final Act Embodying the Results of the Uruguay Round of Multilateral Trade Negotiations, Agreement on Implementation of Article VI of the General Agreement on Tariff and Trade*, GATT Document MTN. TNC/W/FA, December 1991, Art. 2.4.2.
165. Kempton & Stevenson, 'Agreement on the Implement of Article VI of the GATT 1994', 45.
166. Article 17.1 of the ADA.

the panel in *Guatemala- Cement I*,[167] were of the view that Article 17 provided a coherent set of special rules for AD disputes the AB however disagreed.[168] The AB held that the special or additional rules within the meaning of Article 1.2 of the DSM shall prevail over the provisions of the DSU only 'to the extent that there is a difference between the two sets of provisions'.[169] Here, 'difference' was further interpreted as 'conflict', that is, the provisions of the DSU and the special or additional rules and procedures of a covered agreement are 'mutually inconsistent and cannot be read as complementing each other'.[170] The AB did not consider there is a conflict in the case of the ADA. Therefore, with a view to protecting the integrity of the WTO DSM, the AB ruled that Article 17 of the ADA does not replace 'the more general approach of the DSU'.[171]

However, certain special features of Article 17 are undeniable, even though Article 17 cannot replace the general approach of the DSU. Delegation in the ADA therefore can be divided into two parts: non-special provisions, namely Articles 17.1 through 17.3 and special rules, Articles 17.4 through 17.7.[172]

For the non-special provisions, the equivalent provisions can be found in the DSU or other WTO agreements: Article 17.2 has similar wording to Article 4.2 of the DSU; Article 17.3 is considered as the equivalent provision in the ADA to Article XXII and XXIII of the GATT 1994,[173] and closely linked to Article 26 of the DSU. These provisions delegate the same authority to the panel and the AB in settling the AD disputes as in other WTO cases.

Referred to as 'special rules', Articles 17.4 to 17.7 do not have exact equivalents in the DSU or other WTO agreements. Nevertheless, they still can be traced back to the DSU. For instance, Article 17.4 has a similar function to Article 6 of the DSU and was frequently read together with Article 7 of the DSU by both panels and the AB.[174] Although Article 17.4 specially refers 'final action' of three types of AD measures, that is, definitive AD duties, price undertakings and provisional AD measures, this reference does not in AB's view, limit 'the nature of the claims that may be brought concerning alleged nullification or impairment of benefits or the impeding of the achievement of any objective in a dispute under the ADA'.[175] Accordingly, the argument from the US in *US- US Anti-dumping Act of 1916*[176]

167. WTO, *Guatemala – Anti-Dumping Investigation Regarding Portland Cement from Mexico*, Report of the Panel (19 Jun. 1998) WT/DS60/R, para. 7.16.
168. WTO, *Guatemala – Anti-Dumping Investigation Regarding Portland Cement from Mexico*, AB-1998-6, Report of the Appellate Body (2 Nov. 1998) WT/DS60/AB/R, para. 65–68.
169. *Ibid.*, para. 65.
170. *Ibid.*
171. *Ibid.*, para. 67.
172. Appendix 2 of the DSU.
173. WTO, *Guatemala*, WT/DS60/AB/R, para. 64.
174. *Ibid.*, paras 70 and 77.
175. *Ibid.*, para. 79.
176. WTO, *United States – Anti-Dumping Act of 1916, Complaint by the European Communities – Report of the Panel (31 Mar. 2000) WT/DS136/R* para. 5.27 and *United States – Anti-Dumping Act of 1916 – Complaint by Japan*, Report of the Panel (Part 1 and Part 2) (29 May 2000) WT/DS162/R, para. 6.91.

that a WTO member could not bring a claim of inconsistency against national legislation 'as such' was rejected on the grounds that Article 17.4 does not affect a member's right to bring a claim of inconsistency against national AD legislation independently from a claim with respect to one of the three measures identified in Article 17.4.[177]

Article 17.6, the standard of review applicable in AD disputes, has been seen as the most controversial part of Article 17. This provision is more specific than Article 11 of the DSU, the commonly understood legal basis of standard of review in the DSU, and arguably, 'calls for more deference to domestic agency determinations'.[178] With respect to the factual standard of review, Article 17.6(i) requires panels to 'determine whether domestic authorities have properly established the facts and evaluated them in an unbiased and objective manner'.[179] At this point, an AD panel's obligation is not different than those of non-AD panels under Article 11 of the DSU. However, arguably, according to Article 17.6(ii), the established international rules, namely the VCLT, to interpret provisions of the ADA. When a panel applies these rules and finds that there is more than one permissible way to interpret a provision of the ADA, it must 'uphold the domestic agency's determination if it is consistent with one of the permissible interpretation'.[180]

There is a division of opinions among scholars.[181] Some argue that if one follows the first sentence of 17.6, there is always only one permissible interpretation. Therefore, the analysis is over and the second sentence of Article 17.6 has no meaning whatsoever. The opposite side insists that there are, in fact, situations in which 'there exists more than one permissible interpretations'.[182] In such circumstances, the panel and the AB are obliged to defer to national authorities' determination, instead of overturning them, even if they consider that better interpretations are available.

This single sentence of Article 17.6(ii) brought a wide range of far-reaching normative questions from the resistance to hegemony in the multilateral trading system, to the pragmatics of asymmetrical power in WTO decision-making and

177. WTO, *United States – Anti-Dumping Act of 1916 – AB-2000-5 – AB-2000-6*, Report of the AB (28 Aug. 2000) WT/DS162/AB/R, para. 74.
178. United States General Accounting Office (GAO), 'World Trade Organization Standard of Review and Impact of Trade Remedy Rules – Report to the Ranking Minority Member, Committee on Finance, US Senate' GAO-03-824, July 2003 <www.gao.gov/cgi-bin/getrpt?GAT-03-824>, (20 Oct. 2005), 24.
179. WTO, *United States – Anti-Dumping Measures on Certain Hot-Rolled Steel Products from Japan*, AB-2001-2 – Report of the Appellate Body (24 Jul. 2001) WT/DS184/AB/R, paras 55 and 62.
180. US GAO, 'World Trade Organization Standard of Review and Impact of Trade Remedy Rules', 25.
181. J. Jackson, 'The Varied Policies of International Judicial Bodies – Reflection on Theory and Practice', *Michigan Journal of International Law*. 25 (2004): 869, 871.
182. *Ibid.*

judicial branches.[183] The criticism to the panels and the AB's approach to apply Article 17.6(ii) reinforces, in another way, that the expansion of legalization in the AD regime is uneven and unbalanced. This issue will be discussed from different angles in the following sections.

3.1.3 Anti-dumping in the Doha Round

In 2001, the first new round of trade negotiations after the birth of the WTO, the Doha Development Round, was formally launched. The November 2001 Declaration of the Fourth Ministerial Conference in Doha, Qatar, provides the mandate for negotiations on a wide range of subjects, including improving the implementation of the present agreements, such as the ADA.[184] A good opportunity seemed to emerge to significantly enhance the level of legalization in the WTO in general and in AD regime in particular. Eight years later, unfortunately, there is still no definitive answer whether the Doha Round negotiations can improve the level of legalization in the AD regime.

In summary, three features of the Doha Round rules negotiations can be identified as: one, the restricted boundary; two, the emphasis on precision, and three, the divergent positions of parties. The first two features are intertwined in the sense that the restricted boundary of negotiations determines that members only emphasize precision rather than proposing fundamental reform that could change the current level of obligation and delegation.

The restricted subject matters in Doha rule negotiations are the first indicator of how little negotiations can do to move the process of legalization forward. From the beginning of the Doha Round, strict limits were put on what are open to negotiation.[185] Given the strong resistance of the US and the EC to open negotiations on fundamental issues, Article 28 of Doha Ministerial Declaration provided that negotiations were 'aimed at clarifying and improving disciplines' under the ADA, 'while preserving the basic concepts, principles and effectiveness of these Agreements and their instruments and objectives'.[186] This wording points out that 'fundamental concepts' of the ADA, no matter how controversial they might be, must be maintained and the only area of improvements is the effectiveness of the current system.[187] This strict boundary of negotiations disappointed many commentators as they considered that 'the effectiveness of the current system was a function of biased or cumbersome procedures in national institutions' so

183. For example, D. Tarullo, 'The Hidden Costs of International Dispute Settlement: WTO Review of Domestic Anti-dumping Decisions', *Law and Policy of International Business* 34 (2002): 167–172.
184. WTO, 'Negotiations, Implementation and Development: The Doha Agenda', available at: <www.wto.org/english/tratop_e/dda_e/dda_e.htm>, 25 Oct. 2005.
185. Kerr & Loppacher, 'Anti-dumping in the Doha Negotiations', 211.
186. WTO, 'Doha WTO Ministerial Declaration 2001' WT/MIN (01)/DEC/1, 20 Nov. 2001. Also available at: <www.wto.org/english/thewto_e/minist_e/min01_e/mindecl_e.htm>, last visited 25 Oct. 2005.
187. Kerr & Loppacher, 'Anti-dumping in the Doha Negotiations', 215.

that little meaningful reform can be expected from negociations concentrating on improving the efficiency of the existing system.[188]

The second feature, namely focusing only on precision, indicates that Doha negotiations are less likely to create new obligations for WTO members. At the beginning of every submission in rules negotiations, it is clear that the Rules Negotiating Group is expected only to clarify and to improve of the rules of the ADA.[189] Hence, although the issues that covered by rule negotiations in the past eight years were wide ranging they are within the twelve issues identified in Ramsauer Draft Text of the Uruguay Round.[190] Moreover, the issues contained in most members' submissions all have explicit linkages to one or more of the ADA provisions. In some of Friends of Anti-dumping[191] group's submissions, proposals are even organized in the order of articles of the ADA, rather than the order of priority.[192]

Finally, the US and the EC on the one hand, and developing countries on the other have significantly divergent positions in the rules negotiaitions. The US and the EC generally concentrate on increasing the strength and effectiveness of the ADA. The developing WTO members, represented by the Friends of Anti-dumping, who were not satisfied by the Uruguay Round ADA, were 'keen to take this chance to propose changes and negotiate over details of the ADA rules which allegedly disadvantaged them for decades'.[193] They wanted to tighten the discipline and rule out possible abusive interpretations of the ADA.[194] Consequently, most of the contentious substantive issues, such as 'public interest',[195]

188. *Ibid.*
189. For example, WTO, 'Identification of Additional Issues Under the Anti-dumping and Subsidies Agreements', Paper submitted by the United States, 6 May 2003, TN/RL/W/98; and 'Anti-dumping: Illustrative Major Issues', Paper from Friend of Anti-dumping – Brazil, Chile, Colombia, Costa Rica, Hong Kong, China, Israel, Japan, Korea, Mexico, Norway, Singapore, Switzerland, Thailand and Turkey, 26 Apr. 2002, TN/RL/W/6.
190. These twelve issues are (1) use of weighted averages in the calculation of export prices and normal value; (2) sales below cost of production; (3) constructed value: calculation of administrative, selling and other costs and profits; (4) standing; (5) de minimis margins of dumping and negative import volumes; (6) cumulation of imports from multiple countries for determination of injury; (7) sampling; (8) sunset; (9) anti-circumvention; (10) dispute settlement and (11) public interest, see Article 15.7 of the 1979 Code.
191. The members of Friends of Anti-dumping are Brazil, Chile, Colombia, Costa Rica, Hong Kong, China, Israel, Japan, Korea, Mexico, Norway, Singapore, Switzerland, Thailand and Turkey.
192. For example, WTO, 'Second Contribution to Discussion of the Negotiating Group of Rules on Anti-dumping Measures', paper by Friends of Anti-dumping – Brazil, Chile, Colombia, Costa Rica, Hong Kong, China, Israel, Japan, Korea, Mexico, Norway, Singapore, Switzerland, Thailand and Turkey, 28 Jun. 2002, TN/RL/W/10.
193. Kerr & Loppacher, 'Anti-dumping in the Doha Negotiations', 216.
194. WTO, TN/RL/W/10.
195. For example, Friends of Anti-dumping made the following proposals on public interest: TN/RL/W/45, TN/RL/W/174/Rev.1, TN/RL/GEN/53, TN/RL/GEN/142. Hong Kong, China made a further submission, namely Further Explanation of the Public Interest Proposal (TN/RL/W/194) on 17 Nov. 2005. Hong Kong, China and the Separate Customs Territory of Taiwan, Penghu, Kinmen and Matsu made a proposal on 6 Jun. 2006, entitled Economic Effects of Anti-dumping Measures (TN/RL/GEN/142).

'prohibition of zeroing',[196] 'constructed normal value'[197] and 'lesser duty rule',[198] are on the top of their priority list. The ADA provisions corresponding to these issues normally fell into the second or third groups of provisions as discussed in the previous sections, namely the ADA provisions only imposed unspecific obligations with implicit conditions or contingent obligations to the competent authorities. For example, one of Friends of Anti-dumping group's submissions noted that Article 2.2.2 lacked clear guidance on the information to be used in calculating constructed normal value.[199] They argued that such a failure to elaborate on a general principle leads on 'anomalous results' and proposed more comprehensive and representative criteria for the calculation of constructed normal value.[200]

On the other side, the US and the EC paid much more attention to 'transparency, predictability, and adherence to the rule of law' in order to maintain the confidence of the system.[201] The discretion enjoyed by national authorities when deciding major substantive issues, should not be taken away, in their view.[202] There is no need to dramatically change the substantive provisions in the ADA. Instead, procedural issues, such as Article 6.4 maintenance of a public record, Article 6.5 protection and disclosure of confidential information, Article 6.7 and Annex I conduct of verifications, took a large proportion of the US's submissions.

It is worth noting that although there is a contradictory general position between the developed countries and the developing countries, each member was concerned about some special issues in the negotiation. For instance, apart from the general procedural issues, the US has submitted proposals on some of the substantive issues such as the interpretation of domestic production on Article 4.1, causation on Article 3.5 and cumulative assessment of injury on Article 3.3.[203] The Friends of Anti-dumping group also addressed the problem of the expansive use of the exception of sunset review to continue the AD duty (Article 11.3)[204] and the arbitrary introduction of rules, procedures, and methodologies in the reviews

196. For example, WTO, TN/RL/W/6 and TN/RL/W/45.
197. For example, WTO, TN/RL/W/6.
198. For example, the issue of lesser duty rule has been discussed by Members in documents TN/RL/W/4, 13, 22, 25, 26, 28, 29, 34, 45, 47, 54, 55, 56, 62, 65, 66, 73, 74, 79, 86, 94, 99, 101,106, 110, 118,119,121,134, 170 and TN/RL/GEN/1,32,43,58, 99.
199. WTO, TN/RL/W/6, at 2.
200. *Ibid.*
201. WTO, 'Basic Concepts and Principles of the Trade Remedy Rules', Communication from the United States, 22 Oct. 2002, TN/RL/W/27, at 2.
202. Kerr & Loppacher, 'Anti-dumping in the Doha Negotiations', 216.
203. For example, 'Identification of Additional Issues under the Anti-dumping and Subsidies Agreements', Paper submitted by the United States, 6 May 2003, TN/RL/W/98, at 1–2.
204. 'Proposal on Sunset', Paper from Friends of Anti-dumping: Brazil, Chile, Colombia, Costa Rica, Hong Kong, China, Israel, Japan, Korea, Mexico, Norway, Singapore, Switzerland, Thailand and Turkey, 19 Mar. 2003, TN/RL/W/76.

(Articles 9.3, 9.5 and 11.2)[205] in their submissions. In other words, in the Doha Round rules negotiations, every member has some little issues in the ADA that they felt very strong about, which may or may not always link to their general positions in rules negotiations.

As a reflection on the collective effort of rules negotiations so far, on 30 November 2007, the chair of the Negotiating Group on Rules circulated his draft of consolidated texts on AD and subsidies and countervailing measures ('the Chair's text').[206] The purpose of the Chair's text is 'to provide a solid foundation for the future negotiation'.[207] This Chair's text allegedly has 'taken into account the interests of all participants' and is hoped to be a text that 'could facilitate the negotiation of a balanced outcome'.[208] Unfortunately, there have been great controversies surrounding the Chair's text reflecting the divergent positions of WTO members on various major issues. On most hotly debated one is the provision relating to the 'zeroing' methodology.

In the Chair's text, 'zeroing' in original investigations is banned if national authorities take a weighted average-to-weighted average comparison. Draft Article 2.4.3 (i) provides that:[209]

> 2.4.3 When the authorities aggregate the results of multiple comparisons in order to establish the existence or extent of a margin of dumping, the provisions of this paragraph shall apply:
>
> (i) when, in *an investigation initiated pursuant to Article 5*, the authorities aggregate the results of multiple comparisons of a weighted average normal value with a weighted average of prices of all comparable export transactions, they shall take into account the amount by which the export price exceeds the normal value for any of the comparisons.

Nevertheless, draft Article 2.4.3 (ii) and (iii) allow investigating authorities to 'disregard the amount by which export price exceeds normal value for any of the comparison' in case of transaction-to-transaction comparisons or in review investigations. Condemning the Chair's text as a 'step back', 17 WTO members, circulated their joint statement criticizing the inclusion of certain zeroing methods in the Chair's text, warning that this provision would 'nullify the results of trade liberalization efforts'.[210]

205. WTO, 'Proposal on Review', Paper from Friends of Anti-dumping: Brazil, Chile, Colombia, Costa Rica, Hong Kong, China, Israel, Japan, Korea, Mexico, Norway, Singapore, Switzerland, Thailand and Turkey, 25 Apr. 2003, TN/RL/W/83.
206. WTO Press Release Chair Circulates Draft Text on Rules, 30 Nov. 2007, available at: <www.wto.org/english/news_e/news07_e/rules_draft_text_nov07_e.htm>.
207. *Draft Consolidated Chair Texts of the AD and SCM Agreements*, 30 Nov. 2007, TN/RL/W/213.
208. *Ibid.*, 2.
209. *Ibid.*, Art. 2.4.3.(i).
210. Including the Friends of Anti-dumping – Brazil, China, Colombia, Costa Rica, Hong Kong, India, Indonesia, Japan, Mexico, Norway, Pakistan, Singapore, South Africa, South Korea, Switzerland, Taiwan and Thailand.

The debate is still ongoing and a revised text from the chair is expected to be issued.[211]

In sum, the Doha Round negotiations by far have not produced any results to significantly improve the level of legalization of the Ada. The ongoing negotiations involve almost every provision of the ADA, regardless of the nature of obligations. On the positive side, current negotiations that focus on clarification of relevant provisions may result in the improvement of the level of precision of the ADA. However, the restricted scope of negotiations and the divergent positions of parties would likely limit the impact the current negotiations might have on the status of legalization in the AD regime. Given the fact that, lack of specific obligation and consequently precision in the ADA are due to the divergent and frequently contradictory perception of AD rules of different members, rather than a simple failure of draftsmanship, the rules negotiations to produce a more 'legalized' agreement in the near future.

3.2 Surveillance Mechanism and the AD Rules

The surveillance mechanism, which is largely based on the activities of the WTO secretariat, is the most low-profile one among the three pillars of the WTO. One possible explanation for this is the self-declared status of the WTO – a member-driven organization that generally grants no formal power to the secretariat.[212] All powers are vested in the WTO members and they are reluctant to see the emergence of a supranational organization with constitutional rights. The WTO secretariat has therefore been deliberately kept as 'a slim organization with limited resources and formal powers'.[213]

The 'faceless' bureaucracy of the WTO that knows the process inside out, however, exercised considerable influence without formal powers.[214] The influence of the secretariat, although rather indirect, over the AD regime is a clear example of seven types of activities with a view to supporting implemention and administration of the ADA.

First, the secretariat influences the WTO members' AD practice in its efforts to review of actions taken pursuant to the ADA and notifications submitted by members. Under Article 18.5 and 18.6 of the ADA, members are obligated to inform the AD Practice Committee of 'any changes in its laws and regulations and in the administration of such laws and regulations'. The work of the secretariat

---

211. BNA International Trade Reporter 'WTO Members Discuss Services Conference; Doha Rules Chair Promises New Revised Text', 20 Mar. 2008, available at: <http://pubs.bna.com/NWSSTND/IP/BNA/itr.nsf/SearchAllView/259E1C65883BD6B1852574110071B0E8?Open&highlight=ZEROING>, 5 May 2008.
212. H. Nordström, 'The World Trade Organization Secretariat in a Changing World', *Journal of World Trade* 39 (2005): 819.
213. *Ibid.*, 849. The WTO so far has only less than 600 staff, including consultants, and the budget is roughly 160 million Swiss francs.
214. *Ibid.*

to facilitate the practical operation of the ADA is therefore not a 'one-shot' exercise, but a continuous struggle.[215]

The TPRM is another tool to regularly monitor member's trade policies and practices. A detailed description of the TPRM is provided in Chater II above. Anti-dumping, a rather sensitive area, has rarely been the focus of the TPRM. As the example mentioned in the Chapter II, from mid-1990, the US and the EU have entered into a sort of 'unholy alliance' not to criticize each other's AD actions in their public statement. Therefore, even though AD has been considered as the most serious protective device, there was no thorough treatment of this topic in TPRM reports for years.[216]

In-house research and analysis of international AD rules is another activity that the secretariat influences the AD practice of members. In general, in-house research has a relatively low priority in the WTO and 'little policy advice based on independent (self-initiated) research was offered by the secretariat'.[217] In the field of AD, however, the secretariat made serious efforts to clarify the practical aspects of ADA and promoted common or standard practice for investigating authorities. An outgrowth of this effort is *A Handbook on Anti-dumping Investigations*, written by three counsellors in the Rule Division of the WTO secretariat.[218] A handbook of this kind can naturally be considered as policy recommendations from the WTO, even though the authors, make their intentions modest, as being only to 'foster a great understanding of the process related to an anti-dumping investigation' and to 'assist investigators to conduct the required investigation in a manner consistent with the complex multilaterally agreed rules'.[219]

This handbook is divided into three parts, plus four annexes. Part I summarizes the procedural aspects of an AD investigation. Starting AT outlining the multilateral and domestic legal frameworks of an AD investigation and defining key terms in the investigation, the main part of Part I gives a full description of the whole process in chronological order, from pre-initiation, initiation, preliminary determination, final determination, to judicial and administrative reviews. In Part II, the focus moves to the calculation of dumping margin. Based on two case studies, this part goes through methodologies applied in the dumping margin calculation, defining the product concerned, identifying models, determining export price, determining normal value to calculating dumping margin. The last substantive part of the handbook concerns the determination of injury and causation. By providing a 'checklist' of popular injury factors and causations, this handbook makes an effort to further clarify what elements should be taken into account in the determination of injury and causation.

---

215. *Ibid.*, 826.
216. D. Keesing, *Improving Trade Policy Reviews in the World Trade Organization*, (Washington DC: Institute for International Economic, 1998), 5.
217. Nordström, 'The World Trade Organization Secretariat in a Changing World', 833.
218. Czako, Human & Miranda, *A Handbook on Anti-dumping Investigation*.
219. *Ibid.*

The first three annexes are also worth mentioning as they appear to be of practical importance sample applications for the initiation of an AD investigation, sample dumping investigation questionnaires for exporters/foreign producers and sample injury questionnaires for domestic producers, importers, foreign producers and purchasers. It is worth noting that a proposal jointly made by Japan and the EC in the rules negotiations also suggested the use of model/standard questionnaires in investigations.[220] The concern about divergent questionnaires is more than a coincidence. In practice, the excessive collection of information and data in the questionnaires translated directly into huge costs for parties concerned. Worse, these excessive costs do not only arise in relation to the preparation for the questionnaire reply, but also at subsequent stages of the investigation, for example, the preparation for verification and the actual verification visit itself. These sample questionnaires are intending to explore, in a 'soft' way, the possibility of applying more standard rules in AD investigations, which might be more transparent and costs to all parties involved

In a nutshell, although low profile, surveillance activities of the WTO, including overseeing the implementation and administration of the ADA, conducting trade policy reviews and producing policy recommendations based on in-house research, have positive impacts on the development of legalization of the AD regime. In particular, the handbook published by the secretariat demonstrated not only what the rules are, but also, in the view of the WTO, how they should work in practice. It implies the idea of harmonization of national AD laws although in a very soft way, and therefore may be of importance to future legalization of the AD regime.

3.3 Anti-dumping in the Dispute Settlement Mechanism

Anti-dumping is no doubt one of the most litigious areas of the GATT/WTO system. Some commentators depicted the picture as 'WTO panels are "making law" as if they were the Platonic Guardians of trade sitting in secret in Geneva and nowhere is this clearer than in the area of trade remedies.'[221] The number of AD complaints filed during the past decade, the ratio of AD complaints versus other types of complaints and the forceful criticisms to the AD-related panel and AB reports, all manifest the significance of AD in the DSM – not only in terms of quantity but also quality. This section focuses exclusively on the factual and quantitative side of the picture, because the underlying legal issues in relation to delegation in the AD regime has been discussed extensively in previous sections.

220. WTO, 'Proposals on Cost Saving in Anti-Dumping Proceedings', Paper from European Communities and Japan WTO TN/RL/W/138, 17 Jul. 2003, available at: <http://docsonline.wto.org/GEN_searchResult.asp>, 21 Jul. 2004.

221. J. Ragosta, N. Joneja & M. Zeldovich, 'WTO Dispute Settlement: The System Is Flawed and Must be Fixed', *International Lawyer* 37 (2003): 697, 751.

The first two statistical indicators of the importance of AD are the number of AD complaints filed by members during the past ten years and the ratio of AD complaints versus other types of complaints. Of the 391 complaints filed in the WTO from 1995 through 2009, about one fifth (77) of them challenged members' AD measures. The ratio of AD complaints filed versus other types of complaints has generally increased from 1995 to 2000, reaching the peak of one third (11 out of 34) in 2000. After that, the figure slightly dropped down to around one fourth. However, 2004 witnessed a new historical height in the numbers of AD complaints – 8 out of 19, as shown in Figure 4.1. The statistics of original panel reports that have been circulated to members from 1995 to 2008 show a slightly large ratio: 33 out of 121 cases are AD cases.[222]

Figure 4.1 Total Number of WTO complaints versus AD complaints Filed Per Year, 1995–2008

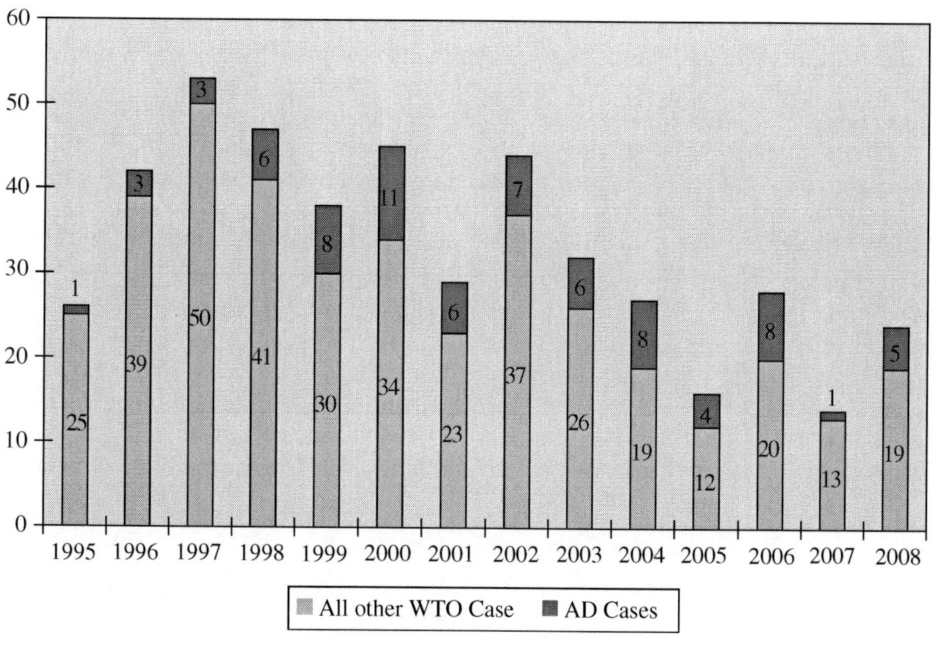

Source: Worldtradelaw.net Dispute Settlement Data

Given the considerable proportion of AD panel or AB reports in the total WTO panel or AB reports, some argue that the panels and the AB have invalidated a large number of AD measuresand consequently stripped away 'much needed protection

222. R. Yerxa & B. Wilson. *Key Issues in WTO Dispute Settlement – the First Ten Years* (Cambridge University Press, Cambridge 2005) 289 (Annex V). The panel and AB reports do not include Art. 21.5 compliance panel reports or appeals.

for domestic industries'.[223] The actual data, however, presents a different picture. From 1 January 1995 to 31 December 2008, of 2,190 AD measures in force worldwide, only 79 of them have triggered the initial step of a request for consultation.[224] Of all these consultations on AD measures, only 33 of these disputes have gone to final panel decisions. There are even less panel reports that have been appealed. Overall, members have challenged a relatively small number of the AD measures that their fellow members imposed and the vast majority of AD measures have never been challenged.[225]

The next indicator demonstrates the importance of AD in the DSM is the wide-ranging participants of the AD cases. The US by far has been the most frequent defendant in the AD cases, followed by Argentina and the EU, while on the other hand, the EU filed the largest number of complaints, as shown in Figures 2 and 3.

Figure 4.2 Most Frequent Complainants in WTO AD Cases, 1995–2009

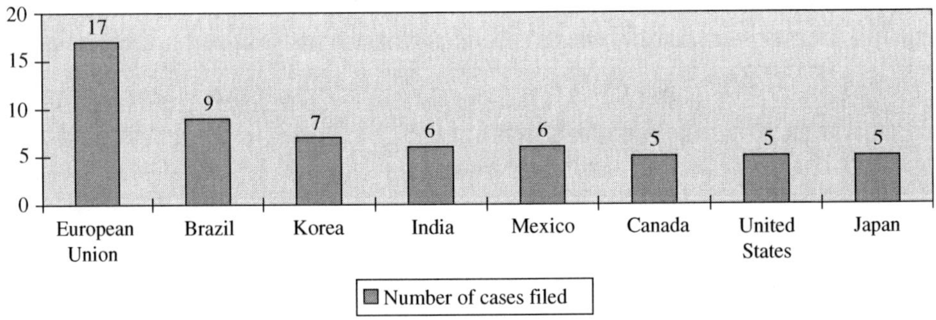

Figure 4.3 Most Frequent Defendants in WTO AD Cases, 1995–2009

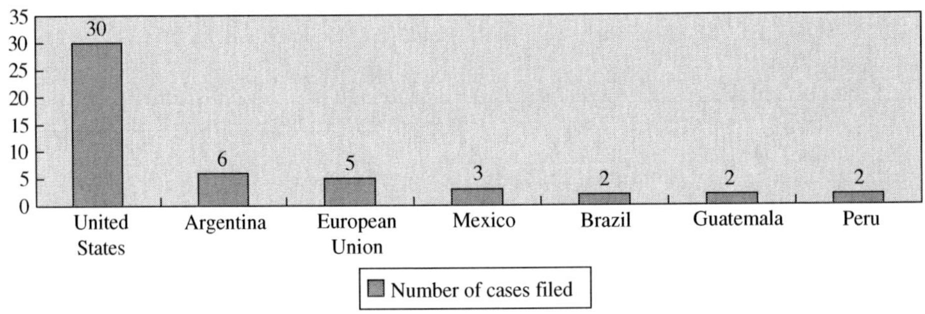

223. J. Durling, 'Deference, But Only When Due: WTO Review of Anti-dumping Measures', *Journal of International Economic Law* 6 (2003): 125, 127.
224. Statistics from Worldtradelaw.net dispute settlement pages.
225. US GAO, 'World Trade Organization Standard of Review and Impact of Trade Remedy Rules', 8.

Although the traditional users, such as the US, the EU and Canada, are fairly active players in the field, the variety of both complainants and defendants illustrated the popularity of AD rules. When Indonesia complained about Korea's AD measure on paper[226] and Bangladesh complained about India's measure on batteries,[227] it is quite clear that AD is moving from a politically sensitive north-south question to a rather technical issue.

Empirical research conducted by economists indicated that there are a number of factors that would determine the members' decision whether to formally challenge AD measures imposed by fellow members.[228] Given the huge amount of AD measures imposed, members 'have to undertake a calculus and only pursue actions in which the expected benefit to a WTO dispute will outweigh the expected cost'.[229] The expected benefit would be jointly determined by the size of import market and the probability of restoration of market access. The expected cost includes the resource cost associated with litigation, as well as the political-economic costs associated with the use of DSM to formally challenge a follow WTO member. Moreover, if 'the litigation were to establish a precedent that would also require the complainant to change the way in which it pursues AD in its own market', the potential complainant might decide not to pursue the case further.[230]

The final indicator of the significance of AD is the overall high success rate of complaints, that is, panels or the AB found in favour of the complainants in almost all cases (with the expectation of *US – Corrosion-resistance Steel Sunset Review*) on at least one claim.[231] This statistic alone may give an impression that 'exporting countries challenging the imposition of AD duties by other countries have prevailed in every case, so that the panel and AB decisions significantly changed the way that Members operate their AD laws'.[232] The reality seems more complex as widely observed. The following three factors portray a more comprehensive picture of the AD jurisprudence by interpreting the high chances of success of AD cases in a different way.

The first issue in assessing the WTO AD jurisprudence is 'self-selection bias at work'.[233] The time, efforts and cost of bringing a case and the potential embarrassment associated with losing a case means that members only bring those cases

226. WTO *Korea – Anti-dumping Duties on Imports of Certain Paper from Indonesia*, Report of the Panel (28 Oct. 2005) WT/DS312/R.
227. WTO *India – Anti-Dumping Measure on Batteries from Bangladesh*, Request for Consultations by Bangladesh, WT/DS306/1, 2 Feb. 2004. India and Bangladesh reached a mutually satisfactory solution on this case.
228. C. Bown, 'Trade Remedies and World Trade Organization Dispute Settlement: Why are So Few Challenged?' *The Journal of Legal Studies* 34(2) (2005): 515, 516.
229. *Ibid.*
230. *Ibid.*, 3.
231. Data from worldtradelaw.net. E. Vermulst & F. Graafsma, 'WTO Dispute Settlement with Respect to Trade Contingency Measures', *Journal of World Trade* 35 (2001): 209, 210; also, Durling, 'Deference, But Only When Due', 131.
232. Tarullo, 'Hidden Costs of International Dispute Settlement', 114.
233. Bown, 'Trade Remedies and World Trade Organization Dispute Settlement', 516 and Durling, 'Deference, But Only When Due, 129.

that 'they believe that they have the highest possibility to win'.[234] This explained why only a tiny fraction of AD measures faces the panel or AB scrutiny – only 'major and meritorious disputes' will proceed in the DSM.[235] It also explains that half of the time losing parties concede that their measures are WTO-inconsistent after the panel reports. Since the decision to appeal largely reflects the losing party's self-assessment of the strength of the legal claim and the significance of the loss, it is sensible to assume 'either that the losing party recognizes a WTO problem with its action, or that the WTO inconsistency can be easily changed in most of these case'.[236]

Second, even in these carefully selected strong cases, the individual claims of exporting countries are not always prevailed. So, the second factor indicating the complexity of the issue is the success rate of individual claims. If the panel or the AB's decision of each case has been broken down by claims, that is, each separate provision raised and addressed is treated as a separate claim, 'a different picture emerges contrary to the rhetoric that importing trade authorities always lose'.[237] As argued, 'it is true that in many cases, the panel found at least one WTO inconsistency; but the overall ratio of successful claim is only about 50%'.[238]

The third factor discussed in the literature, namely the different nature of the claims that the panels or the AB normally uphold or reject, is closely related to the success rate of individual claims. It is well documented that the panel and the AB reports completed between 1995 and 2005, frequently rejected domestic authorities' determinations supporting particular AD investigations. However, the reports upheld the vast majority of the AD laws and regulations that were challenged.[239] The major exceptions are three US laws: the Anti-dumping Act of 1916[240] and two sections of the US Tariff Act of 1930 – section 754 (US Continued Dumping and Subsidy Offset Act of 2000, or commonly referred to as 'Byrd Amendment')[241] and section 735(c)(5) involving calculation of the 'all other' rates.[242] As a US GAO Report recognized, 'very few other rulings so far resulted in many changes to WTO Members' laws, regulation or even uncodified methodologies and procedures of

234. *Ibid.* See also, Vermulst and Graafsma, 'WTO Dispute Settlement with Respect to Trade Contingency Measures', 210.
235. *Ibid.*
236. Durling, 'Deference, But Only When Due', 131.
237. *Ibid.*, 130.
238. *Ibid.*
239. Data from worldtradelaw.net.
240. US GAO, 'World Trade Organization Standard of Review and Impact of Trade Remedy Rules', 24 and WTO, *United States – Anti-Dumping Measures on Certain Hot-Rolled Steel Products from Japan*, AB-2001-2 – Report of the Appellate Body (24 Jul. 2001) WT/DS184/AB/R, paras 55 and 62.
241. WTO, *United States – Continued Dumping and Subsidy Offset Act of 2000* – Report of Panel (16 Sep. 2002) WT/DS217/R, WT/DS234/R.
242. WTO, *United States – Anti-Dumping Measures on Certain Hot-Rolled Steel Products from Japan*, WT/DS184/AB/R, paras 55 and 62. The 'all other' rate is the rate used to calculate AD duties for exporters and producers who are not individually investigated.

competent authorities'.[243] Instead, 'most of the rulings resulted in the onetime case-specific revision to, or removal of, AD measures, that is, majority of domestic agency determinations involved in these cases were rejected by panels or AB'.[244] Frequently, the panel or the AB reports affects the way a national AD legislation was applied in a specific investigation rather than national AD laws themselves. Even the US authorities, the most frequent defendants in the WTO AD cases, admitted that panel and AB decisions did not 'significantly impair their ability to impose AD duties, since 'most rulings did not question US methodologies for determining whether to impose AD duties but have required them to provide fuller explanations and justifications for their decisions'.[245] The US approach to panel and AB reports therefore has been to 'appeal those cases that require a change to a statute or have serious impact on domestic industries', and to work with the panel decisions in those cases when 'the WTO loss having only modest impact'.[246] The appeals often 'reflected the political need to continue fighting, as opposed to any controversial arguments about the legal merits of the claims'.[247]

The status of AD in the WTO DSM was manifested by both the frequency of challenges to national AD measures and the variety of participants of AD cases. The AB and panels have established an impressive record to stringently review AD measures taken by members. Some argue that the AD jurisprudence so far indicates 'an irrevocable trend to progressively standardizing the use of AD rules'.[248] Given the fact-intensive nature of AD investigations, the actual impact of WTO rulings on overall national AD practices is quite limited. In other words, although the DSM dramatically contributes to the increase of precision of international AD rules by identifying WTO-inconsistency in individual cases, it did not successfully achieve the 'standardization' of national AD practices. Moreover, the AD jurisprudence does not necessarily push the value of obligation to a higher level.

4 THE UNEVEN EXPANSION OF LEGALIZATION IN THE AD REGIME

4.1 The Uneven Expansion of Obligation

The discussion above focuses on the current status of legalization in the AD regime, whilst this section focuses on the uneven expansion of legalization in this area. Although certain topics discussed in this section have been touched upon previously, this section approach them from a different perspective.

243. US GAO, 'World Trade Organization Standard of Review and Impact of Trade Remedy Rules', 16.
244. *Ibid.*
245. *Ibid.*
246. Durling, 'Deference, But Only When Due', 133.
247. *Ibid.*, 146–147.
248. Vermulst & Graafsma, 'WTO Dispute Settlement with Respect to Trade Contingency Measures', 225.

In particular, it intends to identify the 'broken links' where uneven expansion of legalization prevents the AD regime from moving to a higher level of legalization and creates long lasting tensions in the system.

Obligation is central to the discussion of legalization in this monograph because the WTO is a treaty-based regime. The obligations in the treaties are the foundation of the system. A close analysis of obligation, which takes into account both the evolution of the formal legal instrument and the 'broader' obligations brought by other activities of the WTO, indicates that the development towards a higher level of obligation in the AD regime is unbalanced.

In the AD regime, the evolution of legal instruments, from GATT Article VI, the 1967 Code, the 1979 Code to the ADA, marked the major turning points that obligation in international AD rules was moving towards the 'hard' law side of commitments. The level of obligation after the ADA has been 'frozen' until the emergence of a new anti-dumping agreement after the Doha Round.

As noted in the previous section, the ADA in fact included four types of different obligations: unconditional and specific, specific with implicit conditions, contingent and principal. Given the interpretation and implementation problems caused by the second and third types of obligation in practice, there is a general trend to move as many of them as possible into the first group, as demonstrated in the evolution of AD instruments. In the ongoing Doha Round rules negotiations, most submissions from members, in particular the Friends of Anti-dumping group, are following the trend, and attempting to clarify the meaning of a particular ADA provision so that national authorities can be clearly instructed. For instance, in the discussion of constructed normal value, Friends of Antidumping group suggested to 'elaborate clearer, more comprehensive and representative criteria when calculations of constructed normal value are made'.[249] As the existing Article 2.2.2 allows investigating authorities to resort to three alternative methodologies for calculating constructed normal value and no clear guidance is provided, they went on to propose the following:

> clarify that the methodology as set out under the chapeau of Article 2.2.2 (i.e., actual data) should be used for determining the amounts for selling costs and profits; when such amounts cannot be determined on this basis, the amounts may be determined only on the basis of the alternative methodology provided for under Article 2.2.2 (i).[250]

One can imagine that if proposals like this are all included in the new ADA after the Doha Round, there will be less room left to national authorities to manipulate the AD investigations. 'Right' behaviour of an investigating authorityunder certain circumstance will be explicitly set out in formal legal instruments and fellow WTO

249. WTO, TN/RL/W/6, at 2.

250. WTO, 'Proposal on Determination of Normal Value', Paper from Friends of Anti-dumping – Chile, Colombia, Costa Rica, Hong Kong, China, Japan, Korea, Norway, Singapore, Switzerland, the Separate Customs Territory of Taiwan, Penghu, Kinmen and Matsu, and Thailand, 16 Apr. 2004, TN/RL/W/150, at 8–9.

members and private parties can legitimately expect them. If an investigating authority cannot follow these instructions exactly, its decisions may be easily challenged in the DSM and they have to change their practice afterwards with embarrassment.

A new ADA with all these specific obligations appears to be desirable to exporting countries that are targeted by AD measures. Two questions, however, must be asked: First, whether the current multilateral negotiations can make ADA specific enough to cover all divergent national practices; and second, even if it is plausible, whether the best solution is to improve the level of obligation in the AD regime.

As to the first question, the reality of Doha Round negotiations, however, does not permit an optimal answer. The positions of members are so different that it is almost impossible to reach a consensus on important substantive issues. If bearing in mind the broader picture of Doha Round negotiations, AD is a contentious area, but not the most politically important one. Therefore, the most possible outcome of rules negotiations will be a compromise or a trade-off rather than a careful drafted legal instrument to cover all practical questions, as experienced before in the Uruguay Round and previous rounds of negotiations.

If the only way of improving obligation in the AD regime is to create an extremely specific ADA, it could be worth the effort irrespective of how difficult it might be. General legal theory, however, suggests the opposite. As discussed in Chapter II, in a highly developed legal system it is generally desirable to have normative directives formulated as precise 'rules', but in many circumstances important directives can be formulated as general 'standards'. In those circumstances, 'determinations have to be made *ex post*, in relation to specific sets of facts, rather than to be decided *ex ante* which categories of behaviour are unacceptable'.[251] 'Standard-like' prescription allows 'judicial bodies to take into account equitable factors relating to particular actors or situations, albeit at the sacrifice of some *ex ante* clarity'.[252] Therefore, it is neither desirable nor feasible to propose a new AD agreement that is specific enough to deprive national authorities of the discretion to make decisions in relation to specific sets of facts and at the same time regulate every single practice of these authorities.

Consequently, another question must be asked: is the institutional context of the WTO legal system sufficiently thick to support the making of obligation beyond the ADA? Two possible routes emerge in the existing institutional structure of the WTO: first, the quasi-judicial bodies adopt an approach similar to domestic courts to effectively use general standards; second, the Ministerial conference and the General Council produce 'authoritative interpretation' under Article IX:2 of the WTO Agreement.[253]

251. Abbott et al.,'The Concept of Legalization', 413.
252. *Ibid.*
253. For more details of authoritative interpretation and general decision-making in the WTO, C. Ehlermann & L. Ehring, 'The Authoritative Interpretation under Article IX:2 of the Agreement Establishing the World Trade Organization: Current Law, Practice and Possible

The first choice has been widely discussed given the proliferation of judicial activities of the panels and the AB in the AD regime. Proponents of the DSM assume that the 'broader' obligations from panel or AB reports are in the making because the panel or AB reports can influence the same practices or regulations of other WTO members in the same issue. The arguments for it are normatively strong as a WTO member has the general obligation of conformity with WTO laws and good faith.[254] It is argued that good faith, including the general obligation of states to 'refrain from acts which would defeat the object and purpose of a treaty to which they are members', can find its way into the WTO jurisprudence as a general principle of international law.[255] One can therefore argue that if a particular national practice has been outlawed by the panel or the AB, it is a clear indication that this practice is WTO-inconsistent so that a WTO member has a duty to act in good faith by bringing its law and practice into conformity, that is, 'removing it from their laws and/or ceasing to apply it as a methodology'.[256]

The counterarguments are, however, equally strong, if not stronger. The formal mandate to the DSM is only to settle the dispute between parties and as such, a report only binds the parties, and only with regard to the case that was settled. Article 19.2 of the DSU explicitly prohibits the panels and the AB to add or diminish rights and obligations of the members.[257] In another words, a panel or AB report does not constitute an 'authoritative interpretation' to impose upon members obligations to which they did not agree.

A description closest to the current practice is that the panel or AB reports themselves do not create broader obligations based on the argument of good faith in a formal legal sense. A challenge of the same or similar legislation of a WTO member or a boldfaced application of the same practice in a future case, nevertheless, would highly likely to be 'won' if it is brought by other WTO members to the DSM. The picture is therefore quite complex: on the one hand, the case at hand does not have the precedent value; on the other hand, 'a series of complaints about the same issue would prevail if the cases were brought'.[258] A perfect example is 'zeroing' cases. After many rounds of challenge by different trading partners (including the EU), 'zeroing' is commonly considered as WTO-inconsistent in AD investigations.[259] By far, it is fair to observe that the possibility of utilizing

Improvements', *Journal of International Economic Law* 8(4) (2005): 803; also C. Ehlermann & L. Ehring, 'Decision-making in the World Trade Organization – Is the Consensus Practice of the World Trade Organization Adequate for Making, Revising and Implementing Rules on International Trade?', *Journal of International Economic Law* 8(1) (2005): 51.

254. For general discussion of good faith in the WTO jurisprudence, H. Zeitler, ' "Good Faith" in the WTO Jurisprudence – Necessary Balancing Element for an Open Door to Judicial Activism?', *Journal of International Economic Law* 8(3) (2005): 721.
255. Ibid., 730.
256. N. McNelis, 'What Obligations Are Created by World Trade Organization Dispute Settlement Reports?', *Journal of World Trade* 37 (2003): 647, 657.
257. Article 19.2 of the DSU.
258. McNelis, 'What Obligations Are Created by World Trade Organization Dispute Settlement Reports?', 666.
259. *Ibid.*, 647.

'zeroing' methodology in major trading partners has been largely obviated even without the amendment of the text of the ADA.

The second possible route to change the obligations in covered agreements without new agreements is the adoption of 'authoritative interpretation' by the Ministerial Conference and the General Council. Article IX:2 of the WTO Agreement reads as:[260]

> The Ministerial Conference and the General Council shall have the exclusive authority to adopt interpretations of this Agreement and of the Multilateral Trade Agreements. In the case of an interpretation of a Multilateral Trade Agreement in Annex 1, they shall exercise their authority on the basis of a recommendation by the Council overseeing the functioning of that Agreement. The decision to adopt an interpretation shall be taken by a three-fourths majority of the Members. This paragraph shall not be used in a manner that would undermine the amendment provisions in Article X.

From a legal point of view, the attribute 'authoritative' distinguishes the interpretation that results from this procedure from the kind of interpretation performed by panels and the AB.[261] Article 3.9 of the DSU makes the distinction clear by stating 'the provisions of this Understanding are without prejudice to the rights of Members to seek authoritative interpretation of provisions of a covered agreement through decision-making under the WTO Agreement or a covered agreement which is a Plurilateral Trade Agreement'.[262] In other words, an authoritative interpretation would be binding to all members and is possible to add or diminish rights and obligations provided in the covered. Although authoritative interpretation could not, without circumventing the amendment procedure, formally 'replace' a set of provisions in a covered agreement with a new or revised legal text, or develop completely new obligations, especially if the area in question was not previously covered by the existing agreements.[263] In other words, the authoritative interpretation cannot create self-standing obligations without a connection to the existing rules.[264]

One might consider that an authoritative interpretation could be a desirable candidate to 'develop' WTO laws especially in areas such as AD, where the existing rules are ambiguous or contain gaps.[265] This tool, however, has never been used to date. In practice, the term 'authoritative interpretation' is most frequently referred to in a negative sense to specify that some explanations, analysis or reports are not 'authoritative interpretation'. For example, the AB has, in a number of reports, referred to the exclusive authority of the Ministerial Conference and the General Council to adopt 'authoritative interpretation' in order to

260. Article IX:2 of the WTO Agreement.
261. Ehlermann & Ehring, 'The Authoritative Interpretation under Article IX:2', 804 and 810.
262. Article 3.9 of the DSU.
263. Ehlermann & Ehring, 'The Authoritative Interpretation under Article IX:2', 811.
264. *Ibid.*
265. *Ibid.*, 810.

distinguish it from what panels and the AB are entitled to do.[266] The only attempt of members to obtain an authoritative interpretation was the EC's request for an authoritative interpretation related to Articles 3.7, 21.5, 22.2, 22.6, 22.7 and 23 of the DSU in 1999.[267] The General Council however did not adopt the requested authoritative interpretation due to, *inter alia* the opposition of the US.[268]

The above discussion on obligation, both within the ADA and beyond, suggests that it is neither effective nor feasible to change all general obligations of the ADA to specific obligations and make the ADA an instrument to cover every single detail AD investigations. There are two potential tools available under the existing WTO system to, fill in the gaps in the ADA and create a network of legal obligations that allows a coherent application of the ADA – through the reports of panels and the AB or the authoritative interpretations. However both tools cannot effectively achieve this goal.

4.2 The Uneven Expansion of Precision

To a large extent, the discussion on precision is indispensable to the discussion of both obligation and delegation. As elaborated above, the basic function of a precise rule is to specify clearly and unambiguously what is expected of a state or other actor in a particular circumstance.[269] From Article VI of GATT 1947, enormous efforts have been made in multilateral negotiations to increase the level of precision of the international AD rules, with a view to providing detailed conditions of application, and spelling out required behaviours in particular situations. To regulate national AD practices by specifying expected conducts and narrowing the scope for reasonable interpretations has always been the underlying theme of multilateral endeavours. Hence, the development of precision in the AD regime is determined by the combination of the intertwined factors: how specific or precise obligations should be *ex ante* and how the quasi-judicial body would interpret them *ex post*.

Precision and obligation are tied together in the sense that the degree of precision of an obligation mainly depends on its function, that is, not every single obligation in a legal instrument is necessary to be highly elaborated or specific: Some obligations are 'intended be general or principal'.[270] Take the example of Article 2.4 of the ADA again. If 'fair comparison' in the first sentence can properly 'inform' the rest of the article, panels and the AB should be able to establish a framework to regulate the calculation of dumping margin – investigating

266. For example, WTO *Japan – Taxes on Alcoholic Beverages*, AB-1996-2 – Report of the Appellate Body (4 Oct. 1996) WT/DS10/AB/R, WT/DS11/AB/R, WT/DS8/AB/R, para. 12.
267. WTO General Council, 'Request for an Authoritative Interpretation Pursuant to Article IX:2 of the Marrakech Agreement Establishing the World Trade Organization – Communication from the European Communities', WT/GC/W/133, 25 Jan. 1999.
268. Ehlermann & Ehring, 'The Authoritative Interpretation under Article IX:2', 814.
269. Abbott et al., 'The Concept of Legalization', 412.
270. *Ibid.*, 413.

authorities may have the discretion to choose a method, but the method affect 'fair comparison' for the overall dumping margin of the like product. There will be no need to elaborate on every possible method that investigating authorities might apply in a particular circumstance., Instead, a network of obligations will narrow the scope of reasonable interpretations.

Another indicator closely related to precision is delegation. The reason that a highly developed legal system tolerates general principles, such as good faith and due process, is because it includes 'well-established courts and agencies to interpret and apply them with more much detailed rules, developing both technicality-intensive secondary legislation and increasingly precise bodies of precedent'.[271] In particular, if *ex post* judicial exercises are capable of coherently carrying out case-by-case interpretations, a certain degree of imprecision in general obligations is not only acceptable, but also necessary. To the contrary, if the judicial exercises are unable to rule out disfavoured conducts, drafters would be forced to be as specific as possible. Yet, the improvement of precision in this way might not be the most effective way of governance for reasons such as 'higher contracting and sovereignty costs in negotiations'.[272] In particular, the consensus-based decision-making mechanism in the WTO, the promotion of precision by way of introducing specific obligation may not be a feasible solution to resolve the challenges facing the AD regime.

In sum, lack of precision is a sign of uneven expansion of legalization in the AD regime and can only be resolved through the systematic improvement of legalization. The level of precision in the ADA cannot be improved by rules negotiations that concentrate on the details of specific provisions of the ADA alone, neither can it be improved by the reports of the panel and AB alone.

4.3 The Uneven Expansion of Delegation

The last dimension of legalization is delegation – the extent to which WTO members delegate authority to its political organs (the Ministerial Conference and the General Council) and to the judicial branch – the DSB – to interpret and implement the ADA.[273] Given serious allegations made against the DSM, members this independent quasi-judicial system, in which norms are clarified and thereby developed, 'has been left out without a political counterweight',[274] it is important to analyse the unbalanced delegation in the AD regime.

At the centre of the contention is a special standard of review provision – Article 17.6 of the ADA. As noted above, Article 17.6 is the only provision in the

271. *Ibid.*, 413.

272. K. Abbott & D. Snidal, 'Hard and Soft Law in International Governance', *International Organization* 54 (2000): 421, 434–436.

273. Abbott et al., 'The Concept of Legalization', 415.

274. For instance, L. Bartels, 'The Separation of Powers in the WTO: How to Avoid Judicial Activism', *International and Comparative Law Quarterly* 53 (2004): 861.

covered agreements in which panels are called upon to apply different (more deferential) standard of review to the interpretation of WTO law.[275] Many argue that under this provision, although a panel's (or the AB's) primary interpretive responsibility is the same as it is under other WTO agreements, broad discretion has been conferred to national authorities and panels or the AB are supposed to defer to their factual determinations.[276] The word 'proper' in Article 17.6(i) 'explicitly carries a considerable margin of discretion in terms of national authority's "establishment" of the facts and its "evaluation" of the facts'.[277]

The locus of the debate is the tension between two sentences of Article 17.6(ii), that is, whether multiple 'permissible' interpretations exist in applying the rules in the VCLT to interpret the ADA. Although the AB has accepted that there are provisions of the ADA that admit of multiple permissible interpretations, the US was still criticized the approach of panels or the AB as 'rendering Article 17.6(ii) a nullity'.[278] The US believed that panels and the AB have not accepted reasonable, permissible interpretations of the ADA. Instead, they used general terms in the ADA to 'extrapolate what the ADA has said about a particular issue', an approach that is inconsistent with the customary rules of interpretation.[279]

Behind this criticism, the underlying issue is what kind of delegation members have agreed when producing the final draft of the ADA. The real point of disagreement between the US and panels and the AB is the role of the ADA and the nature of a panel's (or the AB's) review. In the words of Ehlermann, the ADA gives 'national authorities the responsibility for investigating the facts and making an initial determination'.[280] The role of the panel is, therefore, 'confined to reviewing the investigation and determinations that have been carried out at the national level'.[281] This is obviously a top-down view of the ADA and the panel's review, as it emphasized the uniform application of the ADA and confirmed that the purpose of more intensive review is to make sure that in similar fact situations, the determination of every member to (or not to) apply an AD measure could be the same.

The US's view is quite different. Its underlying argument is that the ADA is only a bottom line for national practices. Beyond that point, something that has never been mentioned in the ADA is at the discretion of a member to act as it considered as appropriate. If one bears in mind the negotiation history of the ADA, that is, a compromise between members with inherent ambiguity, it is difficult to argue that the US is entirely wrong at this point. The deprivation of panel's discretion, however, decreases the level of delegation.

---

275. C. Ehlermann & N. Lockhart, 'Standard of Review in WTO Law', 491, 498.
276. *Ibid.*, 499 and 503.
277. *Ibid.*, 504.
278. WTO, 'Further Issues Identified Under the Anti-dumping and Subsidies Agreements for Discussion by the Negotiating Group on Rules' Communication from the United States, 20 Jun. 2003, TN/RL/W/130, 4.
279. *Ibid.*
280. Ehlermann & Lockhart, 'Standard of Review in WTO Law', 507.
281. *Ibid.*

Powerful members, in particular the US, also firmly opposed another kind of delegation: authoritative interpretation by the Ministerial Conference and the General Council. As previously described, this potentially important tool has remained completely unused, partly because of the US opposition of the EC request in 1999. This signalled that the US is against any kind of further delegation in the decision-making of the WTO, even as modest as an interpretation of existing provisions requiring three-fourths majority of the members. The major concern of the US was that its sovereignty would be undermined by amendments or authoritative interpretations 'forced through by quickly formed majorities'.[282] The US prefers a decision-making structure that contains an in-built preference for the status quo in order to keep its bargaining power would not be reduced in the negotiations.

The skepticism of the powerful members of delegation to political organs could seriously jeopardize the development of legalization in two different ways. First, without delegation to political organs, there is no distinction between rule-making and decision-making, that is, the making of primary rules and secondary rules in the WTO. This will possibly have the result that 'every single rule has to be made on the basis of consensus, regardless its specificity or technicality, and even an overwhelming majority of Members are not able to achieve what they want to decide if at least one Member maintains a veto'.[283] Under this kind of decision-making procedure, whether a breakthrough is possible depends on factors such as the political context of the question at issue and whether trade-offs are made. Hence, it is more difficult to tighten obligations or to improve precision of WTO agreements through the decision-making mechanism. Second, the under-use of delegation to political organs prompts more changes of rules to come from the judicial branch in an informal and allegedly 'inappropriate' way.[284] This, in turn, raises stronger criticisms to the DSM and creates an inherent legitimacy problem for the whole WTO.

To sum up, although it is commonly recognized that a higher level of delegation has been conferred to the WTO DSM, the delegation in the AD regime is unbalanced. Article 17.6 of the ADA specially generates considerable controversies, to what extent panels and the AB are authorized to review the factual determination of national authorities. The absence of delegation to political organs is likely to generate agreements that are made up of compromises rather than precise legal text in the future and stronger criticism to the DSM.

5 CONCLUSION

Similar to other regimes of the GATT/WTO, the multilateral AD regime has been significantly 'legalized' over the past sixty years. The development of legalization

282. Ehlermann & Ehring, 'Decision-making in the World Trade Organization', 62.
283. *Ibid.*, 65.
284. *Ibid.*, 71.

manifested in the AD regime echoes the general trend of legalization of in GATT/WTO. The AD rules have been a hotly debated subject of several rounds of multilateral negotiations. The evolution of legal instruments highlighted the movement towards a higher level of obligation in the AD regime. Also, several 'soft law' devices were developed in the WTO framework to improve the precision of multilateral AD rules and the new DSM of the WTO has been actively engaged in filling the gaps in the legal instruments.

The ongoing process of legalization in the international AD regime is nevertheless unbalanced in many aspects. A fairly large amount of obligations contained in the ADA are unspecific or contingent in nature and this feature of the ADA constrains the development of precision and delegation in the regime. Yet, the current negotiation, surveillance and dispute settlement mechanisms cannot support the improvement of obligation of international AD rules and therefore also limit the space of the improvement of precision and delegation in the regime. Similarly, unbalanced delegation in the AD regime results in greater controversies and further constrains to the process of legalization.

Chapter 5

WTO-transposed and WTO-plus Features of the EU AD Regime

1 INTRODUCTION

The previous chapter discussed the general increase of legalization in the multilateral AD framework, as well as the uneven expansion of legalization in the regime. The rise of legalization in the GATT/WTO greatly shaped the evolutionary trajectory of AD, originally a unilateral trade policy. This chapter examines, from an institutional perspective, the intended and unintended effects of multilateral legalization on domestic systems.

From Article VI of GATT 1947 to the ADA, the negotiation history of international AD instruments displayed the trading partners' general preference of a higher level of legalization – tightened obligations, greater precision, and stronger delegation. Surveillance mechanisms, mainly operated by the GATT/WTO secretariat, contributed to a higher level of precision in the AD regime and the harmonization of national AD rules, although those activities have limited impacts on formal obligation and delegation. The GATT WTO DSM ruled that a considerable number of national AD measures are WTO-inconsistent in the past sixty years, and successfully, albeit controversially, filled in some of the gaps between the provisions of multilateral AD rules. To a large extent, the improvement of delegation in the GATT/WTO advanced the level of precision in AD regime irrespective of whether multilateral negotiations generate new obligations.

The expansion of legalization in the AD regime is, however, uneven, as illustrated by fruitless Doha Round rules negotiations, passive activities of the WTO secretariat and bitter criticisms of the judicial activism of the DSM. In particular, many were worried about the predominance of adjudication and its potentially undesirable consequence.

This chapter examines how legalization of the multilateral AD rules affects national AD regimes, including the evolution of national AD legislation, the administration of AD policies and the judicial review of AD policies. As advocated in the special issue, the understanding of legalization at the international level has to be joined to its consequences at the domestic level by reflexive processes: domestic politics propel legalization at the international level, and multilateral legalization, in turn, shapes the domestic political process.[1] It is widely discussed that the WTO has never had at its disposal an overall regulatory framework capable of sufficiently securing the uniform, coherent, and effective implementation of its rules. The execution of WTO laws is by and large ensured by national authorities that enjoy institutional and judicial autonomy.[2] As discussed in the special issue, legalization at the international level aiming at providing predictability and stability in international trade may or may not have sufficient intervening effects on domestic policies.Following the analysis of the previous chapter on the development of legalization of multilateral AD rules, this chapter adopts a 'bottom-up' approach to enquire how the process of multilateral legalization affects the trade policies of individual WTO members in a formal way. It advances the general observation in Chapter II by exploring how an uncertain economic and political environment at the EU level interacts with the implications of multilateral legalization to shape the EU AD regime.

On the one hand, increased obligation, frequently joined by greater precision and stronger delegation, largely changed the landscape of domestic trade policy-making. Many norms and principles established by the multilateral framework have been transposed into domestic systems and enjoy high authority in the policy-making process. The 'WTO-transposed' provisions establish a framework that national authorities can operate within and to a large extent standardize the way AD investigations are conducted worldwide.

On the other hand, increased legalization is just one factor that interacts with other trade-related interests of domestic actors in the dynamic trade policy-making process. Interest groups with different agendas intend to maximize the possible benefit of domestic institutional settings by creating 'WTO-plus' domestic legal tools. In this monograph, the 'WTO-plus' instruments particularly refer to these practices of national investigating authorities that fall into 'grey areas' of the ADA, namely where WTO disciplines are either non-existent or ambiguous and therefore either unchallengeable or difficult to challenge under the DSM. The introduction of these instruments in national AD legislation enables WTO members to fully comply with their WTO obligations, while still retaining control over the outcomes of AD investigations.

1. M. Kahler, 'Conclusion: The Causes and Consequences of Legalization', *International Organization* 54 (2000): 661, 662.
2. H. Hehl, *Principles of Administrative Procedure in EC Law* (Oxford: Hart Publishing, 1999), 3.

This chapter examines whether the evolution of the EU anti-dumping regime confirms the general observation discussed in Chapter II. It discusses the development of WTO-transposed provisions (including WTO-modified provisions that slightly modified the wording of the corresponding WTO provisions) and WTO-plus provisions, in the EU system. It explores, first, how the development of legalization at the international level changed substantive rules of European AD laws and how EU institutions seek to integrate obligations imposed by the GATT/WTO into their own practices; and second, how the EU builds up WTO-plus features to offer a certain degree of flexibility to the Community institutions and balance European-wide interests. To analyze WTO-plus aspects of the EU system, it compares the EU's laws and practices with WTO laws and jurisprudence in this field, if any, and analyzes how WTO-plus features may change the result of an AD investigation.

This chapter proceeds as follows: Section 2 is devoted to the evolution of the EU's anti-dumping regime, by identifying the response of EU institutions and courts towards the development of legalization at the international level. Section 3 examines three main WTO-plus features of the EU system, namely injury margin, Community interest and anti-circumvention. Section 4 concludes this chapter.

2 WTO-TRANSPOSED FEATURES OF THE EU ANTI-DUMPING REGIME

2.1 EVOLUTION OF COMMUNITY AD INSTRUMENTS

2.1.1 Pre-ADA Community AD Instruments

The most striking trend in the evolution of EU anti-dumping instruments is that the EU always made its intention, to abide by the GATT/WTO AD rule, very clear. In most provisions, the EU basic anti-dumping regulations repeated principles of multilateral AD rules and were 'constructed by identity of structure and large similarity of vocabulary with international rules'.[3] This trend is also evidenced by the coincident appearance of new basic regulations or major amendments to existing basic regulations with new GATT/WTO AD Code or Agreement. As observed, '[T]he GATT negotiating rounds were the principal institutional motor of the periodic changes in EC anti-dumping law' and the GATT 'served not only as a negotiating forum, but also as a study group, mediator and interpreter of norms'.[4] This section provides a brief account on the correlation between the developments of EU basic regulations and pre-ADA GATT codes, that is, how the GATT anti-dumping codes made a 'decisive contribution to the development of

3. D. Pierre, *WTO Trade Instruments in EU Law* (London: Cameron May, 1999), 192.
4. F. Snyder, 'The Origins of "Non-market Economy": Ideas, Pluralism and Power in EC Anti-dumping Law about China', *European Law Journal* 7 (2001): 369.

EC anti-dumping law' The next section examines the role of the EU-specific factors, such as judgments of the ECJ, new accessions to the Community and the codification of the previous practice of the EC.[5]

The initial European Economic Communities (EEC) AD Regulation – 'Regulation 459/68 on Protection against Dumping or the Granting of Bounties or Subsidies by the Countries which are not Members of the European Economic Community'[6] – was adopted in April 1968. It basically translated the 1967 Code into the Community law and 'allocated the tasks of enforcing the new legislation between the Commission, the Council and the Member States'.[7]

This regulation can be considered a positive response from the EU to the first multilateral code dealing with AD. In comparison with the long history of national AD laws of other major trading partners, the EC established its AD framework on the basis of multilateral rules at the beginning. Internally, this regulation also confirmed that after the transitional period, namely since 1968, the Community institutions have exclusive competence to take actions in this field.[8]

From 1968 to 1979, namely, before the birth of the 1979 Code, only minor changes have been made on certain procedural points to the initial regulation.[9] With the accession of Ireland and the UK, the Commission has been empowered to amend or revoke national AD measures of the new Member States.[10]

In 1979, Regulation 459/68 was replaced by Regulation 3017/79 (the 1979 Regulation), as a result of 'incorporating provisions of the 1979 Code of Tokyo Round and codifying the practice of Community authorities and the judgment of ECJ'.[11] Moreover, Regulation 109/70 which set the rule for state-trading countries was repealed by Council Decision 905/79.[12]

Corresponding to the significant modification of the determination of injury in the 1979 Code, the 1979 Regulation first introduced new rules requiring only an indication that dumped or subsidized imports were causing material injury, instead of proving that they are the principal cause of injury. More detailed provisions on confidentiality and publication requirements also have been added into the 1979 Regulation, mirroring amendments made by the 1979 Code to the 1968 Code. Also, by way of codifying the practice of the Commission, the rules were also changed with respect to the determination of normal value of imports from non-market economy countries,[13] the construction of export price, sales made at a loss in the domestic market and allowances to be taken into account when

5. E. Vermulst & P. Waer, *EC Anti-dumping Law and Practice* (London: Sweet & Maxwell, 1996), 5.
6. Regulation 459/68 [1968] OJ L 93/1, Eng Spec. Ed. Series I-68 (1), 80.
7. I .Van Bael & J. Bellis, *Anti-dumping and Other Trade Protection Laws of the EC*, 4th edn (The Hague: Kluwer Law International, 2004), 22.
8. *Ibid.*, 21.
9. Regulation 2011/73 [1973] OJ L 206/3.
10. Regulation 1411/77 [1977] OJ L 160/4.
11. Van Bael & Bellis, *Anti-dumping and Other Trade Protection Laws of the EC*, 22–23.
12. Regulation 905/79 [1979] OJ L 277/10.
13. For details of the origin of non-market economy provisions in the EC, see Snyder, 'The Origins of "Non-market Economy"', 369.

comparing the normal value and the export price.[14] Finally, the amendments to Regulation 489/68 also reflected the European Court of Justice's (ECJ's) ruling in the first ECJ judgment in the AD field, the *Ball Bearings* case.[15] In this case, the opinion of Advocate General Warner that private parties should be given the right to have access to the information used against them was accepted by the ECJ.[16] Accordingly, this principle was incorporated into the 1979 Regulation.

Before the conclusion of the Uruguay Round, the EU anti-dumping rules experienced two more major amendments in 1984 and 1988. In July 1984, Regulation 3017/79 was replaced by Regulation 2176/84.[17] A 'sunset clause' was inserted into the text, providing for the automatic termination of measures five years after the imposition of measures, or five years after last modification or confirmation of measures. Other revisions included a clarification of the meaning of production cost for the purpose of calculating constructed normal value, and the treatment of sales not in the ordinary course of trade.[18] In 1988, Regulation 2423/88 replaced Regulation 2176/84. Additional rules were introduced to clarify or modify the prior practice of the Commission in Regulation 2423/88. For example, the anti-absorption duty, that is, 'the possibility of increasing the duty where it was proven that the exporter bore the cost of it', was introduced.[19] The rules concerning the treatment of discounts and rebates when the normal value and the export price was determined on the basis of price actually paid were clarified.[20]

At the time that the ADA was born, the EU first amended Regulation 2423/88 on the points of decision-making and time limits and then replaced it with Regulation 3283/94,[21] which both consolidated all previous amendments and incorporated provisions of the ADA. The 1994 Regulation was further amended by Regulation 1251/95 to incorporate changes into the ADA in relation to the time limit of the investigation. A consolidated version, incorporating amendments to Regulation 3283/94 as well as certain linguistic changes, was published in March 1996 as Regulation 384/96, the 'Basic Regulation', that is currently applicable.[22] The adoption of the Basic Regulation marked the establishment of the first completely separate AD legislation in the Community law from the anti-subsidy legislation.

Most commentators agreed that the Basic Regulation closely followed the text of the ADA.[23] It follows the structure and provisions of the ADA as far as to adopt most of its terminologies. The EU's approach was 'to transpose the language of the

14. Van Bael & Bellis, *Anti-dumping and Other Trade Protection Laws of the EC*, 23.
15. Case 113/77, *NTN Toyo Bearing Company Ltd and others v. Council of European Communities* [1979] ECR 1185.
16. *Ibid.*, 1212.
17. Regulation 2176/84 [1984] OJ L 201/1, corrected at [1984] OJ L227/35.
18. *Ibid.*
19. Van Bael & Bellis, *Anti-dumping and Other Trade Protection Laws of the EC*, 24.
20. *Ibid.*
21. Regulation 3283/94 [1994] OJ L 349/1, as amended by Council Regulation 355/95 [1995] OJ L 41/2.
22. Van Bael & Bellis, *Anti-dumping and Other Trade Protection Laws of the EC*, 25.
23. For example, Pierre, *WTO Trade Instruments in EU Law*, 18–19 and Van Bael and Bellis, *Anti-dumping and Other Trade Protection Laws of the EC*, 25.

1994 Agreement into the Community legislation to the extent possible and for this purpose, the Agreement, rather than the existing Community legislation . . . has been taken as the basis for the proposed Regulation'. The EU's approach is obviously different from the US approach – the US legislators only modified the existing law where necessary for the purpose of incorporating the ADA to its domestic legislation.[24]

There are, however, a number of areas that the Commission considered as necessary to make additions to the ADA text to meet EU policy demands, which are referred to as 'WTO-plus' provisions in this monograph.[25] The EU's approach has been described in the Commission's Explanatory Memorandum as:[26]

> Additions to the Agreement are few and they have, for the most part, been described to: clarifications where the Agreement is unclear; incorporation of existing provisions on EU's rather unique procedures and decision making, amended to take account of Court judgments; and the amendment or incorporation of EU specific rules on issues such as negligible import volumes, absorption, circumvention and Community interest, on which the Agreement is silent, imprecise or where it merely gives and indication of minima.

The main character of the Basic Regulation – transposing most provisions in the ADA into the Basic Regulation, but adding the Commission's own understanding when necessarily– can be better understood in the context of the process that led to the adoption of these rules. The Community legislative process of the Basic Regulation can be divided into two stages.[27] In December 1994, the Council unanimously approved the results of the Uruguay Round negotiation, including the new ADA.[28] The adoption of the ADA, nevertheless, was followed by two additional conditions: the introduction of a statutory time-limit for an anti-dumping investigation and a reform of the decision-making procedure in the Council – from qualified majority to simply majority, although the latter did not happen immediately following the adoption of the ADA. Both conditions reflected the wish of a number of more protectionist Member States to strengthen the efficiency of the Community's trade deference instruments.[29] Southern Member States, in particular France, considered that the requirement of a qualified majority was 'excessively heavy'. After the accession of Scandinavian countries in 1995, France and other southern Member States were concerned that 'the free-trade camp

24. Uruguay Round Agreements Act, H.R. 5110, 103rd Congress, 2d session, 807.
25. M. Clough & F. Randolph, 'Recent Developments in EC Anti-dumping Practice and the GATT', in *The European Union and World Trade Law – After the GATT Uruguay Round*, ed. N. Emiliou & D. O'Keeffe (Chichester: John Wiley & Sons, 1996), 226.
26. COM (94) (414 find).
27. W. Müller, N. Khan & H. Neumann, *EC Anti-dumping Law – A Commentary on Regulation 384/96* (Chichester: John Wiley & Sons, 1998), 20.
28. Council Decision (of 22 Dec. 1994) concerning the conclusion on behalf of the European Community, as regards matters within its competence, of the agreements reached in the Uruguay Round multilateral negotiations (1986–1994), OJ L 336, 23.12.1994, 1–2.
29. *Ibid.*

comprising the UK, the Netherlands, Germany and Denmark would be reinforced and that an increasing number of AD measures would be defeated through lobbying Member States'.[30] France therefore 'made its approval of the Uruguay Round package conditional upon this amendment of the decision-making system'.[31] Other Member States finally agreed France's condition and the simply majority became the decision-making procedure in the Council for anti-dumping regulations.

In the second half of 1994, the discussion of the Commission's proposal for a new Basic Regulation again drew the attention of both sides. This time, 'the new formula for the Community interest test and the reformulated anti-circumvention provisions' became the most controversial topics.[32] On the issue of the Community interest, MSs were divided into two camps again: southern Member States were concerned that the adoption of a Community interest test could 'lead to a general paralysis of AD actions'; whilst northern Member States opposed amended provisions given the silence of the ADA in this area.[33] Therefore, the final Commission proposal was a trade-off and a solution full of compromises.

In sum, from 1968, the evolution of the EU anti-dumping law could be characterized by the mixture of the transposition of multilateral rules and compromises between interests of different European players including the Member States and the Community institutions. Corresponding to the developments of multilateral rules, a high degree of obligation and precision in substantive rules and a strong emphasis on procedural requirements can be identified in the evolution of the EU basic regulations. The Community institutions, in particular the Commission, have been vested with greater powers and finally taken the 'driving seat' in anti-dumping proceedings.

2.1.2 An Overview of Regulation 384/96 (the Basic Regulation)[34]

As indicated above, the Basic Regulation has an identical structure to the ADA. The Basic Regulation's alignment with the ADA was, on the one hand, generally considered as 'an improvement against the practice prior to the Uruguay Round'.[35] On the other hand, the Community institutions have made efforts to preserve its practices, by either multilateralizing these practices or slightly altering the wording of ADA. It is worth noting that in the Uruguay Round (indeed in all past GATT rounds), the EC, as one of the most powerful trading partners, has essentially

30. Van Bael & Bellis, *Anti-dumping and Other Trade Protection Laws of the EC*, 24.
31. *Ibid.*
32. Müller et al., *EC Anti-dumping Law*, 20.
33. *Ibid.*
34. Council Regulation (EC) No. 384/96 of 22 Dec. 1995 on protection against dumped imports from countries not members of the European Community, OJ L 56/1, 6 Mar. 1996, as amended by Council Regulation (EC) No. 2331/96 of 2 Dec. 1996, OJ L 317/1, 6 Dec. 1996; Council Regulation (EC) No. 905/98 of 27 Apr. 1998, OJ L 128/18, 30 Apr. 1998; Council Regulation (EC) No. 2238/2000 of 9 Oct. 2000, OJ L 257/2, 11 Oct. 2000; Council Regulation (EC) No. 1972/2002 of 5 Nov. 2002, OJ L 305/1, 7 Nov. 2002; Council Regulation (EC) No. 461/2004 of 8 Mar. 2004, OJ L 77/12, 13 Mar. 2004 and Council Regulation (EC) No. 2117/2005 of 21 Dec. 2005, OJ L 340/17, 23 Dec. 2005.
35. Pierre, *WTO Trade Instruments in EU Law*, 33.

succeeded in molding multilateral rules to legitimize its own system, that is, successfully multilateralized various EC practices.[36] This section explains how the Community institutions try to transpose the ADA rules and keep the existing practice alive at the same time.

The first eleven articles of the Basic Regulation were essentially reproduced from the ADA, with slight differences in titles and wording. These articles, referred to as 'WTO-transposed', include rules concerning the determination of dumping, the determination of injury, the definition of Community industry, the initiation of the proceeding, the procedure of investigation, provisional measures, undertakings, retroactivity, the duration of the measure, reviews, and refunds. From Article 12 to Article 24, the Basic Regulation established additional rules, such as, anti-absorption (Article 12), anti-circumvention (Article 13) and the Community interest test (Article 21), which are rather unique for the EU (i.e., the 'WTO-plus' provisions). The only exception is that the EU's non-market economy rule is provided in Article 2(7) of the Basic Regulation.

Many argue that the Basic Regulation does 'not faithfully transpose the WTO rules', on a number of issues.[37] As will be demonstrated below, the transposition of the ADA in the first eleven articles of the Basic Regulation does not necessarily represent a faithful implementation of multilateral rules. Even a tiny dissimilitude between the Basic Regulation and the ADA can make a huge difference in practice. This section, offers two examples to illustrate how WTO-transposed or WTO-modified provisions work in practice.

The first example is the Commission's practice on the computation of selling, general and administrative cost (SG&A) and profit in constructed normal value (CNY). As a subsidiary means of establishing the normal value, the CNV can be calculated if neither the exporter's own domestic prices nor the domestic price of other producers in the exporting country concerned can be used.[38] A CNV of the like product consists of unit costs of manufacture (fixed and variable) in the country of origin plus a reasonable amount of SG&A and profits. Alternatively, instead of CNV, the Commission is allowed to use export prices to a third country as the basis of normal value.[39] In practice, the Commission rarely uses third country exports to determine the normal value.[40] Instead, it routinely establishes very detailed product control numbers (PCNs) in order to compare identical models or types for the purpose of dumping and injury margin calculation. As a result, in virtually every EU anti-dumping investigation, the CNV will be calculated for one or more PCNs. The methodology utilized by the Commission in the calculation of CNV is thus of significance to exporters as it can make a great difference in dumping margins and final AD duties.

---

36. E. Vermulst, 'The 10 Major Problems with the Anti-dumping Instrument in the European Community', *Journal of World Trade* 39 (2005): 105, 107.
37. Van Bael & Bellis, *Anti-dumping and Other Trade Protection Laws of the EC*, 25.
38. Pierre, *WTO Trade Instruments in EU Law*, 84.
39. Article 2(3) of the Basic Regulation.
40. Pierre, *WTO Trade Instruments in EU Law*, 84.

Article 2(6) of the Basic Regulation sets out the rule governing the calculation of one element of normal value, namely the amount of SGA and profits. It outlined four different methods for calculating SGA expenses and the margin of profit. First, as a general rule, the amount of SGA and profits 'shall be based on the actual data pertaining to production and sales, in the ordinary course of trade, of like product, by the exporter or producer under investigation'.[41] If such amounts 'cannot be determined on this basis', the second method may be applied – namely 'the weighted average of the actual amounts determined for other exporters or producers subject to the investigation in respect of production and sales of the like product in the domestic market of the country of origin'.[42] If both of the above methods are not feasible to be used, a third method can be applied by resorting to 'the actual amounts applicable to production and sales, in the ordinary course of trade, of the same general category of products for the exporter or producer in question in the domestic market of the country of origin'.[43] Finally, 'any other reasonable method' can be used, provided that 'the amount of profit so established shall not exceed the profit normally realized by other exporters or producers on sales of products of the same general category in the domestic market of the country of origin'.[44]

Article 2(6) is based on Article 2.2.2 of the ADA, while several changes have been made in the text of this article in comparison with that of Article 2.2.2 of.[45] The first one is the different order of alternative methods. Article 2.2.2 of the ADA listed four methods as well, but putting the third method before the second. This change in the Basic Regulation is considered as 'a signal of the preference for the method in practice. Although no strict legal hierarchy is imposed, the order set out in the Basic Regulation is followed, unless there exists good reasons to the contrary.[46] This codification of previous practices of the Commission is arguably justified on the grounds that there is no hierarchy of the four methods set out in Article 2.2.2, so that 'a degree of flexibility was deliberately reserved for implementing authorities to choose the method which most accurately reflects the expenditure incurred'.[47]

Other changes to the text are neverthless more controversial. For example, whilst Article 2.2.2 of the ADA refers to 'actual costs incurred and realized by other exporters or producers', Article 2(6)(a) uses the wording 'actual amount *determined* for other exporters or producers', clearly indicating that the amount to be used is the same as those which have been determined by the Commission for such exporters. As correctly observed, this change in the wording is 'less innocent' than it looks: 'the amount of SGA and profits determined by the Commission for other exporters will normally be computed on the basis of sales made by the

41. Chapeau of Art. 2 (6) of the Basic Regulation.
42. Article 2(6)(a) of the Basic Regulation.
43. Article 2(6)(b) of the Basic Regulation.
44. Article 2(6)(c) of the Basic Regulation.
45. Van Bael & Bellis, *Anti-dumping and Other Trade Protection Laws of the EC*, 73–74.
46. Pierre, *WTO Trade Instruments in EU Law*, 97.
47. *Ibid.*

exporters in question "in the ordinary course of trade", that is, on the basis of profitable sales only', whilst Article 2.2.2(ii) does not contain such a discrimination.[48] This issue has been addressed by the AB in *EC – Bed Linen*.[49] The AB ruled that an investigating authority could not exclude sales that were not made in the ordinary course of trade when calculating the amount of SGA and profit pursuant to the weighted-average method.[50]

Apart from being inconsistent with the text of Article 2.2.2(i), the addition of 'in the ordinary course of trade' in Article 2(6)(b) makes 'little sense' since the provision refers to SG&A and profits related to the production and sale of the 'same general category of products' in the domestic market of the country of origin as observed. In the absence of detailed model-by-model cost of production data for the general category of products comprising the like product (because detailed cost of production information will only be available for the like product), 'it will be impossible to identify which sales of products within that general category are or are not in the ordinary course of trade'.[51] Consequently, the calculation of CNV according to Article 2(6) is arguably 'unpredictable and arbitrary'.[52]

The second example is the usage of 'zeroing' in the scenario of 'targeted dumping'. 'Target dumping' is normally referring to the situation described in the second sentence of Article 2.4.2 of the ADA, that is, 'a pattern of export prices which differ significantly among different purchasers, regions or time periods'. Article 2.4.2 allows the national authorities to utilize a weighted-average-to-individual-transaction methodology in cases of targeted dumping, provided that there is a reasonable explanation why other methods cannot appropriately establish the dumping margin in such circumstances.

The second sentence of Article 2.4.2 reads as follows:[53]

> A normal value established on **a weighted average basis** may be compared to **prices of individual export transactions** if the authorities find a pattern of export prices which differ significantly among different purchasers, regions or time periods, and if an explanation is provided as to why such differences cannot be taken into account appropriately by the use of a weighted average-to-weighted average or transaction-to-transaction comparison.(Emphasis added)

Article 2 (11) of the Basic Regulation transposes this sentence of the ADA into the EU system. It reads as follows:

> However, a normal value established on a weighted average basis may be compared to **prices of all individual export transactions to the Community**,

48. Van Bael & Bellis, *Anti-dumping and Other Trade Protection Laws of the EC*, 74.
49. WTO, *European Communities – Anti-Dumping Duties on Imports of Cotton-Type Bed Linen from India*, AB-2000-13 – Report of the Appellate Body (1 Mar. 2001) WT/DS141/AB/R.
50. *Ibid.*, para. 6.20.
51. Van Bael & Bellis, *Anti-dumping and Other Trade Protection Laws of the EC*, 74.
52. Vermulst, 'The 10 Major Problems with the Anti-dumping Instrument in the European Community' 108.
53. Article 2.4.2 of the ADA.

> if there is a pattern of export prices which differs significantly among different purchasers, regions or time periods, and if the methods specified in the first sentence of this paragraph would not reflect the full degree of dumping being practised. (Emphasis added)

There is a slight difference in the wording between Article 2(11) of the Basic Regulation and the second sentence of Article 2.4.2 of the ADA. Article 2(11) of the Basic Regulation requires a weighted average normal value to be compared to 'prices of **all** individual export transactions to the Community', but the second sentence of Art 2.4.2 only allows the comparison between a weighted average normal value and 'prices of individual export transactions'. By adding the little word 'all', the EU interpreted the 'individual export transactions' in this sentence differently with the AB. In *US – Zeroing (Japan)*, the AB noted the following:[54]

> The emphasis in the second sentence of Article 2.4.2 is on a 'pattern', namely a 'pattern of export prices which differs significantly among different purchasers, regions or time periods'. The prices of transactions that fall within this pattern must be found to differ significantly from other export prices. We therefore read the phrase 'individual export transactions' in that sentence as referring to **the transactions that fall within the relevant pricing pattern. This universe of export transactions would necessarily be more limited than the universe of export transactions to which the symmetrical comparison methodologies in the first sentence of Article 2.4.2 would apply.** In order to unmask targeted dumping, an investigating authority may limit the application of the W-T comparison methodology to the prices of export transactions falling within the relevant pattern.

According to the Basic Regulation, the Commission is compelled to first compare a weighted average normal value with 'all individual export transactions to the Community' and then utilize a methodology that can reflect 'the full degree of dumping'. Consequently, the Commission argued in various cases that if zeroing is not applied, the result of asymmetrical method would be the same as the symmetrical ones. Hence, the inclusion of the little word 'all' before 'individual export transactions' justified the usage of zeroing in the scenario of 'targeted dumping'. The Commission typically states the following when it applies the 'zeroing' methodology in the scenario of 'targeted dumping':[55]

> The dumping found on these markets would have been inappropriately disguised by the use of a comparison of a weighted average normal value with a weighted average of export prices to all Member States of the European Union, as the prices at dumped levels found for all three exporting producers

54. *United States – Measures Relating to Zeroing and Sunset Reviews*, Report of the Appellate Body, WT/DS322/AB/R, 9 Jan. 2007, para 135.

55. Regulation (EC) No. 355/2006 of 28 Feb. 2006 imposing a provisional anti-dumping duty on imports of certain side-by-side refrigerators originating in the Republic of Korea, OJ L59/12, 1 Mar. 2006, para. 32.

> on the UK and French markets were wholly or partly offset by higher and largely nondumped prices on other Community markets. Such methodology would not, therefore, reflect the full degree of dumping being practised. It was accordingly found appropriate to reflect in the calculation of the dumping the significant differences in the pattern of export prices among different regions.

A number of exporters have challenged this interpretation of the Commission in the court. The Court of First Instance (CFI) nevertheless confirms the reading of the Commission as follows:[56]

> That article provides for the application, in the calculation of the dumping margin, of one of three possible methods, of which two – the symmetrical methods – are the normal methods, and one – the asymmetrical method – is an exceptional method. The condition relating to the existence of a pattern of export prices differing according to the periods, purchasers or regions is only one of the conditions for applying the asymmetrical method. The fact of laying down that condition is therefore in no way intended to allow the institutions to break up the investigation period according to the periods, purchasers or regions, in order to combine, according to those periods, purchasers or regions, one method of calculation with another. The institutions thus could not, in any event, combine the methods for calculating the dumping margin.

However, in the AB's view, the original second sentence of Article 2.4.2 requires the investigating authorities to do otherwise. Here, the AB considers that if the national authorities take a hybrid methodology, namely for targeted dumping transactions, a weighted-average-to-individual-transaction methodology is applied and for other transactions, a weighted-average-to-weighted-average methodology is applied, the 'full degree' of dumping can be reflected.

The slight difference between the wording of the second sentence of Article 2.11 of the Basic Regulation and the second sentence of Article 2.4.2 of the ADA is one of the many examples that reflect the EU's approach. It again indicates that by slightly altering the wording of the ADA, the EC was able to codify the previous practice followed by the Community institutions (in particular the Commission) into the Basic Regulation. The WTO-transposed provisions therefore reflect the compromise between multilateral rules and previously established practices of the Commission.

2.2 Administration of Community AD Rules

2.2.1 The Commission and the Administration of AD Proceedings

The evolution of the Community AD regime is also characterized by the rise of the Commission as the central player in AD proceedings. As most commentators

56. Case T-274/02, Ritek v Council (2006) ECR II-4305, paras 112–113.

recognized, the role of the Commission is 'much greater and more political than a normal executive body'.[57] Indeed, the Commission's attitude could, in many circumstances, determine the result of an AD investigation.

The profound changes in the way that EU anti-dumping rules have been administrated during the past half century can be analyzed from two different perspectives. Outwardly, the Commission's practice has always been regulated and constrained by multilateral rules. The Commission, while following requirements set out in the GATT/WTO laws, constantly compares its practices to its trading partners and justifies them on the grounds that other trading partners were practicing the same.[58] This approach has been described as 'playing the GATT/WTO game', which 'safeguarded the European Market by taking instruments allowed in the GATT/WTO agreement instead of publicly granting protection in the form of AD duties, but developing its methodologies to the maximum'.[59]

Inwardly, the Commission has to balance the divergent interests of different Community institutions, Member States and economic operators.[60] There are three different layers of balance that the Commission has to achieve: Firstly, under the Community interest test, the Commission has to balance different interests of the Community industry, importers, and users; secondly, EC anti-dumping measures have to pass the control of Member States, in the Anti-dumping Committee (the ADC) and in the Council voting; and finally, the Commission administration process is subject to the security of the CFI and the ECJ. The focus of this section is the outward-looking review of the Commission's practices, while the next section concentrates on the inward control by Community institutions, Member States and private actors within the EC.

After the adoption of the 1968 Regulation, during most of the 1970s the primary goal of the Commission in AD investigations appeared to be 'to secure price-revision undertakings from foreign exporters', a practice closely linked to 'voluntary restricted exporting'.[61] It is therefore observed that 'the majority of cases were concluded by the execution of undertakings without having any official determination of the existence of dumping and injury'.[62] The absence of public decisions made it very difficult for interested parties to understand how the AD rule was executed by the Commission. Consequently foreign producers were under

57. For example, C. Stanbrook & P. Bentley, *Dumping and Subsides: The Law and Procedures Governing the Imposition of Anti-dumping and Countervailing Duties in the European Community*, 3rd edn (The Hague: Kluwer Law International, 1996) 13.
58. For example, H. Wenig, 'The European Community's Anti-dumping System: Salient Features', *Journal of World Trade* 39 (2005): 787, 794. The author, as the former leader of the Trade Defence Service of the European Commission's Directorate General for Trade, frequently referred to the practice of other investigating authorities and concluded that 'the EC system scores very well in this respect, as evidenced by the extremely low rate of panel cases brought against the EC in Geneva'.
59. C. Molyneux, *Domestic Structures and International Trade – The Unfair Trade Instruments of the US and the EU* (Oxford: Hart Publishing, 2001), 4.
60. Wenig, 'The European Community's Anti-dumping System', 787.
61. Van Bael & Bellis, *Anti-dumping and Other Trade Protection Laws of the EC*, 41.
62. *Ibid.*

heavy pressure to consent to a price undertaking even 'where the substantive conditions for applying AD measures were not met'.[63]

The Commission significantly improved the process by increasing transparency after the 1979 Regulation due to both the criticism from the ECJ, *inter alia* the judgment of *Ball Bearing*,[64] and the tightening up of procedural obligations to national authorities in the 1979 Code. Exporters and importers subject to investigation were provided the right to request to be informed of 'the essential facts and considerations' on the basis of which the Commission intended to 'recommend the imposition of the definitive duties or the definitive collection of amount secured by way of a provisional duty'.[65] Publication requirements imposed upon the Community institutions also significantly helped to increase transparency as 'the Commission was required to include a summary of the information received in the notice of initiation published in the Official Journal (OJ) and a summary of the reasons for the termination in the notice of termination of proceedings, or where appropriate, information on any undertaking accepted by the Commission'.[66] Moreover, no undertaking could be given unless the Commission has established, at least provisionally, the existence of dumping and injury, according to the requirement in Article 7 of the 1979 Code.

The last ten years, that is, after the establishment of the current EU anti-dumping framework according to the ADA, have witnessed a more rigorous enforcement of the Basic Regulation due to strong domestic interests for a more diligent application of AD rules. This is reflected by a massive increase in the Commission staff, 'from no more than five officials in the early 1970s to around 120 officials in 2003'.[67] When facing the criticisms that EU anti-dumping proceedings were seized by protectionism interest, the Commission always defends its position as 'in strict conformity with the GATT/WTO requirements'.[68] The practice of the Commission, however, has still been condemned for lack of transparency by leading practitioners.[69] For example Vermulst identified the following 11 characteristics of the EC system as symptoms of lack of transparency:[70]

- complaints are treated as confidential until initiation of the proceeding;
- powers of attorney and details of legal representation are treated as confidential;
- questionnaires are made available only to interested parties;
- the public has no access to the non-confidential file;

63. *Ibid.*
64. Case 113/77, *NTN Toyo Bearing Company Ltd and others v. Council of European Communities* [1979] ECR 1185.
65. Van Bael & Bellis, *Anti-dumping and Other Trade Protection Laws of the EC*, 41.
66. *Ibid.*
67. *Ibid.*, 42.
68. Vermulst & Waer, *EC Anti-dumping Law and Practice*, 3.
69. Vermulst, 'The 10 Major Problems with the Anti-dumping Instrument in the European Community', 106.
70. *Ibid.*

- non-confidential questionnaire responses and other submissions often are so vague that they are virtually meaningless;
- verification reports prepared by Commission officials are not provided to interested parties;
- hearings are *ex parte* and no official transcripts or reports are provided to interested parties;
- at the stage of provisional measures, the MSs are informed before the interested parties;
- commission guidelines for applying the AD legislation are considered 'internal' and therefore confidential;
- when disclosure is provided, calculation formulas are normally removed because they are considered as 'confidential'; and
- the decision-making process of the Council and its committees is confidential.

In particular, the Commission has been criticized for monopolizing all factual information and this invites 'leaks and abuse'.[71] For example, it happens often that 'prior to initiation of a proceeding or prior to publication of provisional measures (but after consultation of the Member States by the Commission), information about complaints, respectively provisional findings, leaks out'.[72] This could considerably disadvantage foreign exporters and Community importers since they are normally less organized and less sufficiently represented in Brussels than Community industries. Unfortunately, as admitted by Vermulst, 'most of the intransparencies in the EC system result from insufficient ADA regulation, rather than the deliberate breach of the ADA rules by the Commission'.[73] For example, the EU practice of keeping complaints confidential until the initiation of a proceeding is the preferred option in the ADA, even though it invariably leads to leaks and abuse, as experienced by the EU and other jurisdictions.

In summary, over the years, corresponding to the increasing degree of obligation and precision in multilateral rules, the Community's AD practice has become more and more legalistic and judicialized. However, insufficiencies of the ADA give the Commission considerable room to manoeuvre the rules in order to produce results that are desirable to it and maximize the benefit from alternative methodologies.

2.2.2 Control of Administration within the EU

Although enjoying considerable discretion in administrating AD proceedings, it is fair to observe that the Commission still has to pass three different layers (*ex ante* and *ex post*) of control within the EU framework. These three layers of control in the AD regime illustrate a broader picture of the relationship between the Commission, MSs and private actors in the EU trade policy-making.

---

71. *Ibid.*
72. *Ibid.*
73. *Ibid.*

The first layer of balance is the interest of different Community industries under the Community interest test. Article 21 of the Basic Regulation is entirely dedicated to the notion of 'Community interest'. It provides for a detailed procedural and substantive framework in which the Commission may consider whether it is in the Community's interest to impose a definitive duty, even where dumping and injury have been established. The discussion in this subsection focuses on the dynamic of interested parties in the Community interest test, whilst the next subsection on WTO-plus rules provides more details of the procedural and substantive rules of the Community interest test.

Paragraph 1 of Article 21 established the general principle that a determination shall be based on an appreciation of various interests, and all the parties shall be given opportunities to make their views known.[74] Subsequent paragraphs of Article 21 set out a formal procedure and afford interested parties certain procedural rights, including the right to an oral hearing and the right to access certain information.[75] Finally, paragraph 5 of Article 21 provides that the result of the Commission's analysis of properly submitted information, together with an opinion on their merits, must be submitted to the ADC. The Commission shall take 'the balance of views' expressed by the ADC into account in its proposals.[76]

In practice, the Commission takes the view that this test is a 'non-disproportionate test', that is, 'whether the imposition of measures would place a disproportionate burden on economic operators other than the Community industry.[77] The ultimate intention of this procedure is 'to reassure that the result of AD proceeding is a balancing of economic interests of different operators on the European market, namely exporters, importers, users and consumers'.[78] It dynamically affects the process of an investigation in two ways: first, this test 'influences the structure of the investigation in a way that user and consumer interests or competition aspects are systematically and thoroughly looked into in the course of the investigation'; and second, it has 'repercussions on injury or causation analysis', as information obtained in the process of the Community interest analysis is also relevant there.[79]

Although the Commission has tried to 'professionalize' and 'neutralize' its Community interest determination over time, its established tradition of giving overwhelming weight to the complainants' interest has been criticized. In practice, this exercise of balancing different interests often results in 'findings counted on the fingers of one hand', as described by Vermulst.[80] Three reasons have been identified as relevant: Firstly, complaining industries in AD cases are normally

74. Article 21(1) of the Basic Regulation.
75. Article 21(2)–(4) of the Basic Regulation.
76. Article 21(5) of the Basic Regulation.
77. Wenig, 'The European Community's Anti-dumping System', 791. ('The EC's Anti-dumping System')
78. *Ibid.*
79. *Ibid.*
80. Vermulst, 'The 10 Major Problems with the Anti-dumping Instrument in the European Community', 112.

well organized and easy to be heard comparing to countless end-users or consumers. In AD cases, 'organization means power'.[81] Secondly, the Commission will 'typically find that the interests of the EC-producing industry outweigh those of the EC-processing industry'.[82] Thirdly, where dumping and injury have been found, 'the momentum of those findings will tend to propel the Commission towards proposing AD measures'.[83] The first reason is especially significant if one bears in mind the general position of the Commission in EU policy-making. Compared with other EU institutions, the Commission is widely recognized as being 'receptive and open to interest group representations' in that it is more enthusiastic to seek alliance with influential interest groups to strengthen its position vis-à-vis the Council in the EU system.[84] The alignment towards the interest of highly concentrated Community industries in the Community interest test are therefore not surprising. Statistics suggest that the number of EU anti-dumping investigations against Chinese products for different industry sectors 'does not seem to be related to its relative significance in total import flows', but indicates 'the degree of concentration'.[85] The percentage of EU anti-dumping cases is highest in the chemical sector, representing 37.8% of the total EU anti-dumping cases against China during 1979–2000, while the chemicals sector only represents 3.8% of total EU imports from China.[86]

The second layer of control in the AD administration is the balance of interests between the Commission and MSs as well as between different MSs. At first, the Commission has to confront MSs in the internal Commission procedure.[87] A Commission proposal for the imposition of an AD measure is made only after a careful examination of the result of the investigation by a number of directorate-generals, including those in charge of industry, customs matter and legal affairs. It is then presented to the entire college of Commissioners for adoption. After that, the proposal has to pass 'a strict test' in the ADC.[88] There is a monthly meeting of the ADC in which Commission officials and representatives from all twenty-seven MSs participate. The Commission proposals are discussed and scrutinized by MS in the ADC meetings. It is only after all aspects have been discussed 'in considerable detail and appropriately addressed' that 'a measure is finally adopted by the Council which has the final say on definitive measures as described by the Commission'.[89]

---

81. *Ibid.*
82. *Ibid.*
83. *Ibid.*
84. S. George & I. Bache, *Politics in the European Union* (Oxford: Oxford University Press, 2001), 296.
85. X. Liu & H. Vandenbussche, 'European Union Anti-dumping Cases Against China – An Overview and Future Prospects with Respect to China's World Trade Organization Membership', *Journal of International Economic Law* 36 (2002): 1125, 1132.
86. *Ibid.*
87. Wenig, 'The European Community's Anti-dumping System', 788.
88. *Ibid.*, 789.
89. *Ibid.*

In terms of the Council voting, when qualified majority voting was replaced by simple majority in the Basic Regulation, it is argued that the Commission has been given a better opportunity to 'utilize the conflicting interest of MSs and introduce proposals representing the Community's interest as a whole'.[90] In particular, since 20 March 2004, abstentions count as support, that is, unless fourteen MSs oppose a definitive measure, 'a Commission proposal to impose an AD measure will stand'.[91] Consequently, the scope for interest groups to lobby different MSs to vote in accordance with their wills in AD cases is limited. From an inter-institutional perspective, the Council normally only rubberstamped the Commission's proposal. This also reflects a broader trend in the EU decision-making: the Commission's leadership capacity in the European Integration process gained on popular recognition.[92] Hence, there were always some MSs voting against the Commission's proposal in the ADC and it is difficult for MSs to block the Commission's proposal in most cases.

If one considers that there is a general conflict of interest between the Commission and MSs in the adoption of certain AD measures, there are even bigger conflicts between different MSs on this issue. The emergence of a north liberal bloc and a south protectionism block is recognized from the statistics concerning the voting pattern among MSs in the ADC and the Council.[93] The Northern European states, such as Scandinavia, the United Kingdom and the Netherlands, had tended to vote against the imposition of duties, particularly for products that are used as components and/or inputs for secondary manufacturing. Countries of Southern Europe, such as France, Spain, Portugal, Italy and Greece, almost invariably vote for the Commission's proposals in AD cases. Thus the ADC becomes the place where the different interests of MSs 'clash and are, possibly, reconciled with each other'.[94]

The last layer of control is the judicial review from the CFI and ECJ. Although leading practitioners are of the view that there is an 'absence of meaningful judicial review on substantive issues', the CFI and ECJ jurisprudence still plays an important role in the development of the EU anti-dumping regime.[95]

2.3 Judicial Review of Community AD Policy

While the discussion in the previous two sections demonstrated two basic trends that influenced the evolution of the EU anti-dumping regime (i.e., the development

90. Vermulst, 'The 10 Major Problems with the Anti-dumping Instrument in the European Community', 105.
91. *Ibid.*
92. George & Bache, *Politics in the European Union*, 245.
93. European Commission, Information Note on the Community's Anti-Dumping Instrument and Practice (Jan. 1998), Appendices 7A–7C.
94. Wenig, 'The European Community's Anti-dumping System', 789.
95. Vermulst, 'The 10 Major Problems with the Anti-dumping Instrument in the European Community', 107.

of legalization in the multilateral system and checks and balances within the EU system), the same theme can be found in the AD case law on AD. On the one hand, the CFI and ECJ have to address EU-specific questions, such as *locus standi* of the parties and the principle of good administration in the EU. On the other hand, their review of the application of the basic Regulation inevitably involves the assessment of the Commission's conduct in light of the GATT/WTO laws. Therefore, most AD cases that reach the CFI/ECJ involved two aspects: an EU law aspect and a GATT/WTO law aspect.

On the EU law front, the general impression is that the CFI/ECJ have been 'less enthusiastically intervening in favour of parties suffering detriment through EC anti-dumping initiatives, if compared to the aid given to those who sought to enforce MSs commitments to Community objectives'.[96] Two possible explanations are frequently discussed in the literature: relatively strict requirements concerning *locus standi* for an action for annulment of a Regulation; and the evident reluctance to intervene in administrative actions involving complex economic judgments of the Commission. As argued, the CFI/ECJ adopted 'a more liberal and generous approach to the standing of private parties and are more prepared to double-check the work of the Commission and the Council as far as the observance of procedural rules is concerned'.[97]

The first contestable issue under EU law in early AD cases is the standing of natural or legal persons to challenge AD measures. Since the judicial review of EU anti-dumping or anti-subsidy measures is most frequently sought through an action for annulment under Article 263 of the treaty of the Functioning of the European Union (TEU),[98] the applicants have to prove their direct and individual concerns under a particular Regulation in the first place. Over the years, the ECJ's jurisprudence has developed to the point where it is recognized that, as a general rule, complaints, exporters and importers have standings although, it is still necessary to consider whether or not the measure in question is of direct and individual concern to the applicant.[99]

In terms of the standing of complainants, the ECJ confirmed in cases, such as *Timex* and *FEDIOL*, that complainants have the right to challenge a regulation imposing definitive duties and a decision not to initiate an investigation or terminate an investigation without imposing measures.[100] Complainants can demonstrate their direct and individual concerns if the Community institutions have disregarded any of the rights conferred to them by the Basic Regulation. Moreover, in *Timex*, the ECJ admitted the standing of a main domestic manufacture, although

96. A. Ward, *Judicial Review and the Rights of Private Parties in EC Law* (Oxford: Oxford University Press, 2000), 203.
97. Vermulst & Waer, *EC Anti-dumping Law and Practice*, 161.
98. This provision is ex Article 230 of the Treaty establishing the European Community (TEC).
99. Van Bael & Bellis, *Anti-dumping and Other Trade Prorecrion Laws of the EC*, 467.
100. Case 191/82 EEC, *Seed Crusher's and Oil Processors' Fed'n (FEDIOL) v. Commission* [1983] ECR 2913. (FEDIOL) Case 264/82, *Timex Corporation v. Council and Commission* [1985] ECR 849.

it was not the association that logged the formal complainant, but was one of the Community producers on whose behalf the complaint was lodged.[101]

The ECJ also confirmed the standing of foreign exporters and related importers in various cases. In *Allied Corporation*, the ECJ ruled that foreign exporters are entitled to challenge the imposition of provisional or definitive AD duties regardless of whether they are specifically named in the challenged regulation, provided that they were concerned by the investigation.[102] When the export price is determined on the basis of a constructed export price, related importers involved in the construct export price determination also have standing.[103]

The situation is less straightforward with respect to unrelated importers and traders. Until *Extramet*, independent importers had no standing to bring a direct action for the annulment of AD measures.[104] In *Extramet*, the ECJ, in a departure of its previous case law, ruled that Extramet, an independent importer, had standing to bring a direct action against the contested AD measure under a very special circumstance. Extramet was individually concerned by the contested measure because it established in its application that 'the existence of a set of factors constituting a situation peculiar to it and distinguishing it from all other traders'.[105] Later CFI case law, however, suggested a returning of strict interpretation of the notion of 'individual concern' with respect to independent importers.[106]

The second issue in the judicial review of AD measures under the EU law is the standard of review that CFI and ECJ applied. The CFI and ECJ have been recognized as reluctant to seriously consider substantive challenges to administrative determinations – a signal of 'excessive deference to the Community institutions' unless there has been an infringement of essential procedural requirements in the course of investigations.[107] Beyond essential procedural arguments, the level of review of the Commission's substantive determination, namely its institutional discrection, that can be expected by the potential applicants is less clear. The two cases discussed below demonstrate this unclear position of the CFI and ECJ.

In 1995, one year after AD cases were transferred to the CFI, the CFI delivered its first judgment in this area, *NTN Corporation and Koyo Seiko.*[108] In this judgment, the CFI first repeated the ECJ's finding in *Nakajima* that 'provisions in the basic regulation must be interpreted in the light of Article VI of the GATT and the

101. *Ibid.*, Timex.
102. Case 239, 275/82, *Allied Corporation v. Commission* [1984] ECR 1005.
103. *Ibid.*, Also, Case 113/77, *NTN Toyo Bearing Company Ltd and others v. Council of European Communities* [1979] ECR 1185.
104. Case C-358/89, *Extramet Industrie SA v. Council* [1991] ECR I-2501.
105. *Ibid.*, para. 17.
106. For example, Case C-50/00, *Union de Pequenos Agricultores v. Council* [2002] ECR I-6677. (Union de Pequenos Agricultores)
107. Vermulst, 'The 10 Major Problems with the Anti-dumping Instrument in the European Community', 107.
108. Joint Case T-163, 165/94, *NTN Corporation and Koyo Seiko Co. Ltd v. Council* [1995] ECR II-01381. (NTN Corporation and Koyo Seiko)

1979 Anti-dumping Code'.[109] It went on to examine closely the wording of Article 3(6) of the 1979 AD Code and Article 4(1) of the Regulation 2423/88 in terms of the determination of injury and the facts presented in the contested regulation about injury.[110] After thoroughly examining the factors on which the Council based its finding of injury, the CFI found several paragraphs of the Council's statement were 'incomplete, inaccurate or insufficiently supported', so that they were 'not sufficient to justify a finding of threat of injury within the meaning of Article 4(1) of the basic regulation, a term which must in any event be interpreted in the light of the 1979 Anti-dumping Code and in particular Article 3(6) thereof'.[111] The CFI referred to *FEDIOL* and *Timex* to confirm that it 'may not intervene in the appraisal reserved to the Community authorities by the basic regulation but must exercise its normal power of review over a discretion granted to a public authority'.[112] The CFI concluded that because of the misleading or inaccurate statements of the Council, the contested Regulation should be annulled.[113]

Two months later, the CFI delivered another judgment brought by one of the applicants in *NTN Corporation and Koyo Seiko* against the Council, *Koyo Seiko*.[114] The applicant again challenged the determination of injury in a provisional regulation. The result and the reasoning of the CFI was, however, quite different with the *NTN Corporation and Koyo Seiko*. In particular, when the applicant contested the Council's assessment in terms of other factors that might contribute to the injury and the Council admitted that its statement on this issue was inaccurate, the CFI held that although certain parts of the provisional regulation were 'indeed inaccurate', 'the underlying reasoning adopted by the Community institutions in the regulation at issue proved to be correct'.[115] It then concluded that although the wording of the provisional regulation was misleading, 'that inaccuracy in no way affected either the lawfulness of the regulation at issue or the reasoning underlying it'.[116] The application of annulment was therefore dismissed.

The different results in these two cases indicate a certain degree of uncertainty in the CFI and ECJ's review. The CFI's approach is arguably to examine whether the procedural wrongdoing of the Commission may result in the unlawfulness of the regulation contested. If procedural defects are not manifested, the CFI seems unwilling to annul the regulation in question simply because the Commission does not rigidly follow the procedure. However, it is difficult to draw a conclusive line between the manifest procedural errors and minor errors that have no impact on the results from the CFI/ECJ jurisprudence by far.

With respect to the WTO law, although the CFI/ECJ consistently deny the direct effect of GATT/WTO laws in the Community legal order, due to the

109. *Ibid.*, para. 65.
110. *Ibid.*, paras 66, 67 and 75.
111. *Ibid.*, paras 76, 79, 82 and 106.
112. *Ibid.*, para. 113.
113. *Ibid.*, para. 115.
114. Case T-166/94, *Koyo Seiko Co Ltd v. Council* [1995] ECR II-02129. (Koyo Seiko)
115. *Ibid.*, para. 99.
116. *Ibid.*, 105.

multilateral nature of AD rules, the CFI/ECJ considered that the WTO ADA rule and jurisprudence are relevant in reviewing EU AD measures. WTO laws have been used as 'an aid in interpreting a range of EC legal instruments', including 'both EC domestic law, such as secondary legislation and general principles of law, and international agreements to which the EC is a party'.[117] The ECJ recognized in *Petrotub* that the Basic Regulation is intended 'to transpose into the Community law as far as possible the new and detailed rules contained in the 1994 Anti-dumping', so when it was called to examine the issues such as the determination of dumping and injury, they were obliged to do so in light of the WTO rules'.[118] In *Petrotub*, the applicant complained that the Community institutions did not provide an adequate statement of reason to its practice of zeroing. Therefore, although, as Advocate General Jacobs stated, the practice of zeroing was not itself an issue in the proceeding, the WTO jurisprudence on this issue, *inter alia EC – Bed Linen*, did provide a broader 'multilateral background' for this case.[119] The ECJ held that once Article 2.4.2 of the ADA is transposed by the Community, 'the specific requirement to state reasons laid down by that provision can be considered to be subsumed under the general requirement imposed by the Treaty for acts adopted by the institutions to state the reasons on which they are based'.[120] The CFI thus erred in law in considering that there was no need to take into account Article 2.4.2 of the ADA for the purposes of determining whether the Council has fulfilled the obligation to state reasons.[121] As the contested regulation 'does not contain even the merest reference to the second symmetrical method of Article 2.4.2 or the slightest explanation as to why that method would not enable significant differences in the result', the ECJ held that the Council did not satisfy the requirements of the obligation to state reasons and the contested regulation was declared invalid.[122]

In summary, few challenges to Community AD measures in the CFI/ECJ were successful due to restricted requirements of standing and significant deference to the Community institutions. As time went by, some procedural issues, such as *locus standi*, become less contestable. Deference to the Community institutions on substantive issues, based on the respect for discretion enjoyed by the Community institutions, are still an important rule in the CFI/ECJ review of AD measures. More influences from WTO laws and jurisprudence can be found in the Court's rulings, such as *Petrotub*. In this case, the ECJ, for the first time, linked, or 'subsumed', a provision of the ADA to an EU administrative principle (statement of reason). To some extent, this is a welcome step forward to integrate multilateral rules into the 'interpretation' of the Basic Regulation, which in turn can directly translate to the discipline imposed on the Commission.

---

117. F. Snyder, 'The Gatekeepers: The European Courts and WTO Law', *Common Market Law Review* 40 (2003): 313, 320.
118. Case C-76/00 P, *Petrotub and Republica v. Council of the European Union* [2003] ECR I-89, paras 54–58.
119. Petrotub Opinion of Advocate General, para. 18.
120. *Ibid.*, 58.
121. *Ibid.*, 52.
122. *Ibid.*, 51 and 86.

3 WTO-PLUS FEATURES OF THE EU ANTI-DUMPING REGIME

Although the Commission always claimed that it is its intention to abide by WTO laws, it is widely discussed that certain WTO-plus features characterize the EU AD regime. These WTO-plus provisions enable the Commission to retain certain control over the AD policy, by allowing it to change the result of AD investigations even if the WTO-transposed requirements have been met.

For example, Snyder described the underlying reasons for developing the notion of 'non-market economy', one of the major WTO-plus features of EU AD rules, as follows:[123]

> [T]he principle factors giving rise to this new legal idea were changes in the international anti-dumping repertoire, specific European ideas about comparative economic systems, and perceived new economic threats during the 1970s. They were combined by the European institutions, notably the Commission, in an international context marked by a substantial decline in previous US hegemony. Taken together, they legitimated a more protectionist anti-dumping policy, of which the legal concept of 'nonmarket economy' was an important part.

This section first provides the relevant WTO rules and jurisprudence, and then offers a detailed description of the EU rules and practices for each WTO-plus feature in order to demonstrate how these WTO-plus provisions allow the Community institutions to achieve the balance among different interests within the EU. Three WTO-plus features of EU anti-dumping rules, namely injury margin, community interest and anti-circumvention, are examined in detail in this section. Another main WTO-plus feature, namely the EU's methodology towards non-market economy (NME) countries, will be examined in the next chapter, in the context of the EU-China anti-dumping disputes. Case law is cited to the extent possible to demonstrate how WTO-plus provisions work in practice.

3.1 Injury Margin

3.1.1 Lesser Duty Rule in the WTO

As a general rule, the ADA welcomes investigating authorities to impose AD duty less than the dumping margin. Article 9.1 ADA reads as follows:[124]

> The decision whether or not to impose an anti-dumping duty in cases where all requirements for the imposition have been fulfilled, and the decision whether the amount of the anti-dumping duty to be imposed shall be the full margin of dumping or less, are decisions to be made by the authorities of the importing

123. Snyder, 'The Origins of "Non-market Economy"', 420.
124. Anti-dumping Agreement, Article 9.1.

> Member. It is desirable that the imposition be permissive in the territory of all Members, and that the duty *be less than the margin* if such lesser duty would be adequate to remove the injury to the domestic industry.

In addition, Article 9.3 ADA provides that: '[T]he amount of the anti-dumping duty shall not exceed the margin of dumping as established under Article 2'.[125]

A combined reading of Article 9.1 and Article 9.3 ADA suggests that the absolute maximum of AD duties in investigations is the dumping margin, irrespective of the injury suffered by the domestic industry. The minimum is whatever is needed to eliminate such injury. It is at the discretion of an investigating authority to decide whether to apply the lesser duty rule, provided that the application of this rule is 'desirable'. This is even the case when the product concerned is originating in a developing country.

As a best endeavours clause, the application of the lesser duty rule in an investigation does not justify the breach of obligations deriving from other provisions of the AD Code, as the GATT panel concluded in *EC – Audio Cassette.*[126] The EC in this case stated that certain claims made by Japan before the panel were not proper because of the lack of a legal interest on the part of Japan. The EC argued that even if certain points in the EC's decision have been changed in Japan's favour, it would not affect the level of the AD duties imposed on Japanese imports due to the application of the lesser duty rule. Consequently, no nullification and impairment had been suffered by Japan.[127] It also argued that revocation of the entire Regulation in question on the grounds that part of the dumping calculation was conducted in a GATT-inconsistent manner was inappropriate due to the effect of the lesser duty rule.[128]

The panel did not directly address the EC's argument that, because it had imposed a duty pursuant to the lesser duty rule, the alleged errors of the EC in calculating the dumping margin could have had no impact on the level of duties imposed in this case.[129] Instead, the panel stated that Japan had submitted calculations to the panel relating to one exporter in support of its view that the margin of dumping, calculated in a manner consistent with the Agreement, would have been lower than the duty imposed and the EC did not submit any counter calculation. The panel then stated that its task was to 'review the legal and factual bases for the imposition of an anti-dumping duty in light of the obligations of the Agreement, and not to reach its own determination regarding the existence and extent of dumping'.[130] Therefore, the panel concluded that it was not precluded from considering Japan's claims regarding 'zeroing' and 'asymmetry' on the grounds that Japan has a 'legal interest' in those claims.

---

125. Anti-dumping Agreement Article 9.3.
126. GATT, *EC – Anti-Dumping Duties on Audio Tapes in Cassettes Originating in Japan*, Report of the Panel, 28 Apr. 1995, unadopted, ADP/136.
127. *Ibid.*, para. 15.
128. *Ibid.*, para. 282.
129. *Ibid.*, para. 342.
130. *Ibid.*, para. 345.

Also, in *US – India Plate,* India argued that the US Department of Commerce (USDOC) should have considered applying the lesser duty rule as one form of 'constructive remedy' under Article 15 ADA. However, the panel disagreed with India and stated the following:[131]

> India suggests that the USDOC should have considered applying a lesser duty in this case, despite the fact that US law does not provide for application of a lesser duty in any case. We note that consideration and application of a lesser duty is deemed desirable by Article 9.1 of the AD Agreement, but is not mandatory. Therefore, a Member is not obligated to have the possibility of a lesser duty in its domestic legislation. We do not consider that the second sentence of Article 15 can be understood to require a Member to consider an action that is not required by the WTO Agreement and is not provided for under its own municipal law.

Nevertheless, the application of the lesser duty rule has been considered as an example of a constructive remedy by the Committee of Anti-dumping Practice (the Committee). In its 'Recommendation regarding Annual Reviews of the Anti-Dumping Agreement', adopted on 27 November 2002, the Committee made the following recommendation:[132]

> Developed country Members should include, when reporting anti-dumping actions in the semi-annual report that Members are required to submit under Article 16.4, the manner in which the obligations of Article 15 have been fulfilled. Without prejudice to the scope and application of Article 15, price undertakings and lesser duty rules are examples of constructive remedies that could be included in such Members' semi-annual reports.

The panel in *EC – Bed Linen* further confirmed the status of the lesser duty rule as one form of constructive remedy by stating that:[133]

> The Agreement provides for the imposition of anti-dumping duties, either in the full amount of the dumping margin, or desirably, in a lesser amount, or the acceptance of price undertakings, as a means of resolving an antidumping investigation resulting in a final affirmative determination of dumping, injury, and causal link. Thus, in our view, imposition of a lesser duty, or a price undertaking would constitute 'constructive remedies' within the meaning of Article 15. We come to no conclusions as to what other actions might in

131. WTO, *United States – Anti-Dumping and Countervailing Measures on Steel Plate from India,* Report of the Panel WT/DS206/R and Corr.1, 29 Jul. 2002, DSR 2002:VI, 2073, para. 7.116.

132. WTO Committee of Anti-dumping Practice, Recommendation regarding Annual Reviews of the Anti-Dumping Agreement , 27 Nov. 2002, available at: <www.wto.org/english/res_e/bookspe_e/analytic_index_e/anti_dumping_05_e.htm>.

133. WTO, *European Communities – Anti-Dumping Duties on Imports of Cotton-Type Bed Linen from India,* Report of the Panel, WT/DS141/R, 12 Mar. 2001, modified by Appellate Body Report, WT/DS141/AB/R, DSR 2001:VI, 2077, para. 6.229.

> addition be considered to constitute 'constructive remedies' under Article 15, as none have been proposed to us. (Footnote omitted)

In this case, the EC did consider the application of a lesser duty, although it concluded that such a duty would not be appropriate since the injury margin exceeded the dumping margin for each company.[134] Therefore, the panel did not base its finding that the EC failed to act consistently with its obligations under Article 15 ADA, namely the EC did not apply the lesser duty rule. Instead, the panel stated that 'the failure of the European Communities to respond in some fashion other than bare rejection, particularly once the desire to offer undertakings had been communicated to it, constituted a failure to 'explore possibilities of constructive remedies'.[135]

Hence, WTO rules and jurisprudences establish that, firstly, the application of the lesser duty rule is entirely at the discretion of an investigating authority, even in the context of Article 15 ADA. With respect to investigations against imports from developing countries; secondly, the application of the lesser duty rule does not justify the application of methodologies such as 'zeroing', which may result in miscalculations of dumping margin, and finally, the application of the lesser duty rule qualifies as one form of constructive remedies under Article 15 ADA. Yet, Article 15 ADA imposes no obligation to any member to actually apply such rule. Instead, the obligation is to actively 'consider' the possibility of offering a remedy, which can be the application of the lesser duty rule, prior to the imposition of a definitive duty.

3.1.2 Injury Margin Calculation in the EU

The EU incorporated the lesser duty rule in various provisions of the Basic Regulation and made it mandatory for the Commission to apply this rule in provisional measures, definitive measures and price undertakings. Article 9(4) of the Basic Regulation provides the legal basis for the application of the lesser duty rule in definitive AD measures. It states that:[136]

> Where the facts as finally established show that there is dumping and injury caused thereby, and the Community interest calls for intervention in accordance with Article 21, a definitive anti-dumping duty shall be imposed by the Council, acting by simple majority on a proposal submitted by the Commission after consultation of the Advisory Committee [...]. The amount of the anti-dumping duty shall not exceed the margin of dumping established but it should be less than the margin if such lesser duty would be adequate to remove the injury to the Community industry.

134. *Ibid.*, and European Commission, Information Note on the Community's Anti-Dumping Instrument and Practice (January 1998), Appendices 7A–7C.
135. *Ibid.*, para. 6.230.
136. Article 9(4) of the Basic Regulation.

Article 7(2) of the Basic Regulation addresses the issue of applying the lesser duty rule in provisional measures. The provision reads as follows:[137]

> *The amount of the provisional anti-dumping duty shall not exceed the margin of dumping as provisionally established, but it should be less than the margin if such lesser duty would be adequate to remove the injury to the Community industry.* (Emphasis added)

In addition to the application of the lesser duty rule in provisional and definitive measures, Article 8(1) of the Basic Regulation requests the application of the lesser duty rule in determining the level of a price undertaking. Article 8(1) reads as follows:

> Investigations may be terminated without the imposition of provisional or definitive duties upon receipt of satisfactory voluntary undertakings from any exporter to revise its prices or to cease exports to the area in question at dumped prices, so that the Commission, after consultation, is satisfied that the injurious effect of the dumping is eliminated. Price increases under such undertakings shall not be higher than necessary to eliminate the margin of dumping and they should be less than the margin of dumping if such increases would be adequate to remove the injury to the Community industry.

In light of the above provisions, the level of an AD duty should be equal to either the margin of dumping or the amount necessary to remove injury sustained by the Community industry, whichever is lower. The Community institutions are obliged 'to calculate an injury margin in order to determine the level of duty that is adequate to remove the injury'.[138] The same lesser duty rule applies in connection with price undertakings.

Although no guideline has been provided by either the ADA or the Basic Regulation to foresee how to determine the level of an AD duty at which injury is removed, the Community institutions established, in practice, methodologies to calculate this level of duty by examining the level of price underselling or price undercutting, as the case may be, of dumped imports.[139]

It is now common practice to calculate the injury margin by comparing the price of exporters with the price of the Community industry for the product concerned. More specifically, the calculation of injury margin is normally based on this formula:[140]

$$\frac{\text{Price of the Community industry} - \text{Exporter's Cost, Insurance and Freight (CIF) price}}{\text{Exporter's price 'CIF Community frontier'}} \times 100$$

137. Article 7(2) of the Basic Regulation.
138. Müller et al., *EC Anti-dumping Law*, 404.
139. *Ibid.*, 405.
140. *Ibid.*

The price of the Community industry corresponds to either 'the actual selling price' (in the case of 'price undercutting') or the 'target price', namely 'the price level at which Community producers could sell their product in the absence of dumped imports' (in the case of 'price underselling').[141] The exporter's CIF price can be the actual export price or the export price after adjustment in order to take into account customs duties paid for the imported product, SGA costs and profits of imports, difference in physical characteristics, etc. The difference between the (target) price of the Community industry and the exporter's price, that is, the price underselling amount, represents the injury amount. Such injury amount is converted into an injury margin by expressing such amount as a percentage of the exporter's price at a 'CIF Community frontier, duty unpaid' level.

In the past few years, after some investigations where 'injury margins were based on the undercutting and some others were based on the underselling margin', the practice of Community institutions is 'to opt for the underselling calculation of the injury margin'.[142] This is due to the fact that the exporter's price is often not comparable to the actual price of the Community industry because the latter has been depressed as a result of dumped imports and is no longer made at a profitable or, more accurately, the injury-eliminating level.

The target price is a fictitious price, calculated in order to set the price levels that could 'ensure the complainant industry's long-term viability'.[143] In other words, the target price is an injury-eliminating fictitious price of the Community industry. It is usually computed by increasing the manufacturing costs of the Community producer by the SGA expenses of the same Community producer and a reasonable profit.[144] The determination of such reasonable profit is linked to the level of profit the Community industry could have achieved if imports were not made at a dumped price. However, this is a highly theoretical exercise, as no one can really tell at which price level the domestic industry could have been selling in the absence of dumped imports. In addition, non-dumped imports may equally bring price depression on the market, as they could be much lower than the desirable price of the Community industry. The existence of dumped imports causing injury may form grounds on which an injury margin must be calculated within the EC, but it is not a methodological ground for calculating such injury margin.

In *EFMA v. Council*, the CFI clarified the level of 'reasonable profit' as follows:[145]

> the profit margin [. . .] must be limited to the profit margin which the Community industry could reasonably count on under normal conditions of

141. Van Bael & Bellis, *Anti-dumping and Other Trade Protection Laws of the EC*, 306. ('Anti-dumping and Other Trade Protection Laws')
142. E. Vermulst & F. Graafsma, 'EC Dumping and Injury Margin Calculation Methods: The Major Problem', *Global Trade and Custom Journal* 2 (2007): 27–30.
143. Müller et al., *EC Anti-dumping Law*, 409.
144. *Ibid.*
145. Case T-210/95, *European Fertilizer Manufacturer's Association (EFMA) v. Council of the European Union* [1999] ECRII-3291.

> competition, in the absence of dumped imports', but 'it would not be consistent with Article 4.1 and 13.3 of the basic regulation to allow the Community industry a profit margin that it could not have expected if there were no dumping.

Apart from the establishment of a 'target price', two additional questions arise when the number of export transactions is more than one (which is invariably the case in practice). The first question is how transactions should be treated when their export prices are higher than the Community industry's target sale price (a fictitious injury-eliminating price), when the injury margin is based on price underselling, or the Community industry's actual selling price after adjustment, in case of price undercutting. The question is identical to the problem of 'zeroing' in the dumping margin calculation – in cases where export transactions are not dumped they generate negative dumping.[146] After *EC – Bed Linen*, the EU no longer practices zeroing in the dumping margin calculation, apart from the scenario of 'targeted dumping'.

Despite the abolition of zeroing in the dumping margin calculation, in most cases, the Commission's practice in injury margin calculations remains to zero all transactions where the export price is higher than the Community industry's price or the 'target price'. Although 'zeroing' practice in the dumping margin calculation has been ruled as WTO-inconsistent by panels and the AB on various occasions, no WTO report has ever addressed the WTO consistency of applying zeroing in the injury margin calculation. This is most likely due to the fact that 'lesser duty' is not a mandatory practice in the ADA and, thus, WTO members' voluntary lesser duty rule practice involving zeroing cannot be judged as WTO-incompatible.

The second question is how the result of all individual transactions concerned should be weighted when averaging them in order to calculate a single injury margin.[147] In cases where a producer exports only one model to the Community, the weighted average export price is normally calculated by dividing the overall value by the overall quantity exported. If the exporter exports more than one model of the product concerned, as demonstrated above, export transactions concerning a model for which negative injury was found (i.e., sold at a higher price than the EU target price) will automatically be put at zero in the overall weighing.

A particular problem arises if the models imported into the Community and those produced by the Community industry have different characteristics. Since the Commission's practice is to 'limit the undercutting and underselling comparison to those models produced by the Community producers, which are directly comparable to the imported models'.[148] In case of complex products involving a variety of different characteristics where it is troublesome to select the Community industry's models that are identical to the imported models in order to proceed with the comparison, the Commission usually groups the products by 'closely resembling'

146. Vermulst & Graafsma, 'EC Dumping and Injury Margin Calculation Methods, 31.
147. *Ibid.*
148. Müller et al., *EC Anti-dumping Law*, 407.

types and compares them on a type-by-type basis. Adjustments for differences in physical characteristics may be included.

Finally, in order to compare the price of imported products and the products of the Community industry, the Commission will also typically proceed to adjustments needed for rendering the prices comparable.[149] For example, selling cost allowances should be either deducted or left in the price on both sides: sales of imported products and sales by the Community industry. As to the international commercial terms (Incoterms) applicable, the comparison typically takes place as follows: to compare CIF price of imports with the Ex Works (EXW) price of domestic sales of the Community industry. The rationale for this comparison is that customers should be located somewhere in between the Community border (cf. CIF price of imports) and the factory gates of the Community producers (cf. EXW price of the Community industry).

To sum up, the Commission's methodology on assessing the injury amount and calculating the injury margin is evolving through its practices. Now it is common practice to calculate the injury margin by comparing the exporter's price and the target price of the Community industry. Although 'zeroing' practice in the dumping margin calculation has been abolished by the Commission, it is still applicable in the injury margin calculation where more than one transaction is made or more than one model is compared.

Since the level of injury margin actually determines the level of AD duty in a large amount of AD investigations, the Commission's methodology is of significant practical importance. Unfortunately, to exporting producers, the EU's methodology on the injury margin calculation, no matter what it is, is not challengeable in the WTO.

3.2 Community Interest

3.2.1 Public Interest in WTO Law

The term 'public interest' has never been used in the ADA. The absence of relevant provisions dealing with 'public interest' in the ADA results in lack of consensus among WTO Members on the following three questions: (1) which domestic parties' interest should be considered as part of 'public interest'; (2) what economic factors should be taken into account and how investigating authorities should weight them; and (3) what kind of procedure should be inserted into national AD legislation to allow the interest of various parties to be considered.

Although there is no direct answer for the above three questions in the ADA, two provisions, Article 6.12 and Article 9.1, are generally considered to be of relevance to apply a so-called 'public interest' test in an AD investigation. Article 6.12 ADA warrants the opportunity for presentations regarding the

149. *Ibid.*

evidence of dumping, injury and causality from industrial users and consumer organizations to be considered by the investigating authorities.

It has to be noted that Article 6.12 contains only procedural obligations to an investigation authority. It provides no guidelines on how the information submitted by industrial users and consumer organizations should be considered and imposes no substantive obligation on investigating authorities.

Another provision, Article 9.1, has also been frequently cited as the basis of the inclusion of a 'public interest' test in an AD investigation.[150] Many WTO members who are in favour of including a new 'public interest' provision in the ADA consider Article 9.1 as the legal basis for such a new provision, essentially on the grounds that Article 9.1 recognizes the full discretion of an investigating authority not to impose a definitive measure or not to impose a measure to its fullest extent in the circumstances that it deems appropriate.[151]

However, Article 9.1 does not impose any obligation on a WTO member to establish a domestic procedure to consider presentations made by economic operators other than domestic producers. That is to say, similar to the lesser duty rule, the 'public interest' test is non-mandatory in the ADA and whether and how to consider public interest in an AD investigation is entirely at the discretion of an investigating authority.

3.2.2 Community Interest Test in the EU Law

Among the WTO-plus characterizations of the EU anti-dumping law, the implementation of a public interest test, namely the Community interest test, in AD and CVD investigations is considered to be one of the most important features of the EU system.[152] This addition test, as is believed, makes the EU 'the only WTO Member that consistently applies the public interest test in an elaborated and systematic way' and has 'considerably restricted the use of anti-dumping and anti-subsidy instruments in order to balance the interests of various economic actors'.[153]

With seven sub-paragraphs, Article 21 of the Basic Regulation provides the legal basis for the application of a public interest test under the EU law, both in terms of procedural requirements and substantive criteria.

---

150. It is common understanding in the WTO/EC literature that Art. 9.1 ADA is the basis of the EC's Community interest test. See Van Bael & Bellis, *Anti-dumping and Other Trade Protection Laws of the EC*, 293.
151. For example, Paper from Hong Kong, China and the Separate Customs Territory of Taiwan, Penghu, Kinmen and Matsu, Economic Effects of Anti-dumping Measures, TN/RL/GEN/142, 6 Jun. 2006; and Paper from Canada, Procedures from Adversely Affected Domestic Interested Parties, TN/RL/GEN/111, 21 Apr. 2006.
152. A. Sinnaeve, 'The "Community Interest Test" in Anti-dumping Investigations: Time for Reform?', *Global Trade and Customs Journal* 2 (2007): 157.
153. E. Vyboldina, 'The Green Paper on Trade Defence Instruments: Anti-dumping', *Global Trade and Customs Journal* 2 (2007): 411.

Article 21 (1) sets out the main purpose of the Community interest test, namely to decide 'whether there are compelling reasons not to impose anti-dumping measures in a given proceeding, despite a finding that dumped imports caused material injury to the Community industry'.[154] It directs the Commission to give 'special consideration' to the need to 'eliminate the trade distorting effects of injurious dumping', as well as the need to 'restore effective competition' in the Community market.[155] After the examination, the Commission can decide whether to impose a measure on the basis of the Community interest. Commentators observe that, the test carried out by the Commission is a negative one, namely measures may not be applied only where it can be *clearly* concluded that it is *not* in the Community interest to apply such measure.[156] The Commission is working under the presumption that measures will be applied 'whenever dumped imports caused material injury to the Community industry'.[157] Only if compelling evidence leads to the conclusion that the imposition of a measure would not be in the overall interest of the Community, the Community interest test can provide the legal basis for not imposing duties. The non-imposition of measures on the basis of the Community interest is therefore an exception departing from normal rules and occurs only in special circumstances.

3.2.2.1 *Procedural Aspects of the Community Interest Test*

Article 21(2) clearly stimulates the parties whose interests should be examined and who enjoy various rights in the Community interest test. It provides that complainants, importers and their representative associations, representative users and representative consumer organizations have the right to make themselves known and provide information to the Commission.[158]

It is the view of some commentators that this list is non-exhaustive and 'parties with an economic interest in the product under investigation are meant to be part of the analysis'.[159] Hence, it is a standing practice of the Commission to also consider the interests of other economic actors, such as the suppliers of the Community industry or traders of the product concerned on a case-by-case basis, although they are not explicitly mentioned in Article 21(2).[160] In contrast, parties with non-economic interests, such as environmental organizations, would not be considered as interested parties under Article 21.

Article 21(2), (3), (4) and (6) specifies the procedural rights of interested parties. Those rights include: the right to make submissions; the right to consult

154. Sinnaeve, 'The "Community Interest Test" in Anti-dumping Investigations', 157.
155. *Ibid.*
156. *Ibid.*, and also Müller et al., *EC Anti-dumping Law*, 501.
157. Van Bael & Bellis, *Anti-dumping and Other Trade Protection Laws of the EC*, 294 and Vermulst & Waer, *EC Anti-dumping Law and Practice*, 370.
158. Article 21(2) of the Basic Regulation.
159. Sinnaeve, 'The "Community Interest Test" in Anti-dumping Investigations', 158 and Müller et al., *EC Anti-dumping Law*, 505.
160. *Ibid.*

non-confidential files; the right to respond to submissions; the right to request a hearing; the right to make submissions on the application of a provisional duty; the right to inspect other parties' submissions on the application of a provisional duty and responses; and the right to have a disclosure of final findings.

Article 21(2) also lays down that the interested parties concerned may only submit information on the Community interest within the time limit specified in the initiation notice, which is normally forty days from the date of publication of the notice of initiation of a new investigation, an interim review or an expiry review in the Official Journal (OJ).

3.2.2.2 *Substantive Assessment of the Community Interest*

With respect to substantive assessments, the analysis under the Community interest test consists, first, of an evaluation of likely consequences of applying or not applying the envisaged measure on the Community industry and other interested parties,[161] and second, the weighting and balancing of different interests at stake.[162]

To conduct the first step analysis, the Commission normally goes one step up or down in the chain of economic operators to access the likely effect of taking or not taking the measure upon those operators. Consequently, in addition to the interests of the Community industry, the interests of the upstream industry, users (downstream industries) and sometimes consumers are taken into account the Community interest test.

In comparison with other operators likely to be directly and economically affected by the measure, such as upstream and downstream industries, the standing of consumer organizations in a Community interest test is less straightforward. For products not commonly sold at the retail level, the CFI clarified in *BEUC v. Commission* that consumer organizations are to be involved only if they can demonstrate an 'objective link' with the product concerned.[163] That is to say, in an investigation not concerning consumer products, a customer organization does not automatically qualify as an interested party, yet is not automatically excluded either. An 'objective link', for example, by demonstrating 'the likely effect of a cost increase of the product concerned on the price of further processed products which are sold at the retail level', has to be established on a case-by-case basis to justify the standing of a consumer organization in an AD investigation.[164]

As the second step of the analysis, the Commission weighs all the interests of different parties and balances them against each other. The Commission usually checks whether the negative impact on other interested parties would be clearly disproportionate to the advantages that the imposition is likely to bring to the

161. Case T-132/01, *Euroalliages et al. v. Commission* [2003] ECR II-2359, para. 47.
162. Sinnaeve, 'The "Community Interest Test" in Anti-dumping Investigations', 159–160.
163. Case T-256/97, *Bureau Europeen des Unions de Consommateurs (BEUC) v. Commission* [2000] ECR II-101.
164. Sinnaeve, 'The "Community Interest Test" in Anti-dumping Investigations', 59.

Community industry. In practice, as observed in the vast majority of cases, the Commission considers 'the positive effects of measures for the Community industry outweigh the possible negative effects on users and consumers'.[165] Therefore, unless overwhelming evidence suggests otherwise, that is, the imposition of a measure would 'not bring any benefit to the Community industry, for instance, in cases where the Community industry is not viable anymore and the imposition of measures could not be expected to allow its return to viability', the imposition of measures will not be considered as disproportionate.[166]

Due to methodological difficulties, the Commission does not quantify the interest of each economic factor in the process of weighting different interests. Hence, even though the Commission tries to balance various interests, these interests are not weighed against each other in a mathematical equation. In other words, 'the assessment of Community interest is not a cost-benefit analysis in the strict sense and the Commission enjoy a large degree of discretion to conduct a qualitative appreciation instead of a quantitative analysis'.[167]

Also, interests that can be taken into account in the Community interest test vary from one interested party to anther. For the Community industry, factors that are normally recognized as relevant in a Community interest test include the objectives 'to prevent the future aggravation of an already precarious situation for the Community industry or even of its disappearances'; 'to prevent investment and rationalization in the sector concerned being put in jeopardy'; 'to safeguard sufficient earnings of the Community industry in order to fund necessary levels of investment'; 'to prevent the loss of the Community industry's competitiveness in terms of technology'; 'to prevent the distortion of competition arising from dumping on the Community industry', and so on.[168]

Similarly, certain arguments put forward by upstream industries and users are frequently taken into account by the Commission. Protection of upstream industries in the Community, especially if a loss of technology is imminent, can be an argument that supports the imposition of a measure, whereas the points made by users with regard to potential price increases to be borne by the user industry and difficulties to make sure sufficient supply of the product concerned in the Community can provide significant support to the argument in favour of termination of an investigation without the measure imposed.

For example, in *Synthetic staple fibres of polyesters (PSF)* case, the Commission terminated the investigation due to strong opposition from the user industry.[169] In particular, the Commission considered the following arguments made by users: shortage of supply; price increases of PSF; cost impact of the

165. Vermulst & Waer, *EC Anti-dumping Law and Practice*, 371.
166. Sinnaeve, 'The "Community Interest Test" in Anti-dumping Investigations', 159.
167. Müller et al., *EC Anti-dumping Law*, 501.
168. *Ibid.*
169. Commission Decision of 19 Jun. 2007 terminating the anti-dumping proceeding concerning imports of synthetic staple fibres of polyesters (PSF) originating in Malaysia and Taiwan and releasing the amounts secured by way of the provisional duties imposed, OJ L 160/30, 21 Jun. 2007.

proposed measure; price increases for downstream products and consequence for employment in the Community market. The Commission, after taking into account the submissions made by various interested parties, concluded that:[170]

> The overall advantages to be gained by the Community industry must be weighted against the probable disadvantages, in particular for users and, to some extent for consumers. The volume and the variety of supply offered by Community producers are deteriorating. This is due, among other reasons, to the industrial conversion of Community producers from PSF to other products (for example la Seda de Barcelona) and the financial difficulties of Tergal. There is a supply problem in the Community market for certain types of fibres and the Community producers cannot or are not willing to make the necessary efforts to meet the demand. Furthermore, it is likely that the imposition of duties will lead to substantial price increases of certain types of PSF which are not available in sufficient quantities in the Community. Moreover, account should be taken of the fact that certain users of PSF (in particular the bedding industry) have very low profit margins and will have to pass on to consumers any price increase in PSF or abandon their activities in case competition from third countries would not allow them to increase their prices.

Other important considerations for the Commission in a Community interest test include the elimination of trade-distorting effects resulting from dumped imports and to restore effective competition in the Community market. In this regard, the Commission normally rejects the argument from exporters, users or consumers that the adoption of AD measures would exclude producers outside the Community to supply the Community market.

However, in two situations, the Commission examines the competition argument with special care. The first is when 'the possible danger of reducing competition or even creating an monopolistic market structure as a result of the imposition of an anti-dumping measure'.[171] The second is where the Community industry has been the subject of measures sanctioning anti-competitive behaviour.[172] Yet, the mere existence of these situations does not automatically result in the termination of the investigation on the grounds of Community interest.

---

170. *Ibid.*, retrial 40.

171. For example, in a potassium chloride case, the form of the measure has been changed on the grounds of Community interest. Council Regulation (EC) No. 969/2000 of 8 May 2000 imposing a definitive anti-dumping duty on imports of potassium chloride originating in Belarus, Russia and Ukraine, OJ L 112, 4, recitals 123 and 125.

172. For example, Commission Regulation (EC) No. 617/1999 of 23 Mar. 1999 imposing a provisional anti-dumping duty on imports of stainless steel wires with a diameter of 1 mm or more originating in India, OJ L 79, 13, recitals 27 and 76. Also, Commission Decision of 28 May 1999 terminating the anti-dumping proceeding concerning imports into the Community of certain stainless steel heavy plates originating in Slovenia and South Africa (notified under document number C (1999) 1383), OJ L 135, 95 and Council Regulation (EC) No. 348/2000 of 14 Feb. 2000 imposing a definitive anti-dumping duty on imports of certain seamless pipes and tubes of iron or non-alloy steel originating in Croatia and Ukraine and collecting definitively the provisional duty imposed, OJ L 45, 1, at recitals 30 and 39.

3.2.2.3 Reflections on Green Paper

On 6 December 2006, the Commission adopted a *Green Paper for Public Consultation on Europe's Trade Defence Instruments in a Changing Global Economy* ('Green Paper') to launch reflections on the application of the EU Trade Defence Instruments (TDI) in light of 'emerging new realities from the application of TDI as well as in a context of globalization'.[173]

Two issues related to the Community interest test, namely the weighting of different EU interests and the form, timing and duration of AD measures, were raised in the Green Paper consultation. These issues were emanated from high profile investigations involving consumer products, such as footwear,[174] in which the concept of 'Community interest' took the centre stage.[175] During these investigations, stakeholders started to question whether the balancing of interests should be rethought or whether the scope of analysis of Community interest should be enlarged, in order to reflect the reality of the changing global economy.

For instance, in the footwear investigation, deep divisions among different stakeholders were provoked. One feature of the EU leather footwear sector is its significant degree of outsourcing. Although some EU companies still maintain their production in Europe, a large number of footwear companies have outsourced their production to China and Vietnam, while keeping other functions, such as design and marketing, in the EU. These outsourcing companies are subject to the AD measure and suffer negative consequences from this measure. Similarly, consumers suffer price increases as a result of the imposition of the duty. Therefore, questions were raised on 'whether and how to better reflect the interests of those outsourcing EU companies and consumers in an anti-dumping investigation'.[176]

During the process of the Green Paper consultation, possible changes to the existing law and practice of Community interest have been discussed in more than 500 submissions made by interested parties around the world.[177] Three proposed changes, which have already been practiced by the Commission in certain cases but have not yet been codified, draw the most attention.

The first proposed change is to codify the Commission's practice in modulating the level of AD measures. The current Community interest test leads to either a positive or negative conclusion, namely whether a measure should be imposed or

173. Communication from the Commission, *Global Europe: Europe's trade defence instruments in a changing global economy – A Green Paper for public consultation,* COM (2006) 763 final, Brussels 6 Dec. 2006.
174. Council Regulation (EC) No. 1472/2006 of 5 Oct. 2006 imposing a definitive anti-dumping duty and collecting definitely the provisional duty imposed on imports of certain footwear with uppers of leather originating in the People's Republic of China and Vietnam, OJ L 275, 1, recital 301.
175. F. Graafsma & J. Comelis, 'The EC's Green Paper on Trade Defence Instruments: Guillotine on Anti-dumping or Smokescreen for More Basic Predicaments?', *Global Trade and Customs Journal* 2 (2007): 255.
176. Sinnaeve, 'The "Community Interest Test" in Anti-dumping Investigations', 162.
177. Bulletin Quotidien Europe No. 9548, 'Peter Mandelson Gives Himself Extra-time before Submitting His New Revision Proposals', 22 Nov. 2007.

not. The Commission therefore considers that more flexibility might be appropriate, in particular in cases 'where the balance of interest is not a clear-cut and a lower level of duties might alleviate the negative impact on certain economic operators'.[178]

The Commission's practice in the footwear case was an experiment in modulation of the level of AD measures. In this case, the Commission adopted a new approach to incorporate the concept of a non-injurious import volume in the calculation of the injury margin.[179] The Commission calculated new underselling margins based on the size of non-materially injurious import value amounts. For this purpose, the cumulated import values of 2003 were regarded as non-materially injurious. These import values were then allocated to China and Vietnam on the basis of their share of import volumes during 1 April 2004 – 31 March 2005. These adjusted non-injurious import values were subsequently expressed as a percentage deducted from the underselling margin to arrive at a revised lower underselling margin. Consequently, and also as a result of the lesser duty rule, the definitive AD duty imposed by Regulation 1472/2006 was lower than the dumping margin and injury margin calculated under 'normal' rules.

Despite potential positive effects of the flexibility to modulate the level of AD measures, it is argued that its implementation may reveal a number of difficulties.[180] Among them, lack of criteria or methods to define the modulation could be one of the most serious risks. Criticism of modulation lays the fact that this rule can make the outcome established by the precise and sophisticated methodology of dumping and injury margin to be modulated according to non-precise parameters, that is, the Community interest test.

The second hotly debated proposal is the shorter duration of AD measures. The application of AD measures for a shorter period of time than the normal five-year period is rare, but not exceptional. Again, in the footwear case, the Commission experimented with a definitive AD measure for two years, instead of the normal five years as stipulated in the Basic Regulation, in order to gain sufficient political support from Member States.[181]

The Community institutions argue that this practice of the Commission has been confirmed by the CFI in *Cecom v. Council*.[182] In this case, the CFI held that a shorter duration of measures provided by Article 11(2) of the Basic Regulation is allowed, since Article 11(2):

> [m]ust be structured as allowing the Council a discretionary power to fix at less than five years the period of application of definitive anti-dumping duties adopted following a procedure for the review of the measures initially adopted if, . . . , such a limitation best serves to protect the differing interests of the

178. Sinnaeve, 'The "Community Interest Test" in Anti-dumping Investigations', 175.
179. Council Regulation (EC) No. 1472/2006 of 5 Oct. 2006, OJ L 275, 1, recital 301.
180. Sinnaeve, 'The "Community Interest Test" in Anti-dumping Investigations', 176.
181. *Ibid.*
182. Case T-232/95, *Committee of European Copier Manufactures (Cecom) v. Council of the European Union* [1998] ECR II-2679.

parties to the procedure and maintain the equilibrium between those interests which the basic regulation seeks to establish.

However, the legitimate and long-standing practice of the Commission has not yet been codified in the Community law and no guideline has been provided to clarify how a shorter duration of AD measures can be applied in each investigation.

In the absence of a clear legal framework, the Commission's practice to shorten the duration of AD measures in both original investigations and expiry reviews causes fierce controversy, as proven by the *Compact Fluorescent Lamps (CFL-i)* case.[183] In this case, the Community institutions extended the measure for another year (instead of five years), after an expiry review. The EU's decision has been challenged by both sides, that is, the complainant, Osram, and some exporters/importers.[184] Osram essentially argued that the Basic Regulation mandates the Community institutions to extend the measure if the likelihood of a concurrence of dumping and injury is established for five years following an expiry review. The Community institutions have no flexibility to extend the measure for another year under the Basic Regulation. Unfortunately, Osram withdrew the case before the CFI delivered its judgment. So the CFI's opinion on whether the institutions have the discretion to shorten the AD measures remains uncertain by far.

The third proposal concerns the possibility of excluding certain product types from the application of AD measures in order to balance the interests of producers, importers, retailers, distributors and consumers. Again, the case best demonstrated the Commission's experiment is the footwear case. During the course of the investigation, the Commission excluded, both at the provisional stage and the definitive stage, *Special Technical Athletic Footwear* (STAF) from the product scope on the grounds that STAF has distinctive technical features.[185]

The proposal to allow certain flexibility to exclude certain product types from the application of AD measures received less criticism than other proposals, as it is easier to operate. However, it has been pointed out that the main concern is 'that this proposal is likely to increase the risk of circumvention'.[186]

In conclusion, the EU's Community interest test is unique among WTO members in the sense that it establishes a systematic instrument to look into the wider economic impact of AD measures and consider whether the application of a measure is in the 'public interest' in light of its potential impact on different economic operators. In applying the Community interest test, the Commission exercises its wide discretion and makes an overall appreciation under the principle of proportionality. The practice to date shows that the current threshold is very high

183. Note of initiation of an expiry review of the anti-dumping measures applicable to imports of integrated electronic compact fluorescent lamps (CFL-i) originating in the People's Republic of China OJ C 167/13, 19 Jul. 2006.
184. Case T-466/07, *Osram v. Council*. Two further appeals of the same regulation, from export/importers, are: Cases T-459/07, *Hang zhou Duralamp v. Council* and T-469/07 *Philips Lighting Poland, Philips Lighting v. Council.*
185. Council Regulation (EC) No. 1472/2006 of 5 Oct. 2006, OJ L 275, 1, recital 15.
186. Sinnaeve, The 'Community Interest Test' in Anti-dumping Investigations', 176.

for concluding that the negative effects of the measure would outweigh the benefit and an investigation should be terminated on the grounds of Community interest. However, as discussed above, the availability of the Community interest test gives the Commission certain flexibility to balance the interests of different economic operators in the EU and allows it to take actions if the interests of a particular industry need to be protected. The proposals discussed in the Green Paper may achieve more transparency, effectiveness and workability, but may equally risk opening the door to a politicization of AD investigations. It remains to be seen how the Commission will address these challenges in its future practice.[187]

3.3 Anti-circumvention

3.3.1 Anti-circumvention in the WTO

The issue of circumvention arises when an exporter, which is subject to an AD duty, avoids the duty by misclassifying or altering the goods, trans-shipping them through a third country as a product of that country or sending components of the product concerned to the importing country for assembly into a finished product that otherwise would be subject to anti-dumping duty.[188]

Forms of circumvention include:

- carrying out the final assembly in the importing country or a third country;
- altering the product without economic justification so that it falls under a different tariff code, which is not subject to dumping measures;
- trans-shipment via other third countries;
- repackaging;
- re-channelling the sales via exporters with lower duties;
- incorrect origin declarations; and
- importation of parts or knock-down kits.

Neither the Kennedy Round nor the Tokyo Round AD Codes contained any provisions on circumvention. The introduction of multilateral rules on this subject in the Uruguay Round was one of the negotiation objectives of the EU and the USA, but these rules were not adopted in the end.

The 'Dunkel draft' contained separate provisions for importing country circumvention and third country circumvention.[189] Article 12 provided that 'under specific circumstances, anti-dumping duties could be extended, in the case of circumvention operations consisting of assembling or completing a like-product

---

187. MLex TDI package slips from commission agenda, 4 Dec. 2007, available at: <www.mlex.com/list3.aspx?jobid=5254>.

188. Van Bael & Bellis, *Anti-dumping and Other Trade Protection Laws of the EC*, 482.

189. GATT Secretariat, *Draft Final Act Embodying the Results of the Uruguay Round of Multilateral Trade Negotiations*, MTN.TNC/W/FA/F-21 (20 Dec. 1991).

in the importing country from components originating in the country subject to the duties'.[190]

The US found this draft provision insufficient, so it filed a proposal to extend AD duties in case of third-country and minor alternation circumventions.[191] The majority of GATT Contracting Parties rejected this proposal. As there was no strong political interest in the adoption of multilateral anti-circumvention provisions, no final agreement was reached and Article 12 of the Dunkel Draft was deleted.[192]

Nevertheless, the Final Act embodying the result of the Uruguay Round (the Final Act) included the following statement:[193]

> Noting that while the problem of circumvention of anti-dumping duty measures formed part of the negotiations which preceded the Agreement on Implementation of Article VI of GATT 1994, negotiators were unable to agree on a specific text,
>
> Mindful of the desirability of the applicability of uniform rules in this area as soon as possible,
>
> Decide to refer this matter to the Committee on Anti-Dumping Practices established under that Agreement for resolution.

3.3.2 Anti-circumvention in the EU Anti-dumping Law

Despite the absence of international rules, several WTO members have adopted anti-circumvention legislation, *inter alia* the EU.[194] These members, including the EU, interpreted the declaration in the Final Act as permitting individual members

190. *Ibid.*, Art. 12.1. These specific circumstances include cases in which it has been established that: (1) the product assembled/completed had to be a like-product with regard to a product which was subject to a definitive dumping measure; (2) the assembly/completion operation had to be carried out by an entity which was related to the original dumping exporter; (3) the components used in the assembly/completion operation had to be, directly or indirectly, sourced by the dumping exporter; (4) the assembly/completion operation had to have started or expanded substantially after the initiation of the anti-dumping investigation; (5) the total costs of the components used in the assembly/completion operation had to be no less than the 70% of the total cost of all the parties used in the operation, with the exception that no anti-dumping measure should be extended if the value of the assembly/completion operation was greater than 25% of the ex-factory cost of the like-product; (6) there had to be evidence of dumping concerning the difference between the priced of the product in the importing country and the normal value of the product when subject to the original definitive anti-dumping duty; and (7) there had to be evidence that the extension of the anti-dumping measures to the components was within the scope of the definitive anti-dumping duty in order to prevent the injury to a domestic industry with regard to the like-product.
191. Communication for the United States, Proposal for Improvements to the Anti-Dumping Code, MTN.GNG/NG8/W59 of 20 Dec. 1989.
192. K. Aamantopoulos & D. Notaris, 'The Future of the WTO & the Reform of the Anti-Dumping Agreement: A Legal Perspective', *Fordham International Law Journal* 24 (2000): 30, 32.
193. WTO *Final Act Embodying the Results of the Uruguay Round of Multilateral Trade Negotiations* LT/UR/A/1, 15 Apr. 1994.
194. Australia, Canada, Japan, Mexico, New Zealand, as well as the EU and US have adopted anti-circumvention measures.

to adopt provisions unilaterally, pending a multilateral solution within the framework of the WTO. For example, the Council stated in *Polyethylene Terephthalate Film* that, as 'the Final Act of the Uruguay Round contained a Decision on anti-circumvention referring the matter to the Committee on Anti-Dumping Practices, and as this decision was made knowing that several WTO members already had their own anti-circumvention legislation, the European Community interpreted it as permitting individual members to adopt or maintain provisions in this respect, pending the adoption of multilaterally agreed rules'.[195]

Provisions on anti-circumvention were first introduced by the EU in 1987 as Article 13(10) of Regulation 1761/87[196] and were aimed at covering assembly operations within the Community, namely the EU circumvention, where a very high proportion of the components used were from countries whose export AD measures had been imposed. Article 13(10) fell into disuse, however, after the GATT panel found that this provision was not consistent with the Community's obligations under the GATT, in Panel Report *EEC – Parts and Components*.[197] Third country circumvention was dealt with under the rule of origin.

When implementing the result of the Uruguay Round, the EU introduced new circumvention procedures into the Basic Regulation that were subsequently amended in 2004.

Article 13(1) of the Basic Regulation provides that:[198]

> Circumvention shall be defined as a change in the pattern of trade between third countries and the Community or between individual companies in the country subject to measures and the Community, which stems from a practice, process or work for which there is insufficient due cause or economic justification other than the imposition of the duty, and where there is evidence of injury or that the remedial effects of the duty are being undermined in terms of prices and/or quantities of the like product, and where there is evidence of dumping in relation to the normal values previously established for the like product, if necessary in accordance with the provisions of Article 2.

Article 13(2) expressly deals with circumvention as regards assembly. In accordance with paragraph 2 of the provisions, operations involving assembly operations may be caught where:[199]

> a) The operation started or substantially increased since, or just prior to, the initiation of the anti-dumping investigation and the parts concerned are from the country whose exports are subject to measures; and

195. Regulation 1975/2004 [2004] OJ L 342/1.
196. Council Regulation (EEC) No. 1761/87 amending Regulation (EEC) No. 2176/84 on protection against dumped or subsidised imports from countries not members of the European Economic Community, OJ L 167, 26 Jun. 1987, 9.
197. GATT *European Economic Community – Regulation on Imports of Parts and Components*, Report of the Panel, ('EEC – Parts and Components'), adopted 16 May 1990, BISD 37S/132, 152.
198. Article 13(1) of the Basic Regualtion.
199. Article 13(2) of the Basic Regulation.

b) The parts constitute 60% or more of the total value of the parts of the assembled product; however circumvention will not be considered to be taking place where the value added to the parts brought in, during the assembly or completion operation, is greater than 25% of the manufacturing cost; and

c) The remedial effects of the duty are being undermined in terms of the prices and/or quantities of the assembled like product and there is evidence of dumping in relation to the normal values previously established for the like or similar products.

Given the variety of circumvention practice, the EU's practice in the anti-circumvention is in fact established by case law, as discussed below, which provides meaningful interpretation to the wording of the Basic Regulation.

3.3.2.1 Change in the Pattern of Trade

A 'change in the pattern of trade' is not defined in the Basic Regulation. The Commission consistently interprets it as: a decrease in the imports of the product concerned from the country whose exports are subject to measures and an increase in imports from a third country that is not subject to measures; or an increase in imports of parts of the product concerned or slightly altered product without being economically justified. The following cases illustrate the Commission's practice.

In *Certain tube and pipe fittings of iron and steel (China)*,[200] a change in the pattern of trade was established on the basis that exports to the Community from cooperating exporters in a third country increased by 300% and, in relation to the non-cooperating exporters, the increase in imports from the third country was substantially higher.

In *Tungsten electrodes*,[201] some companies were assigned individual AD duty rates, which were significantly lower than the residual duty rate. The Commission stated that where the exports by the companies benefiting from lower individual duty rates increased significantly in volume after the imposition of the measure, such an increase in volume could be considered as constituting a change in the pattern of trade.

In *Ring Binder Mechanisms*,[202] AD duties were extended where duties imposed on imports of ring binder mechanisms (RBM) from China were being circumvented by means of trans-shipment through Vietnam. The replacement of exports of RBM from China with imports of the same product from Vietnam was considered a clear change in the pattern of trade, irrespective of whether exports from China were replaced immediately or only after a certain time period. The Commission stated that the mere fact that exports from China ceased prior to the start of operations in Vietnam did not have any impact on the conclusion whether there had been a change in the pattern of trade.

---

200. Regulation 763/2000 [2000] OJ L 94/1, recital 12.
201. Regulation 260/2007 [2007] OJ L 72/1.
202. Regulation 1208/2004 [2004] OJ L 232/1, recital 23.

3.3.2.2 *Practice, Process or Work*

A variety of activities may potentially be considered a *'practice, process or work'*, ranging from simple 'operations' such as: trans-shipment; repackaging; wrong origin declarations; imports of knockdown kits; reversible product alterations; slightly altered goods, to more complex activities. For example, in *Ring-Binder Mechanisms*,[203] a circumventing 'practice, process or work' was considered to have occurred where both machinery and equipment used in Vietnam had been transferred from related companies dealing with RBMs that were located in China or in Indonesia. Also, the transfer of equipment took place immediately prior to the imposition of definitive measures.

In *Integrated Electronic Compact Fluorescent Lamps (CFL-i)*,[204] the assessment of circumvention was undertaken by analysing successively whether there was a change in the pattern of trade between third countries and the Community by the consignment of the product concerned via third countries. It was found that imports from China more than halved after the imposition of measures in 2001, that is, decreased from 85 million units in 2000 to 37 million units in 2002. Although imports recovered partially after 2002, their level in 2004 was still more than 20% below the level before the imposition of measures. In the meantime, imports from Vietnam, Pakistan and the Philippines, which were practically non-existent prior to 2001, increased significantly after the imposition of measure. Exports from China to the Philippines had increased consistently since 2000 and dramatically in 2003; at the same time import statistics from the Philippines showed consistently higher volumes than export statistics from China to the Philippines. The Commission therefore concluded that the difference between the statistics corresponded to the volumes exported from the Philippines to the EU, indicating that goods may have been trans-shipped from China via the Philippines to the EU.

3.3.2.3 *Insufficient Due Cause or Economic Justification*

The Commission normally investigates the criterion '*insufficient due cause or economic justification other than the imposition of the anti-dumping duty*' for the change in the pattern of trade by examining import patterns, the functions of the product concerned, their marketing, packaging, and expected uses.[205]

In *Coumarin*,[206] the company stated that the main reason for exporting coumarin originating in China was because of insecurity of supply, namely the risk of strikes, in India. However when the Commission considered the facts of the case , it did not consider the threat of strikes to be an economic justification.[207]

---

203. *Ibid.*
204. Regulation 866/2005 [2005] OJ L 145/1.
205. *Ibid.*, recital 15.
206. Regulation 2272/2004 [2004] OJ L 396/18.
207. During the IP, the volume of coumarin that was subject to further purification by Atlas (the cooperating Indian company) was 75% of Atlas' total production volume, the remaining

The economic justification criterion was accepted in *Imports of certain zinc oxides originating in the People's Republic of China by imports of certain zinc oxides consigned from Kazakhstan.*[208] In this case, AD duties had been imposed on zinc oxides originating in China from 2002. It was alleged that there was a change in the pattern of trade by a significant increase in imports of the same product from Kazakhstan. The reasonable economic grounds, other than the imposition of definitive duties, for the change in the pattern of trade shown by Kazakstan, were accepted.

3.3.2.4 *Remedial Effects of the Duty*

Notwithstanding the existence of circumvention, in order to extend duties to third country exporters, the Commission must also establish that the remedial effects of the duty are being undermined in terms of price and/or quantity of like product being exported. The un-dumped export price of the original product (export price, plus customs and duties) is compared with the average EU sales price of the new product. An estimate is then made to determine the extent to which imports of the new product have replaced those of the original.

In *Integrated Electronic Compact Fluorescent Lamps (CFL-i)*,[209] in order to assess whether the imported products had, in terms of quantities and prices, undermined the remedial effects of the measures in force, quantities and prices to unrelated customers in the Community of imports consigned from the three countries under investigation were used where available. The prices so determined were compared to the injury elimination level established for Community producers in the original investigation.

3.3.2.5 *Like Product*

The product that is allegedly circumventing the duties must be like the product concerned in the original investigation. The term 'like product' is defined in Article 1(4) of the Basic Regulation as a product that is identical, that is, alike in all respects, to the product under consideration, or in the absence of such a product, another product which has characteristics closely resembling those of the product concerned.

In *Polyester staple fibre/polyester filament tows*[210] the Commission noted that polyester staple fibre (PSF) and polyester filament tows (PFT) shared the same

---

volume of 25% represented genuine production in India. In addition, the CN code used for the coumarin imported from the PRC was the same as the one used for the further purified coumarin re-exported by Atlas to the Community. The product re-exported to the Community thus retained its Chinese origin. The cost of further purification of coumarin was not high, it consisted of a slight modification and the value of coumarin lost in the purification process was incurred at the moment the product was purchased, it could not thus be considered as a cost generated by the purification process itself.

208. Regulation 465/2006 [2006] OJ L 83/6.
209. Regulation 866/2005 [2005] OJ L 145/1.
210. Regulation 2513/97 [1997] OJ L 346/1, recital 8.

basic physical and chemical characteristic. The only difference between PFT and PSF resulted from a simple cutting process. The imported PFT was therefore viewed as a product that has been slightly altered in order to avoid the AD measure applicable to PSF. Differences of this nature, which could be created or eliminated by minor alterations, could lead to the conclusion that PSF and PFT were essentially 'like product'. Thus, the Commission decided that although the alteration process from PFT into PSF was not, as such, an assembly operation, it was of such a nature that it had to be considered as a practice which was carried out to avoid the measures in force.

In *Gas-fueled, non-refillable pocket flint lighters and disposable refillable pocket flint lighters,*[211] the Commission found that an ineffectual addition to a product does not affect its likeness. In that case, disposable, refillable flint lighters from China were identical in all respects to the disposable, non-refillable flint lighters covered by the AD duty, except for the addition of a refill valve. The Commission was therefore determined that these were alike the lighters subject to the existing measure.

3.3.2.6 The 60% Value of Parts Test and the 25% Value-added Test

In determining the existence of circumvention, the Commission also carries out a 60% value of parts test and a 25% value-added test. In *Electronic weighing scales (Japan, Singapore) assembled in the Community*[212] the circumvention consisted of imports of parts, which were used for the assembly in the Community, for use in the retail trade. The investigation established that an assembly operation was conducted by three Dutch companies (CTW, Keylard and Digi Nederland) acting in close cooperation and belonging to the same corporate group. The value of the parts incorporated by the Dutch companies, was established on the basis of the purchase price of the parts when delivered to the assembler's premises, that is, an into-factory basis.

In view of the fact that CTW, Keylard and Digi Nederland were found to be related and functionally interdependent in the assembly of REWS, they were considered to be part of a single economic entity. Consequently, parts were identified and their value determined when first entering this single economic entity. Intra-group transfers of parts and semi-finished or finished products were disregarded for the purpose of the value added test.

In this case the Commission established that the prices charged by the exporters of REWS parts to the assembler were at arms length, that is, above cost of production plus a reasonable profit for parts produced by the exporter or above the exporters' own purchase price and allowing for a reasonable profit. It also established that the value of parts originating in Japan and Singapore was found to be higher than 60 % of the total parts value of the assembled REWS during the IP.

211. Regulation 119/97 [1997] OJ L 22/1, recital 10.
212. Regulation 984/97 [1997] OJ L 141/57.

In the same case, the average value-added established during the investigating period was found to be above the 25% threshold. The value-added to parts was determined as the sum of labour costs and factory overheads incurred within the single economic entity. SG&A expenses, profit and parts that allegedly acquired the Community origin were not considered to be value-added within the meaning of Article 13(2)(b) of the Basic Regulation. The value-added established was then expressed as a percentage of the manufacturing cost. Given the fact that the value-added to parts by the three Dutch companies exceeded 25%, the Commission concluded that the assembly operation could not be considered to constitute circumvention.

In conclusion, the Basic Regulation allows the Community institutions to extend AD duties to third country producers if circumvention is found. Despite the absence of multilateral framework, the EU established a comprehensive legal framework to cover assembly, third country circumvention and minor modification.[213] The EU is reportedly a main user of anti-circumvention rules. For example, the EU initiated 13 anti-circumvention investigations against Chinese producers from 2003 to 2005, which represented 76% of all anti-circumvention investigations initiated by WTO Members against China in that period of time.[214] Hence, the anti-circumvention provision in the Basic Regulation provides an additional layer of protection to the Community industry after the imposition of AD measures.

4 CONCLUSION

The rise of legalization in the international AD regime provides a rich arena to examine the intervening effect that multilateral legalization has on domestic systems. The evolution of the EU anti-dumping regime in the past sixty years demonstrates how the phenomenal rise of legalization in the trade regime interacts with other factors to shape the AD regime of Europe.

The development of the EU anti-dumping regime is an illustrative example of both the effects of the legalization process on domestic systems and the limit of its effects. On the one hand, most of the EU anti-dumping instruments are constructed based on the basic principles of GATT/WTO AD rules. On the other hand, a close look of them suggests that those instruments are in fact a mixture of the transposition of multilateral rules and the compromise between interests of different Member States, Community institutions and economic operators. Similarly, although the administration of AD policy in the EU has always been regulated and constrained by multilateral rules, the Commission, as the key player, has to balance divergent interests within the EU. The CFI and ECJ, also key players in the EU trade policy-making, have a more ambivalent attitude towards multilateral legalization – although to a large extent they admitted the impact of multilateral

213. Y. Yu, 'Circumvention and Anti-circumvention in Anti-dumping Practice: A New Problem in China's Outbound Trade', *JWT* 41 (2007): 1015, 1023.
214. WTO, Anti-dumping semi-annual reports from WTO Members, available at: <www.wto.org>.

legalization on the EU's trade policy-making, they refused to completely substitute European legalization with multilateral legalization. Hence, the impact of multilateral legalization on the EU system is more complex than the similarity between the Basic Regulation and the ADA suggest.

Meanwhile, the EU introduced a number of WTO-plus provisions to provide the Community institutions more flexibility to handle uncertain economic and political situations and balance different interests within the EU. Injury margin calculation, Community interest, anti-circumvention and non-market economy provisions are representative of the WTO-plus features of the EU system. These provisions, although indeed offering additional protection to the Community industry from time to time, do not necessarily favour domestic protectionists all the time. Instead, the key function of these provisions is to give additional flexibility to the system so that the imposition of AD measure can be 'a balanced act'.

The next chapter will examine whether one of the EU's WTO-plus features, the non-market economy provision, can be challenged in the WTO dispute settlement, in the context of China's AD-related activities.

Chapter 6

China's AD-related WTO Activities

1 INTRODUCTION

This chapter examines another consequence of legalization, namely the impact of the multilateral legalization on the utilization of the DSM. The rise of legalization in the GATT/WTO, which is characterized by tightened obligation, greater precision and stronger delegation, creates stronger incentives for WTO members to utilize the DSM for the purpose of protecting trade interests and strategically advancing trade claims. One commentator describes the trend as '[W]hen officials from different countries disagree about trade policy, some say "see you in Geneva!" meaning "see you in court" '.[1] Although this formal legal representation is arguably just one aspect of the trade regime and there are many other ways that GATT/WTO law affects global governance, it is commonly agreed that '[T]he crowning achievement of the WTO, . . . , is its codified legal obligations and a dispute settlement system more active than any other international tribunal'.[2]

It is, however, not an easy task to use the more 'legalized', and consequently more complicated, DSM to the full extent. Various reasons are propounded for lack of effective uses of the DSM by some WTO members, in particular the developing ones.[3] The reasons include:

> a lack of sufficient awareness of WTO rights and obligations; inadequate coordination between the government and private sector; difficulty in

---

1. R. Wolfe, 'See You in Geneva? Legal (Mis)representations of the Trading System', *European Journal of International Relations* 11 (2005): 339.
2. *Ibid.*
3. Relevant literature includes, for example, J. Lacarte-Muró & P. Gappah, 'Developing Countries and the WTO Legal and Dispute Settlement System: A View from the Bench', *Journal of*

> determining the existence of undue trade barriers and the feasibility of legal challenge; financial and human resource constrains in lodging dispute; and an oft-cited lack of political will to pursue trade disputes due to fear that trade preferences or other forms of assistance will be withdrawn, or some form of retaliatory action will be taken.[4]

Among the factors listed above, the shortfall of resources, frequently due to the absence of institutional arrangements to enable a government to obtain necessary support for its actions in the DSM, is presented as one of the main obstacles for WTO members to utilize the DSM. It is widely observed that to litigate a trade dispute in Geneva can 'take up to three years' and 'cost more than half a million dollars in legal fees, as well as requiring significant time commitment for a bureaucracy that may already be severely under-resourced'.[5] With the inequality of power and size of WTO members in mind, it is understandable that not all WTO members can afford to litigate in Geneva. This phenomenon has been rightly described as '[N]otionally equal litigation rules provide unequal opportunity for WTO Members'.[6]

Apart from resources and institutional arrangements, the low level of legalization in some covered agreements also presents obstacles to the utilization of the DSM. As discussed in Chapter II and IV, given the uneven expansion of legalization, the status of obligation and precision in a large number of provisions in the covered agreements remains low. Coupled with the textual approach adopted by the panels and the Appellate Body (AB), it is unfeasible for a WTO member to challenge a foreign trade barrier in the DSM in many occasions.

The rise of legalization hence has mixed effects on the utilization of the DSM. On the one hand, the development of legalization in the GATT/WTO, although uneven and unbalanced in many aspects, provides systematic incentives for governments to overcome the above-mentioned obstacles and to more effectively utilize the DSM. The gradually 'legalized' system first incentivizes governments to coordinate with private sectors to secure resources in order to challenge undue trade barriers in the DSM, that is, 'engaging the private sector'. In the meanwhile, tightened obligation and greater precision in many of the covered agreements provide possibilities for WTO members to challenge more foreign trade barriers, including those that are perceived as 'unchallengeable' due to the lack of 'good' textual basis in the covered agreements in the past. To a large extent, 'engaging the private sector' describes the institutional response of WTO members to a higher level of legalization, in particular in terms of delegation, whilst 'litigating the

---

International Economic Law 5 (2000): 395; C. Bown & B. Hoekman, 'WTO Dispute Settlement and the Missing Developing Country Cases: Engaging the Private Sector', *Journal of International Economic Law* 8 (2005): 861; and G. Shaffer, 'The Challenges of WTO Law: Strategies for Developing Country Adaptation', *World Trade Review* 5(2) (2006): 177.

4. H. Nordström & G. Shaffer, 'Access to Justice in the World Trade Organization: The Case for a Small Claims Procedure – A Preliminary Analysis', (2007) ICTSD Issue paper No. 2.
5. *Ibid.*, 1.
6. *Ibid.*, 3.

unlitigatable' is a more direct response to tighter obligation and greater precision in the covered agreements.

On the other hand, the uneven and unbalanced expansion of legalization still poses restraints on the utilization of DSM by WTO members. This is in particular demonstrated by the difficulties WTO members experience when litigating matters where the degree of legalization in the covered agreement is low.

Again, the mixed effects of legalization on the utilization of the DSM need to be understood in a reflexive process: the more WTO members utilize the DSM to 'litigate' foreign trade barriers, the more chances they could find that the matters they are litigating have no 'textual' basis in the covered agreements. Consequently, on more occasions, the panels and/or the AB have to adjudicate matters on the basis of provisions in the covered agreements that have a low level of legalization, that is, with less specific obligations and/or less precise language. Nevertheless, as discussed in Chapter II above, there is a risk that the more the panels and the AB fill the gap judicially between the covered agreements, the more criticism they will attract. This, in turn, may cause the WTO members to be less willing to return to the negotiation tables in order to tighten obligations and improve the level of precision of the covered agreement.

China's AD-related dispute settlement activities nicely illustrate the complicated effects of legalization on a WTO member's utilization of the DSM.

China has been chosen as the example due to its unique position on AD issues. It has been the main target of AD measures worldwide for the past two decades.[7] Before China's accession, many hoped that after joining the WTO, China would be less vulnerable to foreign AD investigations. However, the WTO secretariat reported that during the period of 1 July to 31 December 2008, China remained the most frequent target of new investigations initiated worldwide, with 34 initiations directed at its exports out of 120 new investigations.[8]

There could be many possible explanations for China's vulnerability to foreign AD measures. Economists argue that China a target of foreign AD measures is much more likely to be 'because of the intrinsic economic features of her exported products (differentiation level and oligopolistic markets) than because it was not a WTO Member'.[9] Many also blame the huge trade surplus China enjoys against its trading partners.

Legally, the specific, but vaguely drafted, non-market economy (NME) provisions in the WTO accession protocol of China (the Protocol) could also be an important reason for which China has difficulties in minimizing its exposure in foreign AD investigations and reducing the damages. The NME provisions grant wide discretion to investigating authorities and create considerable obstacles for China

7. P. Messerlin, 'China in the WTO: Anti-dumping and Safeguards', in *China in the WTO: Accession, Policy Reform, and Poverty Reduction Strategies*, ed. D. Bhattasali, S. Li & W. Martin (World Bank and Oxford University Press, 2003), 29.
8. WTO, 'WTO Secretariat Reports Increase in New Anti-dumping Investigations', 7 May 2009, available at: <www.wto.org/english/news_e/pres09_e/pr556_e.htm>, (10 Jul. 2009).
9. Messerlin, 'China in the WTO: Anti-dumping and Safeguards', 35.

to challenge many 'unfair' practices of these authorities in the DSM.[10] At the time when China accessed the WTO, although lacking specific rules in the multilateral agreements such as the ADA concerning the NME, major trading partners ensured that the methodologies towards NME countries in their national laws were 'legitimated by specifically articulated provisions in the Protocol'.[11] Irrespective of the fact that chief negotiator Long Yongtu ranked stricter AD rules second among China's priorities in the WTO accession negotiations, these NME provisions in the Protocol and the Working Party Report have a noticeably low level of obligation and precision. This low level of legalization reduces legal options available to Chinese exporters and the Chinese government when they feel that the result of an AD investigation is 'unfair' to them. The broad discretion conferred by the NME provisions to investigating authorities and the slim possibilities for their practices to be challenged in the DSM, allow investigating authorities to be more responsive to their domestic industries, which are normally in a better position to lobby their governments.

China's eight years experience in the WTO hence presents a mixed picture. On the one hand, the much-anticipated WTO membership of China does not significantly reduce the number of foreign AD measures targeting it for the past eight years. The ambiguous language in the Protocol concerning NME enables importing WTO members to 'grandfather' their NME methodologies, which systematically disadvantage Chinese firms in the AD investigations.

On the other hand, the frequent use, or misuse in China's view, of the AD instruments against Chinese exports worldwide forces China to take steps to strategically utilize the DSM to protect its interests. The overall development of legalization in the WTO system, in particular the tighter obligations and greater precision of the covered agreements, also provides incentives for China to litigate matters which are important to it, yet are widely perceived as 'un-litigable' due to the lack of 'a sound' textual basis in the relevant agreements. China's recent consultation requests against both the US and the EU concerning their NME methodologies clearly indicate that China is determined to litigate the 'un-litigable'. China's experience therefore shows how a relatively new WTO member struggles to deprive benefit from the rise of legalization in the trade regime, and at the same time fights the restrains imposed by the uneven expansion of legalization.

This chapter proceeds as follows. Section 2 depicts how the Chinese government engages the private sector in AD cases, by examining the *Regulation on Responding to Anti-dumping Investigations of Products Exported from China* and ad hoc public-private networks formed in previous AD cases. Section 3 outlines the GATT/WTO rules on NME and national laws of the EU and the US towards NME. Section 4 analyses the double-remedy issue that arose in the *US – Definitive Anti-dumping and Countervailing Duties on Certain Products from China* and how

10. For details of special rules governing AD investigations against Chinese products, see para. 151 of the Report of the Working Party on the Accession of China (1 Oct. 2001) WT/ACC/CHN/49.
11. F. Snyder, 'The Origins of the "Nonmarket Economy": Ideas, Pluralism and Power in EC Anti-dumping Law about China', *European Law Journal* 7 (2001): 369.

the level of legalization in the relevant agreements/protocol affects the arguments from both sides. Section 5 concludes the chapter.

2 ENGAGING PRIVATE SECTORS

2.1 BACKGROUND OF CHINA'S AD PROBLEMS

From the late 1990s, Chinese exporters were becoming formidable competitors in the world market, exporting a wide range of products, from inexpensive textiles, televisions and bicycles, to higher priced electronic equipment. In 2008, China's trade volume reached USD 2561.63 billion, up by 17.8% from 2007 and the trade surplus reached USD 295.46 billion, up by 12.7%.[12] The huge trade surplus resulted in intense trade frictions between China and its trading partners and increased political pressure for trade protection in major trading partners. The Ministry of Commerce (MOFCOM), which is responsible for China's trade policy, pointed out in its annual Foreign Market Access Report, '[W]ith the rapid growth of China's economy and foreign trade, some of our trading partners and industry groups in those countries are increasingly using various trade and investment barriers against Chinese products in order to protect their domestic industry and home market.'[13]

Among all foreign trade barriers, the use (or misuse) of the AD instrument by trading partners is one of the first major trade barriers that Chinese exports encountered. Since 1979, when the first AD case against China was initiated by the EU, for almost two decades, China has been the main target of worldwide AD investigations.[14] After China's accession, the MOFCOM felt the pressure to take steps to actively utilize the DSM to address AD issues in order to maintain market access abroad and advance China's trade interests. It had two options: First, it could follow other large developing countries, such as India and Brazil, to aggressively initiate AD investigations against imports; and second, it could minimize its own AD use and invest its resources in effectively responding to foreign AD investigations in front of foreign investigating authorities and possibly the DSM. With a huge trade surplus and strong export dependant industries at home, the Chinese government opted for the second one, by reducing the number of new initiations in the past few years and putting significant efforts on fighting foreign AD charges.[15]

12. Ministry of Commerce of People's Republic of China (MOFCOM) 'Foreign Market Access Report 2009', 12 Apr. 2008, available at: <http://henan.mofcom.gov.cn/accessory/200804/1176368802629.pdf>.
13. *Ibid.*, 2.
14. For example, X. Liu & H. Vandenbussche, 'European Union Anti-dumping Cases Against China – An Overview and Future Prospects With Respect to China's World Trade Organization Membership', *Journal of World Trade* 36 (2002): 1125. The author confirmed that from 1979 to 2002, China has been the most accused country in EU AD charges.
15. For example, as reported by WTO Secretariat, Chile, China, Colombia, Malaysia, Pakistan, and Chinese Taipei, each of which had reported new initiations during the second half of 2006, no new initiations were reported during the corresponding period of 2007.

MOFCOM's efforts focus on two areas: Formally, it institutionalizes legal mechanisms to support exporters curtailing the abuse of AD instruments by trading partners. In this regard, a regulation has been promulgated and upgraded to effectively organize resources and to improve the response rate and the quality of cooperation of exporters in AD investigations targeting China.[16] Informally, it worked closely with trade associations, enterprises and their lawyers to increase the awareness of AD rules. For example, as early as 2001, the Shanghai People's Municipal Government set up a professional, non-governmental consulting organization, the Shanghai WTO Affairs Consultation Centre, to provide legal and policy advice on WTO affairs, as well as WTO-related trainings.[17] AD-related research and trainings are among their main activities.

2.2 Regulation on Responding to Anti-dumping Investigations[18]

As discussed above, the MOFCOM exercises a legal tool to solicit industry support in advancing its AD agenda, namely '*Regulation on Responding to Anti-dumping Investigations of Products Exported from China*' (the Regulation). In order to help Chinese firms more effectively defend themselves in foreign AD investigations, the MOFCOM upgraded the Regulation in August 2006 and repeated the one issued in December 2001.[19]

With only twenty articles, the Regulation is relatively brief. It nevertheless clarifies the rights and obligations of key players including the MOFCOM, trade associations, and private firms, when responding to foreign AD charges,. Article 2 of the Regulation provides that it is an obligation of exporting producers under investigation to actively respond to foreign AD investigating authorities. It also emphasizes the role of trade associations and gives more respect for the market-based decisions of individual firms, whilst limiting the role of MOFCOM to provide key information and guidelines pertaining to AD procedures.[20]

Unlike the previous version, the Regulation clearly states that each respondent in the AD investigation has the right to decide how it wishes to respond to an

16. Non-cooperation or not sufficient cooperation in AD investigations was one of the major problems that China has in the EC anti-dumping cases. *Ibid.*, 1135.
17. B. Gong, 'Shanghai's WTO Affairs Consultation Centre: Working Together to Take Advantage of WTO Membership', in *WTO Managing the Challenges of WTO Participation: Case Studies – Case study 2: An Early-warning System for Anti-dumping Disputes in China*, at <www.wto.org/english/res_e/booksp_e/casestudies_e/case11_e.htm>.
18. This section is reproduced from the author's work, Y. Luo, 'Engaging the Private Sector: EU – China trade Disputes Under the Shadow of WTO Law?', *European Law Journal* 13, no. 6 (November 2007): 800–817.
19. MOFCOM, 'Decree No. 12, 2006 of the Ministry of Commerce of the People's Republic of China, Promulgating the Regulations on Responding to Anti-dumping Cases of Export Products', 29 Aug. 2006, at <http://english.mofcom.gov.cn/aarticle/policyrelease/gazettee/200608/20060803009941.html>.
20. *Ibid.*, Arts 4 and 6.

investigating authority and to select its legal counsel.[21] If a respondent believes it has been discriminated against during the investigation, the firm may file a complaint with the MOFCOM.[22]

The MOFCOM is responsible for formulating policies to promote effective responses in foreign AD investigations.[23] It is also responsible for providing information to exporting producers during the investigations.[24] However, it no longer directly bears the responsibility of day-to-day coordination and organization of exporting producers in an AD investigation.

Articles 4 and 12 provide that trade associations are playing key roles in responding to foreign AD investigations. Among other things, they are responsible for building up databases to collect export data and trade remedy information; assisting firms under investigation on issues such as non-market economy, individual treatment and verification; organizing firms to participate in hearings and negotiations; providing assistance on negotiating price undertakings and making proposals to the MOFCOM where government involvement is necessary; and assisting firms to seek judicial remedies in the importing country.[25] Trade associations are required to consult with the MOFCOM under certain circumstances, such as those investigations involving a large amount of exports or critical exporting markets or where the investigating authority acted discriminately.[26]

The emphasis of trade associations' role in AD investigations is expected to improve the leverage of individual Chinese firms in AD cases and to allow small- and medium-sized enterprises to enjoy downstream benefits from collaborations spearheaded by larger organizations. Although it is well established in developed countries that firms can enhance their chances of successfully challenging foreign trade restrictions when they coordinate their activities through a trade association, in previous AD proceedings, Chinese firms rarely organized themselves to present a united industry front through trade associations.[27] The Regulation aims to change this and brings collective benefits to Chinese firms. Also, through trade associations acting as diplomatic middlemen, the MOFCOM hopes to differentiate the new public-private networks from the old state interference and distance itself from the Chinese firms' market-orientation decisions.

2.3 Ad hoc Public-private Networks in Responding to Foreign AD Investigations

In practice, the Chinese government, Chambers of Commerce (trade associations) and private exporters develop ad hoc networks to organize themselves in responding to foreign AD investigations.

21. *Ibid.*, Art. 9.
22. *Ibid.*
23. *Ibid.*, Art. 5.
24. *Ibid.*, Art. 6.
25. *Ibid.*, Arts 4 and 12.
26. *Ibid.*, Art. 16.
27. Liu & Vandenbussche, 'European Union Anti-dumping Cases Against China', 1125.

The process of responding to a foreign AD investigation normally starts with the publication of the initiation of a foreign AD investigation by the MOFCOM in its website, *China Trade Remedy Information.*[28] The relevant Chambers of Commerce then notifies its members who have been targeted in the investigation and organizes meetings with those exporting producers. Normally, the meetings are divided into two parts: the exporters firstly hold close door discussions to form a joint defence position and then invite outside counsels to present on the legal aspects of the case. Exporters who are involved in the investigation are free to hire their own legal representatives and make submissions to the investigating authority. Throughout the investigation, Chambers of Commerce and the MOFCOM work closely with targeted exporters by providing them information and guidance.

In the meanwhile, the MOFCOM frequently involves WTO Affairs Consultation Centres to analyze underlying legal issues and 'educate' potentially targeted exporters. Recognizing that 'many Chinese exporters lack the knowledge of the trade rules or the financial resources required to defend their interests', WTO Affairs Consultation Centres throughout the country are developing mechanisms that aim to provide 'practical assistance to Chinese manufacturers and exporters'.[29] One project that the Shanghai WTO Affairs Consultation Centre developed to help potentially targeted exporters is an early warning system. The system is described as follows:[30]

> [I]n its first stage, the V 1.0 system covers 189 varieties of export goods in eighteen categories (mainly textiles, home appliances, steel and furniture) which are contained in the items accounting for some 60 per cent of China's annual total exports to the United States. Registered companies receive information on the quantity, future prices and dumping margins of Chinese products exported to the United States. Companies can also obtain monitoring reports on US trade remedy measures, and receive training services to help them respond to anti-dumping investigations or charges.

After several years of effort, Chinese exporters are now more willing to actively participate in foreign AD investigations. For example, on 6 February 2006, eight Chinese firms involved in the EU's footwear investigation voluntarily formed an ad hoc association to coordinate their activities and consolidate the industry position after the EU refused to give any of the thirteen sampled firms the market economy status (MES).[31] The association issued a Position Paper, which specifically stated that it would support further government actions on this

28. <www.cacs.gov.cn/>.
29. Gong, 'Shanghai's WTO Affairs Consultation Centre', Case Study 2.
30. *Ibid.*
31. 'An Association Established in Guangzhou in Response to the EU's Footwear Anti-dumping Investigation', News Release, Bureau of Foreign Trade and Economic Cooperation of Guangzhou Municipality, at <www.gzboftec.gov.cn/articles/2006-2/17214.htm>.

matter.[32] Later, more than 200 Chinese firms joined this association and it was still functioning after the definitive measure has been imposed by the EU. This move of the private sector indicates that Chinese firms are increasingly aware of the importance of organizing themselves and cooperating with the government in addressing their trade claims, echoing the thread of the Regulation.

In short, China's institutional capacity building, which is represented by the emergence of a strong public-private network for responding to foreign AD investigations, illustrates one of the effects that the rise of legalization has had on the utilization of the DSM, namely, mobilizing domestic export groups. As discussed in Chapter II, by increasing transparency and information available to domestic export groups, the legalization process provides strong incentives for pro-trade industries to utilize the legal tools available to push the enforcement of trade agreements and maintain market access abroad. By the same token, Chinese exporting industries are also keen to support the efforts of the Chinese government to tighten up AD disciplines at the WTO level.

3 LITIGATE THE UNLITIGATABLE: NON-MARKET ECONOMY (NME)

3.1 NME in China's WTO Accession Protocol and the Working Party Report

With additional resources and the backing of stronger public-private networks, the Chinese government has made great efforts to utilize the DSM in recent years. To precisely interpret the vaguely drafted NME provisions with a view to limiting the discretion of foreign investigating authorities in AD investigation targeting China is one of the biggest challenges China facing in litigating AD cases in the DSM.

This section provides a brief account of the origins of NME in the GATT/WTO and analyzes the relevant provisions in China's WTO Accession Protocol (the Protocol) and the Working Party Report. In particular, it discusses the scope of obligations imposed on China and other WTO members, as well as the scope of exceptions offered by the Protocol and the Working Party Report when handling AD investigations involving Chinese products.

The special treatment of state-trading and non-market economy in the GATT/WTO has a long history – long before China emerged as a major player in international trade.[33] Stemming from the idea that 'free trade' only exists if trading

32. *Ibid.*

33. For background on the legal concept of 'non-market economy', F. Snyder, 'The Origins of the "Nonmarket Economy": Ideas, Pluralism and Power in EC Anti-dumping Law about China', *European Law Journal* 7 (2001): 369; and H. Detlof & H. Fridh, 'The EU Treatment of Non-Market Economy Countries in Anti-dumping Proceedings', *Global Trade and Customs Journal* 2 (2007): 265.

partners operate 'free markets', essentially capitalist non-regulated markets, GATT Contracting Parties have made the distinction between market and non-market economies since the very beginning.[34] The US Department of State defines NME in a glossary of trade terminology, *The Language of Trade*, as follows:[35]

> **NONMARKET ECONOMY (NME)** – A national economy in which the government seeks to determine economic activity largely through a mechanism of central planning, as in the former Soviet Union, in contrast to a market economy, which depends heavily upon market forces to allocate productive resources. In a nonmarket economy, production targets, prices, costs, investment allocations, raw materials, labor, international trade, and most other economic aggregates are manipulated within a national economic plan drawn up by a central planning authority. Hence, the public sector makes the major decisions affecting demand and supply within the national economy.

GATT Contracting Parties, led by the US, considered at the time that AD rules expressed in Article VI of the GATT should not apply to NME countries.[36] This is based on the idea that comparing market prices on different markets would be meaningless when markets do not actually set the prices. For this purpose, an interpretative note was added to the first paragraph of GATT Article VI in 1955. The supplementary provision to Article VI reads as follows:[37]

> It is recognized that, in case of imports from a country which has a complete or substantially complete monopoly of trade and all domestic prices are fixed by the State, special difficulties may exist in determining price comparability for the purpose of paragraph 1, and in such cases importing contracting parties may find it necessary to take into account the possibility that a strict comparison with domestic prices in such a country may not always be appropriate.

It is argued that despite the fact that this interpretative note, in theory, could be applied only to countries where all prices are fixed by the State, and despite the fact it did not affirm the use of prices or costs in a surrogate country as the basis of the normal value calculation, the provision remains the only reference to NME in the covered agreements (with the exception of protocols of accession).[38] Practitioners

34. *Ibid.*, Snyder, 'The Origins of the "Nonmarket Economy" ', 381.
35. US Department of State International Information Programmes, in Glossary of *The Language of International Trade*, available at: <http://usinfo.state.gov/products/pubs/trade/glossjr.htm#nonmarkeco> (last accessed 15 Jul. 2008).
36. Snyder, 'The Origins of the "Nonmarket Economy" ', 381 and Detlof & Fridh, 'The EU Treatment of Non-Market Economy Countries in Anti-dumping Proceedings', 268. Also, A. Polouektov, 'Non-market Economy Issues in the WTO Anti-dumping Law and Accession Negotiations Revival of a Two-tier Membership', *Journal of World Trade* 36 (2002): 1.
37. GATT *Contracting Parties – Ninth Session – Report of Review Working Party III on Barriers to Trade other than Restrictions or Tariffs*, L/334, 1 Mar. 1955, Annex 1, para. 10.
38. Detlof & Fridh, 'The EU Treatment of Non-Market Economy Countries in Anti-dumping Proceedings', 268.

therefore argue that '[T]here are very few, if any, countries left where the government controls 'all' prices, thus any WTO Member is entitled to normal MES treatment under the WTO Anti-dumping Agreement, unless it has agreed otherwise'.[39]

China's Accession Protocol is the most recent example that the NME treatment is 'agreed otherwise'. In its First Written Submission to the Panel in *United States – Definitive Anti-dumping and Countervailing Duties on Certain Products from China ('US – AD and CVD on Chinese Products')*,[40] the US describes what it considers are the reasons for the existence of the NME provisions as follows:

> 21. In light of the fact that China's economy was still heavily dominated by the state, Members carefully considered and insisted upon numerous provisions that would permit effective remedies against unfairly traded imports from China. While China initially insisted that there be no rules specific to Chinese products, Members insisted upon, and ultimately obtained, such rules in the areas of safeguards, AD and CVDs.
>
> 22. The commitments in the areas of AD and CVDs reflected Members' recognition that prices and costs in China were not necessarily market-based. Therefore, the normal AD methodologies used to measure price discrimination, which rely on market prices and costs, could not be applied so as to arrive at accurate and reliable dumping margins. Similarly, normal CVD methodologies, which measure subsidy benefits in reference to the marketplace, would likely be difficult to apply. Therefore, special rules and flexibilities for both the AD and CVD remedies needed to be agreed upon in the Accession Protocol if these traditional mechanisms were to have any meaningful and practical applicability.

To reflect the concerns of WTO members, section 15 of China's Accession Protocol, entitled 'Price Comparability in Determining Subsidies and Dumping', reads as follows:[41]

> Article VI of the GATT 1994, the Agreement on Implementation of Article VI of the General Agreement on Tariffs and Trade 1994 ('Anti-Dumping Agreement') and the SCM Agreement shall apply in proceedings involving imports of Chinese origin into a WTO Member consistent with the following:
>
> (a) In determining price comparability under Article VI of the GATT 1994 and the Anti-Dumping Agreement, the importing WTO Member

39. J. Maloney & G. Horlick, 'Market Economy Status for Ukraine in Anti-dumping Cases in the United States and European Union', *Global Trade and Customs Journal* 1 (2006): 49.

40. *United States – Definitive Anti-dumping and Countervailing Duties on Certain Products from China (WT/DS379)*, the First Written Submission of the United States, 27 May 2009, available at: <www.ustr.gov/trade-topics/enforcement/dispute-settlement-proceedings/wto-dosîte-settlement/definitive-anti-dump-1>, paras 21–22.

41. Paragraph 15 of the Protocol on the Accession of People's Republic of China (1 Jan. 2002) WT/L/432.

shall use either Chinese prices or costs for the indstry under investigation or a methodology that is not based on a strict comparison with domestic prices or costs in China based on the following rules:

(i) If the producers under investigation can clearly show that market economy conditions prevail in the industry producing the like product with regard to the manufacture, production and sale of that product, the importing WTO Member shall use Chinese prices or costs for the industry under investigation in determining price comparability;

(ii) The importing WTO Member may use a methodology that is not based on a strict comparison with domestic prices or costs in China if the producers under investigation cannot clearly show that market economy conditions prevail in the industry producing the like product with regard to manufacture, production and sale of that product.

(b) In proceedings under Parts II, III and V of the SCM Agreement, when addressing subsidies described in Articles 14(a), 14(b), 14(c) and 14(d), relevant provisions of the SCM Agreement shall apply; however, if there are special difficulties in that application, the importing WTO Member may then use methodologies for identifying and measuring the subsidy benefit which take into account the possibility that prevailing terms and conditions in China may not always be available as appropriate benchmarks. In applying such methodologies, where practicable, the importing WTO Member should adjust such prevailing terms and conditions before considering the use of terms and conditions prevailing outside China.

(c) The importing WTO Member shall notify methodologies used in accordance with subparagraph (a) to the Committee on Anti-Dumping Practices and shall notify methodologies used in accordance with subparagraph (b) to the Committee on Subsidies and Countervailing Measures.

(d) Once China has established, under the national law of the importing WTO Member, that it is a market economy, the provisions of subparagraph (a) shall be terminated provided that the importing Member's national law contains market economy criteria as of the date of accession. In any event, the provisions of subparagraph (a)(ii) shall expire 15 years after the date of accession. In addition, should China establish, pursuant to the national law of the importing WTO Member, that market economy conditions prevail in a particular industry or sector, the non-market economy provisions of subparagraph (a) shall no longer apply to that industry or sector.

Legally speaking, section 15 is vaguely drafted. With respect to AD investigations where NME methodologies applies, it touched upon two different but interrelated issues: (i) the establishment of market economy status of China as a whole, or a particular Chinese industry or a particular Chinese producer and (ii) a special methodology to calculate the dumping margin, if China as a whole or a particular Chinese industry/producer cannot prove that they are operating under the market economy conditions. Section 15 provides a clear answer to neither of them. It does not offer the importing WTO members any criteria on the establishment of 'market economy conditions' in an investigation. Neither does it 'give any guidance as to which methodology can be used when a strict comparison with domestic prices or costs is inappropriate'.[42] Instead, it only gives the permission to an importing country to disregard Chinese 'domestic prices and costs' in case it considers China cannot be treated as a market economy, that is, if Chinese producers cannot demonstrate that market economy conditions prevail in the industry 'producing the like product'.

Concerned about 'past measures taken by certain WTO members that had treated China as a non-market economy and imposed anti-dumping duties on Chinese companies without identifying or publishing the criteria used, without giving Chinese companies sufficient opportunity to present evidence and defend their interests in a fair manner, and without explaining the rationale underlying their determinations, including with respect to the method of price comparison in the determinations', China tried to tighten up the discipline in the Working Party Report and obtained the following commitments from its trading partners:[43]

> In response to these concerns, members of the Working Party confirmed that in implementing subparagraph (a)(ii) of Section 15 of the Draft Protocol, WTO Members would comply with the following:
>
> (a) When determining price comparability in a particular case in a manner not based on a strict comparison with domestic prices or costs in China, the importing WTO Member should ensure that it had established and published in advance (1) the criteria that it used for determining whether market economy conditions prevailed in the industry or company producing the like product and (2) the methodology that it used in determining price comparability. With regard to importing WTO Members other than those that had an established practice of applying a methodology that included, *inter alia* guidelines that the investigating authorities should normally utilize, to the extent possible, and where necessary cooperation was received, the prices or costs in one or more market economy countries that were significant producers of comparable merchandise and that either were at a level of economic development comparable to that of China or were otherwise an appropriate source for the prices or costs to be utilized in light of the nature of the industry under investigation, they should make best efforts to ensure that their methodology for determining price comparability included provisions similar to those described above.

---

42. J. Cornelis, 'China's Quest for Market Economy Status and its Impact on the Use of Trade Remedies by the European Communities and the United States', *Global Trade and Customs Journal* 2 (2007): 105, 109.
43. Report of the Working Party on the Accession of China (1 Oct. 2001) WT/ACC/CHN/49, para. 151.

(b) The importing WTO Member should ensure that it had notified its market-economy criteria and its methodology for determining price comparability to the Committee on Anti-Dumping Practices before they were applied.
(c) The process of investigation should be transparent and sufficient opportunities should be given to Chinese producers or exporters to make comments, especially comments on the application of the methodology for determining price comparability in a particular case.
(d) The importing WTO Member should give notice of information which it required and provide Chinese producers and exporters ample opportunity to present evidence in writing in a particular case.
(e) The importing WTO Member should provide Chinese producers and exporters a full opportunity for the defence of their interests in a particular case.
(f) The importing WTO Member should provide a sufficiently detailed reasoning of its preliminary and final determinations in a particular case.

On the one hand, paragraph 151 provides, to a certain extent, useful guidelines on the methodology of price comparability in case China is treated as an NME and reassures a few procedural rights of Chinese producers under investigation. On the other hand, some commentators consider that this paragraph validates the approaches of the EU and the US in terms of using analogue country data to calculate the dumping margin.[44]

To read section 15 and paragraph 151 together, one may reasonably consider that in handling cases involving China, an investigating authority is free: first, to establish criteria to determine whether market economy conditions prevailed in the industry or company producing the like product ('NME criteria'); and second, to establish a methodology to calculate normal values in case the industry or the producer cannot prove that market economy conditions prevail ('NME methodology'). In applying the NME methodology to calculate the normal value, investigating authorities are allowed to disregard domestic prices and costs in China, but are required to use 'the prices or costs in one or more market economy countries that were significant producers of comparable merchandise and that were either at a level of economic development comparable to that of China or were otherwise an appropriate source for the prices or costs to be utilized in light of the nature of the industry under investigation'.[45]

In other words, section 15 and paragraph 151 provide two exceptions, 'NME methodology' and 'NME criteria'. These two exceptions give an importing WTO member the freedom to depart from Article 2.2 of the ADA – the provision that sets out the rule to establish normal values in investigations not involving Chinese products. The exception – the NME methodology is more explicit to section 15 is entitled 'Price Comparability in Determining Subsidies and Dumping', whilst the NME criteria exception is more implicit – section 15(d) states that China has to

44. Cornelis, 'China's Quest for Market Economy Status and its Impact on the Use of Trade Remedies by the European Communities and the United States', 109.
45. Report of the Working Party on the Accession of China (1 Oct. 2001) WT/ACC/CHN/49, para. 151.

establish itself as a market economy 'under the national law of the importing WTO Member'. This could indicate that an importing WTO member can set its own rules to determine the NME of a Chinese industry or producer and Chinese producers have to follow these rules.

In order to determine the scope of the two exceptions provided by section 15 and paragraph 151, two questions have to be asked: First, should the interpretation of NME criteria be bound by the general interpretative approach of the WTO even if they are by nature domestic laws? Second, apart from the two exceptions, namely NME criteria and NME methodology, should an investigating authority be bound by general rules in the ADA in other parts of the investigation, such as adjustment, sampling, the treatment of export price and the combined imposition of AD and countervailing duty (CVD)?

There are different views on these two questions. The traditional view, and the view taken by investigating authorities such as the US Department of Commerce (US DOC) and the Commission, is that the establishment of NME criteria and NME methodology are purely matters of national law and investigating authorities enjoy full discretion offered by national legislation. Some commentators conclude that 'the WTO does not give much guidance on these issues, and Member States are not forbidden to set their own parameters'.[46] As such the answers to both questions are 'no'.

This monograph, however, considers that section 15 and paragraph 151 can be interpreted differently and offer a 'yes' answer to the second question, whilst the WTO jurisprudence may confirm the wide discretion investigating authorities enjoy in interpreting the NME criteria.

With respect to the second question, the argument in favour of China can be that in an NME investigation, although the laws that apply to establish the NME criteria and the NME methodology are national laws, those parts of the investigation, that are not covered by the exceptions provided by section 15 and paragraph 151 should be conducted in a WTO-consistent manner. In other words, the purposes of section 15 and paragraph 151 are, in investigations targeting Chinese products, to permit the investigating authority to use alternative methodologies to calculate normal value than these set forth in Article 2.2 of the ADA and to give a WTO member the discretion to establish certain criteria in order to determine when it can do this. The general rules of the ADA still govern other parts of the investigations.

The Panel's statement in *US – 1916 Act* supports this argument. The Panel stated that 'Article VI:1 of the GATT 1994, interpreted in accordance with the Vienna Convention, must be understood as applying to any situation where a Member addresses the type of transnational price discrimination defined in that Article'.[47] Therefore, unless an exception is provided for by other WTO agreements, the

46. Detlof & Fridh, 'The EU Treatment of Non-Market Economy Countries in Anti-dumping Proceedings', 280.

47. WTO, *United States – Anti-Dumping Act of 1916, Complaint by the European Communities*, Report of the Panel, WT/DS136/R and Corr.1, adopted 26 Sep. 2000, upheld by Appellate Body Report, WT/DS136/AB/R, WT/DS162/AB/R, DSR 2000:X, 4593.

general rules of Article VI of the GATT and the ADA apply to any AD investigations, that is, 'any situation where a Member addresses the type of transnational price discrimination defined in that Article'. Whether an investigation involves products of Chinese origin should not be a factor that affects the application of the ADA in such investigation.

Consequently, it is crucial to determine the scope of the two exceptions provided for by section 15 and paragraph 151. These two exceptions can be elaborated as follows: the first exception allows a WTO member to disregard domestic prices and costs of Chinese producers under investigation in calculating their normal value and the second exception allows a WTO member to establish its own rules to decide when they may (or may not) disregard Chinese prices and costs. If these two exceptions are read in the context of ADA, one can reasonably argue that in any AD investigation involving Chinese products, a WTO member can choose not to conduct the investigation in accordance with Article 2.2.1.1 and 2.2.2 and reject the 'domestic costs and prices of Chinese producers' despite the fact that those costs and prices are kept in records 'in accordance with the generally accepted accounting principles' (Article 2.2.1.1) and are 'actual data pertaining to production and sales' (Article 2.2.2).

Apart from these two exceptions, other provisions of the ADA are still binding on the investigating authorities. Section 15 and paragraph 151 do not offer investigating authorities the liberty to conduct parts of the investigation other than the determination of normal value in a ADA-inconstant manner. For example, an investigating authority still has to fulfil its obligations under Articles 2.3, 2.4 and 3 of the ADA to ensure that, *inter alia,* the comparison of the export price and the normal value is fair, the export price is appropriately established and the injury and causation are properly determined. Their conduct in these aspects is subject to scrutiny of the DSM in the same way as in any other investigations that do not involve Chinese products.

The investigating authorities have developed a number of 'associated practices', which are essentially beyond the exceptions offered by the Protocol and the Working Party Report in investigations involving Chinese products. A non-exhaustive list of these practices includes the EU's sampling in the Market Economy Treatment (MET) test, the EU's ndividual treatment practice and the US's combined AD and CVD case. A textual reading of the two exceptions suggests that although the Protocol is vaguely drafted and does not provide a sound textual basis on many points, it is still possible for China to invoke the ADA provisions other than Articles 2.2.1 and 2.2.2 to challenge associated practices. In other words, the fact that section 15 and paragraph 151 provide for exceptions in AD investigations targeting Chinese products, does not affect China's right to challenge the associate practices. This is so, if, by applying the associated practices, an investigating authority is in breach of its obligations under other provisions of the ADA. This issue will be examined in the following two subsections in great details.

The answer to the first question is somewhat different and the WTO jurisprudence is less favourable towards China. The NME criteria of WTO members are rightly considered as provisions of national laws and these provisions, irrespective of their contents, do not breach any WTO rule. Irrespective of how 'unfair' China considers these NME criteria to be, by having its own NME criteria and following these criteria in investigations involving Chinese products, a WTO member does not breach its obligations under the ADA and the Protocol.

Against this background, even if an investigating authority does not adopt the interpretative approach followed by the panel and the AB, it does not necessarily violate WTO law. China may politically argue that it has been treated less favourably or 'unfairly'. However, it is difficult to legally argue that an importing WTO member, by interpreting the NME criteria in its national law as less favourable towards China, fails to meet its obligations under the WTO.

The WTO jurisprudence cannot provide much help to China in this regard. In previous cases, the WTO panels and the AB examined municipal laws only for a specific purpose, namely 'in accessing the conformity of that domestic law with the relevant GATT/WTO obligations'.[48] Moreover, the panels and the AB repeatedly held that they do not interpret national laws 'as such', or in the same way that they interpret the provisions of a covered agreement. Hence, under the assumption that the NME criteria themselves cannot be inconsistent with the ADA or the Protocol, it is not surprising that a panel may decline to rule that an importing WTO member breaches its WTO obligations by interpreting its NME criteria in a way that is less favourable towards China or by not following the interpretative approach of the panel or the AB.

The next subsection, by taking examples of the US and the EU's NME practice towards China, further demonstrates the complexity of the issue discussed above.

3.2 AD Methodology towards Non-market Economy in National Laws

3.2.1 The US

This subsection describes the law and practice of the USDOC in AD investigations involving NME countries. Although China is the most important trading partner that the US DOC is currently treating as an NME country, the methodology of a normal value (NV) calculation in an NME case is not China-specific. The China-specific controversy occurred when the US DOC decided to depart from its previous practice and to apply the combined CVD and AD to China. More details of the simultaneous AD and CVD proceedings which were conducted by the US DOC and the underlying WTO issues are to be found in the next subsection.

The legal basis for the US DOC to use the NME methodology to calculate NV for cases involving NME countries instead of the standard NV methodology

48. WTO, *India – Patent Protection for Pharmaceutical and Agricultural Chemical Products*, Report of the Appellate Body, WT/DS50/AB/R, adopted 16 Jan. 1998, DSR 1998: I, 9, para. 78.

applicable to market economies is section 771(18) of the Tariff Act of 1930 (section 771(18)). Section 771(18)(A) first defined NME as follows:[49]

> The term 'nonmarket economy country' means any foreign country that the administering authority determines does not operate on market principles of cost or pricing structures, so that sales of merchandise in such country do not reflect the fair value of the merchandise.

Section 771(18)(B) provides five criteria on which the US DOC can rely to make a determination to treat a trading partner as an NME:[50]

> In making determinations under subparagraph (A) the administering authority shall take into account:
>
> (i) the extent to which the currency of the foreign country is convertible into the currency of other countries;
> (ii) the extent to which wage rates in the foreign country are determined by free bargaining between labor and management,
> (iii) the extent to which joint ventures or other investments by firms of other foreign countries are permitted in the foreign country,
> (iv) the extent of government ownership or control of the means of production,
> (v) the extent of government control over the allocation of resources and over the price and output decisions of enterprises, and
> (vi) such other factors as the administering authority considers appropriate.

In the Code of Federal Regulations, the methodology of NV calculation in an NME case is clarified as follows:[51]

> In identifying dumping from a nonmarket economy country, the Secretary normally will calculate normal value by valuing the nonmarket economy producers' factors of production in a market economy country. (See section 773(c) of the Act.)

The 'factors of production' approach is codified in section 773(c) of the Tariff Act of 1930, which requires the US DOC 'normally' to calculate NV using market economy (surrogate country) prices to value the NME country 'factors of production' used to produce the product concerned.[52] The list of factors include, for example, hours of labour required; quantities of raw materials employed; amounts of energy and other utilities consumed; representative capital costs, including depreciation, etc.[53] For the purpose of the NV calculation, to these factor costs, the US DOC also adds amounts for factory overheads, SG&A expenses, profits and

49. 19 U.S.C. 1677 (18) (A).
50. 19 U.S.C. 1677 (18) (B).
51. 19 CFR 351 408.
52. 19 U.S.C. 1677 b (c).
53. United States Department of Commerce, *Import Administration Antidumping Manual*, 1997 edition, Ch. 8, 87–90, available at: <http://ia.ita.doc.gov/admanual/index.html>.

packing. As a established practice, the US DOC measures material inputs in the number of physical units used in the production of the product, that is, tons, pounds, gallons; labour in terms of hours (distinguished between direct and indirect labour); and energy in terms of the quantities used, for example, BTUs (gas), kilowatt hours (electricity), gallons (fuel oil).[54]

The US described the three-step process in its First Written Submission to the panel in *US – AD and CVD on Chinese Products* as follows.[55]

> Under the NME methodology provided for in Ad Note 2 to Article VI:1 of the GATT 1994, normal value need not be based on a strict comparison with domestic prices and costs of the exporting country. In such cases, Commerce normally calculates normal value through a three-step process:
>
> (a) First, it determines the quantities of the factors of production (essentially, inputs) used to produce the product subject to investigation. In other words, Commerce determines the amount of raw materials, labor, energy and other inputs used to produce the merchandise.
> (b) Second, Commerce values these inputs in the surrogate, market economy country. For example, 3 kilowatt hours of electricity in China, valued at a price in India of 50 rupees per kilowatt hour, would yield an electricity cost of 150 rupees for the merchandise. It is important to note that the actual cost of electricity in China may be either higher or lower than the surrogate value used for electricity.
> (c) Third, Commerce adds amounts for factory overhead, selling, general and administrative ('SG&A') expenses, and profit, calculated on the basis of the ratios of these costs to the costs of the other inputs in the surrogate country.

By filing the NME questionnaire, exporters in the NME provide information on the quantity of inputs actually used to produce the product concerned. Nevertheless, it is a long-standing policy of the US DOC that not all exporters in NME cases are assigned their individual duties. Only those exporters who can have sufficient autonomy over their export activities qualify for an individual dumping margin. The US DOC's practice is to examine whether exporters pass a 'separate rate' test in order to decide whether they can receive their own, individual dumping margins.[56]

In a number of cases, the US DOC sets out the elements of this separate rate test. It essentially requires that an exporter demonstrates that its export activities, on both a *de jure and de facto* basis, are not subject to government control.[57]

54. *Ibid.*, 88.
55. *United States – (WT/DS379)*, the First Written Submission of the United States, 450.
56. *Ibid.*, 91.
57. For example, US DOC '*Final Determination of Sales at Less than Fair Value: Sparklers from the People's Republic of China*', 56 Federal Register, 20588 (6 May 1991), and *Final Determination of Sales at Less than Fair Value: Silicon Carbide from the People's Republic of China ('Silicon Carbide')*, 59 Federal Register, 22585 (2 May 1994).

Evidence, such as 'an absence of restrictive stipulations associated with an individual exporter's business and export licenses' and 'any legislative enactments devolving central control of export trading companies', can support, yet not guarantee, a finding of *de jure* absence of government control over export activities.[58] Other evidence, such as 'whether the export prices are set by or are subject to the approval of a government authority', 'whether the respondent has the authority to negotiate and sign contracts and other agreements', 'whether the respondent has autonomy from the government in making decisions regarding the selection of management'., can be taken into account in a *de facto* determination.[59]

One formal exception to the US DOC's standard approach to calculate NV in an NME is the market-oriented industry (MOI) standard. Section 773(C)(1) of the Tariff Act of 1930 allows the US DOC, in certain circumstances, to use the market-economy methodology described in section 773(A) to determine NV in an NME case.[60] Under the current MOI test, an affirmative finding of an MOI requires:[61]

> For the merchandise under investigation or review, there must be virtually no government involvement in setting prices or amounts to be produced. For example, state-required production or allocation of production of the merchandise, whether for export or domestic consumption in the non-market-economy country, would be an almost impossible barrier to finding a MOI.
>
> The industry producing the merchandise under investigation or review should be characterized by private or collective ownership. There may be state-owned enterprises in the industry, but substantial state ownership would weigh heavily against finding a MOI.
>
> Market determined prices must be paid for all significant inputs whether material or non-material (e.g., labor and overhead) and for all but insignificant proportions of all the inputs accounting for the total value of the merchandise under investigation or review. For example, an input price will not be considered market-determined if the producers of the merchandise under investigation or review pay a state-set price for the input or if the input is supplied to the producers at government direction. Moreover, if there is any state-required production in the industry producing the input, the share of state-required production must be insignificant.

If these conditions are not met, the industry under investigation will be treated as NME producers and the NV will be calculated under the 'factors of production' approach. Although consistently used in practice, this test has not been codified in

---

58. *Ibid.*
59. *Ibid.*
60. 19 U.S.C. 1677 b (c) (1).
61. For example, *Preliminary Determination of Sales at Less Than Fair Value: Sulfanilic Acid From the People's Republic of China*, 57 Fed. Reg. 9,409, 9,411 (DOC., Mar. 18,1992); *Notice of Final Determination of Sales at Less Than Fair Value and Negative Final Determination of Critical Circumstances: Certain Colour Television Receivers From the People's Republic of China*, 69 Fed. Reg.20,594, 20,595 (DOC, 16 Apr. 2004).

US DOC's regulations, due to US DOC's concerns that 'the test did not succeed in 'identifying situations where it would be appropriate to use domestic prices or costs in an NME as the basis for normal value'.[62]

Upon China's accession, the US negotiated 'the right to treat China as an NME country for fifteen years from the date of China's accession'.[63] Ever since, China has started to request that WTO members grant it market economy status or at least to recognize that some of its industries or producers are market-oriented and thus can benefit from the market economy treatment. Over the years, the US DOC has found that the vast majority of exporters in China qualify for a separate rate. Nevertheless, no industry in China has succeeded in meeting the MOI test in the past fifteen years.

The US NME criteria and methodology themselves, though having been fiercely criticized as 'unfair', are difficult to challenge in the DSM since the US has pushed China to accept most of its practices in the Protocol and US – China bilateral agreement.[64] Hence, although it has long been argued that the US DOC practices on the selection of surrogate values and calculation of the country-wide rate in NME cases are discriminatory, China for many years did not challenge the US practices.[65] It was when the US decided to depart from its tradition, that is, not to apply anti-subsidy laws to China, that China considered the US practice can no longer hide behind the curtain of NME and is challengeable in the WTO. The details of China's request of consultation, the ongoing panel proceeding and the underlying legal issues concerning double remedy, will be discussed extensively in the next subsection.

3.2.2 The EU

The EU, over the years, has established a similar system as the US to handle AD cases involving NME countries. According to Article 2(7)(a) of the Basic Regulation, the normal value in an NME should be determined on the basis of:

> the price or constructed value in a market economy third country, or the price from such a third country to other countries, including the Community, or where those are not possible, on any other reasonable basis, including the price actually paid or payable in the Community for the like product, duly adjusted if necessary to include a reasonable profit margin.[66]

---

62. *Antidumping Duties; Countervailing Duties; Final Rule*, 62 Fed. Reg. 27,295, 27,364 (DOC., 19 May 1997) (citation omitted).
63. The White House Office of Public Liaison, 'Summary of US-China Bilateral WTO Agreement', 17 Nov. 1999, available at: <www.uschina.org/public/991115a.html>, (last accessed 15 Jul. 2008).
64. K. Tracey, 'Non-market Economy Methodology Under US Anti-dumping Laws: A Protectionist Shield from Chinese Competition', *Current: International Trade Law Journal* 15 (2006): 81, 90–91.
65. For example, J. Greenwald & G. Horlick, 'Dumping Margin Calculation Problems in the United States', *Global Trade and Custom Journal* 2 (2007): 67, 68–69.
66. Council Regulation (EC) No. 384/96 of 22 Dec. 1995 on protection against dumped imports from countries not members of the European Community, OJ L 56/1, 6 Mar. 1996, as amended

In other words, the EU methodology of calculating an NV in an NME case also bases on the price or constructed NV in an analogue country. The similarity between the US and the EU systems nevertheless ends here. In the EU system, no 'factors of production' approach is used to calculate the NV, that is, the quantity of inputs used to produce the product concerned by an exporter in an NME country is irrelevant to the calculation of the NV in a EU investigation.

Moreover, in 1998, the Basic Regulation was amended to reflect the changes of economic conditions in Vietnam and in China so that they were no longer automatically considered as NMEs.[67] This amendment significantly changed the EU system. Individual companies in China and Vietnam now have the opportunities to apply for market economy treatment (MET). A company that is granted MET is treated the same way as a company from a market economy, namely their NV will be calculated based on their own home market prices and costs. It is therefore different from the US system, which grants MOI status to industries, instead of individual companies.

Article 2(7)(c) specifies conditions that must be fulfilled in order for a company to qualify for MET as follows:

> (c) A claim under subparagraph (b) must be made in writing and contain sufficient evidence that the producer operates under market economy conditions, that is if:
>
> – decisions of firms regarding prices, costs and inputs, including for instance raw materials, cost of technology and labour, output, sales and investment, are made in response to market signals reflecting supply and demand, and without significant State interference in this regard, and costs of major inputs substantially reflect market values;
> – firms have one clear set of basic accounting records which are independently audited in line with international accounting standards and are applied for all purposes;
> – the production costs and financial situation of firms are not subject to significant distortions carried over from the former non-market economy system, in particular in relation to depreciation of assets, other write-offs, barter trade and payment via compensation of debts;
> – the firms concerned are subject to bankruptcy and property laws which guarantee legal certainty and stability for the operation of firms; and
> – exchange rate conversions are carried out at the market rate.
>
> A determination whether the producer meets the abovementioned criteria shall be made within three months of the initiation of the investigation, after

---

by Council Regulation (EC) No. 2331/96 of 2 Dec. 1996, OJ L 317/1, 6 Dec. 1996; Council Regulation (EC) No. 905/98 of 27 Apr. 1998, OJ L 128/18, 30 Apr. 1998; Council Regulation (EC) No. 2238/2000 of 9 Oct. 2000, OJ L 257/2, 11 Oct. 2000; Council Regulation (EC) No. 1972/2002 of 5 Nov. 2002, OJ L 305/1, 7 Nov. 2002; Council Regulation (EC) No. 461/2004 of 8 Mar. 2004, OJ L 77/12, 13 Mar. 2004 and Council Regulation (EC) No. 2117/2005 of 21 Dec. 2005, OJ L 340/17, 23 Dec. 2005.

67. Council Regulation (EC) No. 905/98 of 27 Apr. 1998, OJ L 128/18, 30 Apr. 1998.

> specific consultation of the Advisory Committee and after the Community industry has been given an opportunity to comment. This determination shall remain in force throughout the investigation.

It has long been argued that although the five MET criteria look straightforward, 'EC case handlers have broad administrative discretion to interpret whether a company meets each of the conditions, particularly with respect to the first three'.[68] In numerous cases, the Commission has applied these criteria to examine hundreds of Chinese companies and rejected the MET for the majority of them.[69] As demonstrated below, although Article 2(7)(c) itself can hardly be considered as WTO-inconsistent, the Commission's interpretation and application of these five criteria have caused significant controversies.

Also, the Commission had developed a few practices associated with its MET methodology, such as individual treatment and sampling, and consistently applies them in AD investigations involving Chinese products.

The first established practice associated with MET is the individual treatment. As another important exception of one-country-one-duty rule, if a company does not qualify for MET, it can apply for the individual treatment, which allows their own export prices to be used to calculate the dumping margin. Individual treatment is similar to the US's 'separate rate' test, although with slightly different conditions. Article 9(5) of the Basic Regulation stipulates the conditions as follows:[70]

> Where Article 2(7)(a) applies, an individual duty shall, however, be specified for the exporters which can demonstrate, on the basis of properly substantiated claims that:
>
> (a) in the case of wholly or partly foreign owned firms or joint ventures, exporters are free to repatriate capital and profits;
> (b) export prices and quantities, and conditions and terms of sale are freely determined;
> (c) the majority of the shares belong to private persons. State officials appearing on the board of Directors or holding key management positions shall either be in minority or it must be demonstrated that the company is nonetheless sufficiently independent from State interference;
> (d) exchange rate conversions are carried out at the market rate; and
> (e) State interference is not such as to permit circumvention of measures if individual exporters are given different rates of duty.

The second practice that often arises in an NME investigation is sampling. In cases where a large number of respondents need to be investigated and the Commission does not have the resources to conduct the investigation, it resorts to sampling

68. E. Vermulst & F. Graafsma, 'Recent EC Anti-dumping Practice towards China and Vietnam: The Great Leap Backward?', *International Trade Law Review* 5 (2006): 124.
69. Detlof & Fridh, 'The EU Treatment of Non-Market Economy Countries in Anti-dumping Proceedings', 276.
70. Council Regulation (EC) No. 2117/2005 of 21 Dec. 2005, OJ L 340/17, 23 Dec. 2005., Art. 9(5).

techniques.[71] Yet, as is widely discussed, the sampling practice can have 'peculiar consequences' for the companies not selected in the sample, since their status (MET, individual treatment or non-market economy) is unknown.[72] The Commission once introduced a desk-check analysis to remedy the problem of sampling. The system is described as follows by commentators:[73]

> If a desk-check system is utilized, companies outside the sample will be checked in detail on the merits of their application, but will not be investigated on the spot. These non-selected companies will then, in due course, be provided their status and attributed the weighted average duty of each status group of companies (MET, IT or NME).

The practice of the Commission with the desk-check system is that in the initial stage of the investigation, the Commission requests exporting producers to supply sampling information and MET/individual treatment requests at the same time. After examining and verifying both sampling and MET/individual treatment information, it merges the two sets of information and makes decisions. The sampled producers that obtained MET and/or IT will normally receive individual dumping margin based on their own data. For producers that are not included in the sample, those that were granted MET after desk-check will be awarded the weighted average dumping margin of the sampled MET producers and those that were granted individual treatment after desk-check will be awarded the weighted average dumping margin of the sampled individual treatment producers. Companies that were neither granted MET, nor individual treatment, received the country-wide dumping margin.

The Commission, however, stopped applying the MET desk-check system after the *Footwear* case. In the footwear case, it granted only one MET from 154 cooperating Chinese exporting producers and rejected the MET application from all non-sampled companies, up to 140 companies.[74]

For more than a decade, Chinese exporting producers criticized the Commission's approach to interpret five criteria in Article 2(7)(c), its individual treatment practice and its sampling practice in various AD cases, and challenged some of these practices in the CFI and ECJ.[75] The focus of this subsection is however whether these issues are litigatable in the DSM. The following analysis, by taking

71. Vermulst & Graafsma, 'Recent EC Anti-dumping Practice towards China and Vietnam', 128.
72. *Ibid.*
73. *Ibid.*
74. Council Regulation (EC) No. 1472/2006 of 5 Oct. 2006 imposing a definitive anti-dumping duty and collecting definitely the provisional duty imposed on imports of certain footwear with uppers of leather originating in the People's Republic of China and Vietnam, OJ 275/1, 6 Oct. 2006.
75. For example, Detlof & Fridh, 'The EU Treatment of Non-Market Economy Countries in Anti-dumping Proceedings', 281 and Vermulst & Graafsma, 'Recent EC Anti-dumping Practice towards China and Vietnam', 129. For ECJ challenge, for example, Case T-138/02 *Nanjing Metalink v. Council* [2006] ECR II-4347; Case T- 35/01 *Shanghai Teraoka Electronic v. Council* [2004] ECR II-3663.

the examples of the first criterion of Article 2(7)(c), intends to shed some light on the question.

3.2.2.1 First Criterion of Article 2(7)(c): 'State Interference'

The first criterion of Article 2(7)(c) requires that the 'decision of firms regarding prices, costs and inputs, . . . are made in response to market signals reflecting supply and demand, and without significant State interference in this regard, and costs of major inputs substantially reflect market values'. Although the five criteria of Article (7)(c) are cumulative, meaning that, the companies applying for MET must fulfil all five of them, statistics show that 'the main reasons that MET is refused is that companies are either under state influence, or that they do not keep adequate accounts', since '[F]ifty eight per cent of the companies who failed MET, failed upon each of these grounds'.[76] State interference is therefore one of the key reasons that the Commission rejects MET applications by Chinese companies.

In the past, the Commission has, for various reasons, considered that state interference existed in Chinese companies. Among these widely varied reasons, three types of state interference are frequently cited, namely, 'direct state ownership or ownership by state owned companies', 'limitations on sale and export targets', and 'restrictions on imports and exports'.[77]

Due to limited space, this analysis cannot discuss every type of state interference in the numerous AD investigations against China. It takes the Commission's interpretation of state ownership or ownership by state-owned companies as an example. Chinese exporting producers in more than a dozen AD cases argued that majority state ownership or ownership by state-owned companies should not be a factor automatically disqualifying the MET status of a company, yet none of them was successful.[78]

The key question is how the first criterion should be interpreted. It can be interpreted as requiring that (1) the company's business decisions are made in response to market signals, and (2) that these business decisions are made without significant State interference in this regard. This is to say that if the state interference is not such as to prevent the business decisions from being made in response to market signals with respect to price, costs and inputs, this kind of state interference does not fall within this criterion. Also, this state interference needs to be 'significant'. Therefore, Chinese exports could argue that the relevant factors in assessing whether a company fulfils the first criterion are: (1) through the state ownership, whether the State has interfered with the company's business decisions so as to prevent the business decisions from being made in response to market signals and (2) whether the State interference is 'significant', although the exact

76. Detlof & Fridh, 'The EU Treatment of Non-Market Economy Countries in Anti-dumping Proceedings', 276.
77. *Ibid.*, 277.
78. For example, Commission Regulation (EC) 255/2001 [2001] OJ L 38/8, recital 16; Regulation 950/2001 [2001] OJ L 197/4, recital 22; Regulation 1612/2001 [2001] OJ L 214/3, recital 20; Regulation 306/2004 [2004] OJ L 52/5, recital 60–64; Regulation 538/2005 [2005] OJ L 89/4, recital 46–54 and Regulation 552/2005 [2005] OJ L 93/6, recital 24–25.

scope of the term 'significant' is not defined in the Basic Regulation. In other words, evidence of past significant State interference is sufficient to disqualify the company's MET application, yet the mere possibility that the State may influence the future decision-making of the company is not sufficient. Whether State interference affects business decisions so that they do not reflect demand and supply must be verified.

This line of argument has been nicely elaborated upon in a recent judgment, *Zhejiang Xinan Chemical Industrial Group Co. Ltd v. Council*, as follows:[79]

> It submits that the wording of that provision requires the Community institutions to assess whether the evidence produced by the exporting producer is sufficient to show that its business decisions respond to market signals and are taken without significant State interference. Thus, the absence of 'significant State interference' must be assessed, objectively and factually on the basis of the evidence, 'in regard' to each aspect of the business decisions encompassed in the first indent of Article 2(7)(c) of the basic regulation. In the applicant's submission, in view of the meaning of the term 'interference', a situation in which the State is not involved in the business decisions, or is involved but does not prevent them from responding to market signals reflecting supply and demand, does not constitute 'interference' within the meaning of the first indent of Article 2(7)(c) of the basic regulation. The applicant observes, moreover, that that provision accepts a situation of State interference unless that interference is 'significant'.
>
> On that point, Audace adds that, in English, the concept of 'interference' clearly refers to 'an element of meddling, tampering or actual contamination'. It states that it is a 'transitive concept' and that the State must interfere 'with' a particular decision or action, which must fall within one of the categories mentioned in the first indent of Article 2(7)(c) of the basic regulation. The wording of that provision in the other official languages confirms that interpretation ('intervention significative' in the French version and 'Staatseingriffe' in the German version). According to Audace, that concept cannot be validly assimilated to the concepts of 'control' or 'influence' which are 'intransitive concepts', the State being able to exercise a degree of influence without, thereby, actually tampering with decisions or actions. Moreover, the use of the phrase 'in this regard' ties such interference to decisions on prices, costs and inputs.
>
> More particularly, the applicant notes that it is not control which constitutes the criterion provided for in the first indent of Article 2(7)(c) of the basic regulation and submits, consequently, that the State's minority shareholding is not a factor from which it could be inferred that the condition set out in that provision was not satisfied. It claims, also, that no published decision has ever denied MES to a company by reason of a minority shareholding held by the State or by State owned companies and that the Commission itself must have formed the opinion, during the investigation, that such shareholding was not

79. Case T-498/04, *Zhejiang Xinan Chemical Industrial Group Co. Ltd v Council of the European Union*, ECR II-0000, paras 49–51. The contested regulation is Regulation 1683/2004.

> an obstacle to the grant of MES since, otherwise, the on-the-spot verification it carried out would have been meaningless.

This is nevertheless not the Commission's approach. The Commission considers that if the State exercises control over a Chinese company, this company does not fulfil the first criterion. Evidence, such as the State has a blocking majority; other shareholders are so fragmented that the State as the majority shareholder can exercise influence; and several members of a company board were appointed by the State or state-owned parent company, can be considered as proof that the company is controlled by the State and operates with significant State interference.[80]

Hence, in the Commission's view, the first criterion of Article 2 (7)(c) refers to past State interference or the possibility of State interference in the future. In *trichloroisocyanuric acid*,[81] the Commission stated its interpretation as follows:

> The aim of the investigation, is *inter alia* to assess to which extent the State could interfere in business decisions, and which measures were taken by the company to prevent such interference.
>
> In this regard, it was found that the State held the majority of the Director posts on the Board of Directors, and that there were no restrictions on the State-appointed Directors' voting rights on the Board (minority protection). The company failed to demonstrate that appropriate measures have been taken to prevent such State interference in the future.

Moreover, in *Zhejiang Xinan Chemical Industrial Group v. Council*, the Council defended its position as follows:[82]

> Furthermore, the Council disputes the existence of an established practice whereby the institutions examine in detail the measures to prevent State interference adopted by the exporter under investigation. In any event, the Council submits that the applicant did not show in the investigation that it had in fact taken measures to prevent State influence. It observes that measures that could be relevant in that regard are, for example, measures concerning the composition of the board of directors (whose members would be neither State officials nor persons having links with the State) or measures relating to voting rules (no minority blocking vote for the State shareholder, which would enable the majority non-State shareholders to control the company). However, the only measure referred to by the applicant is the Chinese company law which is not a measure adopted by the applicant. In the Council's submission, if the Chinese company law alone could preclude State influence, all State-controlled companies could, on the basis of such a law, apply for MES, which would render the assessment of MES virtually meaningless.

---

80. For example, *ibid.*, Regulation 538/2005 and Regulation 1683/2004 [2004] OJ L 303/1, recital 13.
81. Regulation 538/2005, *ibid.*, recital 47–48.
82. Case T-498/04, Regulation 1683/2004, paras 72 and 74.

> The Council adds that it depends on the circumstances of each case whether the State participation in overall decision-making is of sufficient weight to constitute 'interference' within the meaning of the first indent of Article 2(7)(c) of the basic regulation. In the present case, the institutions concluded that the grounds of refusal set out in the contested regulation, 'taken together', were sufficient to conclude that the applicant had not shown that it operated free of State interference.

The CFI, although acknowledged that State control existed in this specific case, interpreted Article 2(7)(c) of the Basic Regulation as follows:[83]

> It is clear from the wording of that provision that the question of whether or not there is significant State interference must be assessed in the light of the way that 'decisions of firms regarding prices, costs and inputs' are made. It requires the exporting producer concerned to show that its decisions are made both 'in response to market signals' and 'without significant State interference'. In addition, the use of the words 'in this regard' further accentuates the connection between the relevant decisions and the State interference. Consequently, conduct by the State which is not such as to influence those decisions cannot constitute 'significant State interference' within the meaning of the first indent of Article 2(7)(c) of the basic regulation.
>
> Furthermore, in view of the wording, purpose and context of that provision, the concept of 'significant State interference' cannot be assimilated to just any influence on the activities of an undertaking or to just any involvement in its decision-making process, but must be understood as meaning action by the State which is such as to render the undertaking's decisions incompatible with market economy conditions.
>
> The very use of the expression 'significant . . . interference' is evidence of the Community legislature's intention to allow a certain degree of State influence over an undertaking's activities or of State involvement in its decision-making process if it has no effect on the manner in which its decisions concerning prices, costs and inputs are made.

Based on this statement and other evidence, the CFI reached the conclusion that '[w]hilst State control over an undertaking is a matter which may be possibly taken into account, it is not sufficient, by itself to demonstrate the existence of 'significant State interference' within the meaning of that provision' and thus the contested Regulation should be annulled in so far as it concerns the applicant.[84]

A hypothetical question is raised as to whether a WTO panel will support this kind of argument from the Chinese exporter and in light of the WTO laws and jurisprudence, whether China should bring such a matter to a panel. The answer can hardly be straightforward.

83. *Ibid.*, paras 84–86.
84. *Ibid.*

On the one hand, it has to be noted that the first sentence of Article 2(7)(c) uses the present tense 'are'. If one intends to strictly follow the general rule of interpretation followed by the AB and panels, that is, Article 31 of the VCIL, the use of the present sense in the first sentence of Article 2(7)(c) suggests that State interference, if any, must be in existence or in progress. By using the present tense, it is arguable that the ordinary meaning of the first sentence of Article 2(7)(c) is that, as long as a Chinese firm's decision is made in response to market signals and without significant State interference in this regard, it fulfils the requirement of the first sentence of Article 2(7)(c), unless there is evidence to the contary. The determination of whether the first sentence of Article 2(7)(c) is fulfilled by a Chinese company should not be connected to the future action or behaviour of this company. In addition, the Chinese companies are certainly not required to 'take measures to prevent State influence' as is argued by the Council.

On the other hand, a WTO panel may consider that although the Commission interprets Article 2(7)(c) in a different way that either a panel or the AB might have, to apply a different interpretative approach itself does not necessarily constitute a violation of the EU's WTO obligation. The fact that Article 2(7)(c) is not a provision in a covered agreement, and Article 2(7)(c) itself does not breach any WTO rules, creates a different situation from the Panel and the AB's examination and interpretation of Indian law in *India – Patents (US)*, where the AB stated as follows:[85]

> It is clear that an examination of the relevant aspects of Indian municipal law and, in particular, the relevant provisions of the Patents Act as they relate to the 'administrative instructions', is essential to determining whether India has complied with its obligations under Article 70.8(a). There was simply no way for the Panel to make this determination without engaging in an examination of Indian law. But, as in the case cited above before the Permanent Court of International Justice, in this case, the Panel was not interpreting Indian law 'as such'; rather, the Panel was examining Indian law solely for the purpose of determining whether India had met its obligations under the TRIPS Agreement. . . . .
>
> Previous GATT/WTO panels also have conducted a detailed examination of the domestic law of a Member in assessing the conformity of that domestic law with the relevant GATT/WTO obligations. For example, in United States – Section 337 of the Tariff Act of 1930, the panel conducted a detailed examination of the relevant United States' legislation and practice, including the remedies available under Section 337 as well as the differences between patent-based Section 337 proceedings and federal district court proceedings, in order to determine whether Section 337 was inconsistent with Article III:4 of the GATT 1947. This seems to us to be a comparable case.

85. WTO, *India – Patent Protection for Pharmaceutical and Agricultural Chemical Products*, Report of the Appellate Body, WT/DS50/AB/R, adopted 16 Jan. 1998, DSR 1998:I, 9, paras 65–67.

The Panel in *US – Section 301 Trade Act* repeated the AB's finding and stated that it would not 'interpret US law "as such", the way we would, say, interpret provisions of the covered agreements'.[86] Rather, the panel held that it was instead 'called upon to establish the meaning of Sections 301–310 as factual elements'.[87] This panel also makes statements with respect to the different interpretations between WTO law and municipal law as follows:[88]

> We note, finally, that terms used both in Sections 301–310 and in WTO provisions, do not necessarily have the same meaning. For example, the word 'determination' need not always have the same meaning in Sections 304 and 306 as it has in Article 23.2(a) of the DSU. Thus, conduct not meeting, say, the threshold of a 'determination' under Sections 304 and 306, is not by this fact alone precluded from meeting the threshold of a 'determination' under Article 23.2(a) of the DSU. By contrast, the fact that a certain act is characterized as a 'determination' under domestic legislation, does not necessarily mean that it must be construed as a determination under the covered agreements.

Although the above-mentioned quotes do not preclude China from arguing that by interpreting Article 2(7)(c) in a way that is not consistent with the 'ordinary meaning' of the provision, the EU breaches its WTO obligations, it obviously increases the difficulty of challenging the Commission's practices in the DSM, although the same practice has been condemned by the CFI.

3.3 *US-AD and CVD on Chinese Products*

3.3.1 Background of *US-AD and CVD on Chinese Products*

On 14 September 2007, China formally requested consultations with the US concerning the preliminary AD and CVD determinations made by the US DOC on 29 May 2007 and 2 April 2007, respectively, in relation to coated free sheet paper from China.[89] As the first request of consultation filed by China alone after its accession to the WTO, China made this move in a hope to stop 'a trend' that could develop after the US DOC's decision to levy preliminary duties of 23.19%–99.65% on coated paper imported from China.[90] This request for consultation did

86. WTO *United States – Sections 301-310 of the Trade Act of 1974*, Report of the Panel, WT/DS152/R, adopted 27 Jan. 2000, DSR 2000:II, 815, para. 7.18.
87. *Ibid.*
88. *Ibid.*, para. 7.20.
89. WTO, 'United States – Preliminary Anti-dumping and Countervailing Duty Determinations on Coated Free Sheet Paper from China, Request for Consultation by China', WT/DS368/1, G/L/826, G/SCM/D77/1, G/ADP/D72/1, 18 Sep. 2007.
90. Competition Law 360 'Disgruntled with US Duties, China Goes to WTO', 14 Sep. 2007, available at: <http://competition.law360.com/>. See also, MOFCOM, 'China Seeks WTO Resolution over Paper Disputes with US', 17 Sep. 2007, available at: <http://melbourne2.mofcom.gov.cn/aarticle/chinanews/200709/20070905127303.html>.

not lead to the establishment of a panel since the US International Trade Commission (ITC) found on 21 December 2007 that the imports were not materially injuring or threatening material injury to the US industry and there is no definitive duty imposed.[91] Nevertheless, the US imposed the combined CVD and AD duties to Chinese exports in a number of subsequent investigations.[92]

China therefore again requested consultations with the US on 19 September 2008 concerning the definitive AD and CVD duties imposed by the US in four combined investigations.[93] In the Request for Consultation, China made seven categories of claims, which cover the substantive claims under the Agreement on Subsidies and Countervailing Measures (ASCM) and the ADA, and procedural claims. The dispute finally reached the panel stage after the consultations failed to resolve the dispute.[94] On 20 January 2009, the DSB established a panel pursuant to the request of China and the Director-General composed a panel on 9 March 2009.[95]

Among all of the claims that China made in its request for consultation, the one most relevant to this study is the so-called 'double remedy' issue, which arises when the US authorities use 'a non-market economy (NME) methodology for the purpose of determining the existence and amount of alleged dumping under Article VI of the GATT 1994 and the AD Agreement, simultaneously with the determination of subsidization and imposition of countervailing duties on the same subject merchandise'.[96]

China claimed in the Request for Consultation that the US authorities, by imposing combined AD and CVD duties, are in breach of the following provisions in the covered agreements:

(a) the failure of the US authorities to ensure that the final affirmative determination of subsidization, and the imposition of countervailing duties, were based on the amount of subsidy found to exist, as required by Article 19.4 of the SCM Agreement;
(b) the use by the US authorities of a specific action against subsidization that is not in accordance with the GATT 1994, as interpreted by the SCM Agreement, in violation of Article 32.1 of the SCM Agreement;

---

91. ITC, 'Coated Free Sheet Paper from China, Indonesia, and Korea Does Not Injure US Industry, says ITC', <www.usitc.gov/ext_relations/news_release/2007/er1120ee1.htm>.
92. Competition Law 360 'PRC Imports: Countervailing Duties, US Trade Policy', 19 Dec. 2007, available at: <http://competition.law360.com/>.
93. WTO, 'United States – Definitive Anti-dumping and Countervailing Duties on Certain Products from China, Request for Consultation by China', WT/DS379/1, G/L/845, G/SCM/D78/1, G/ADP/D74/1, 22 Sep. 2008.
94. WTO, 'United States – Definitive Anti-dumping and Countervailing Duties on Certain Products from China, Request for the Establishment of a Panel by China', WT/DS379/2, 12 Dec. 2008.
95. WTO, 'United States – Definitive Anti-dumping and Countervailing Duties on Certain Products from China, Constitution of the Panel Established at the Request of China', WT/DS379/3, 11 Mar. 2009.
96. Page 5 of WTO, 'United States – Definitive Anti-dumping and Countervailing Duties on Certain Products from China, Request for Consultation by China', WT/DS379/1, G/L/845, G/SCM/D78/1, G/ADP/D74/1, 22 Sep. 2008.

(c) the US authorities' failure to take all necessary steps to ensure that the imposition of countervailing duties was in accordance with Article VI of GATT 1994 and the SCM Agreement, as required by Article 10 of the SCM Agreement;
(d) the US authorities' levying of anti-dumping and countervailing duties in excess of the 'appropriate amounts,' in violation of Article 9.2 of the AD Agreement and Article 19.3 of the SCM Agreement, respectively;
(e) the US authorities' failure to ensure a fair comparison between the export price and normal value, in violation of Article 2.4 of the AD Agreement; and
(f) the failure of the US authorities to ensure that the final affirmative determination of dumping, and the imposition of anti-dumping duties, were based on the amount of dumping found to exist, as required by Article 9.3 of the AD Agreement.

Given the limited space available, this subsection will not examine China's claims under the ASCM. Instead, it will focus on the parties' arguments that are related to the ADA.

It should be noted that the comments in this subsection only concern the legal arguments raised by parties as summarized in the US's Written Submissions and is made without any knowledge of factual backgrounds of the contested investigations. Given that the Panel proceeding of *US – AD and CVD on Chinese Products* is still ongoing, China's submissions (written submissions and oral statements) and the panel's communication to the parties are not publicly available. Hence, the primary source of information is the US's Written Submissions, which are made available by the Office of the United State Trade Representatives (USTR) in its website. Also, due to limited information, this subsection will only discuss the GATT/WTO rules on simultaneous AD and CVD investigations, the US's arguments in its two Written Submissions and possible arguments under Article 2.4 of the ADA with respect to double remedy (which the US has not rebutted in its two Written Submissions).

3.3.2 Double Remedy and Fair Comparison

3.3.2.1 GATT/WTO Rules on Simultaneous AD and CVD Investigations

As discussed in Chapter IV above, the purpose of AD duties is to offset dumping, which is defined in GATT Article VI:1 as being the introduction of products originating in one country into the territory of another country at less than the normal value of these products. By imposing AD duties or undertakings, the price of dumped imports is increased to non-dumped levels, exporting producers are committed to sell above a minimum price, which is set at a non-injurious level.

Subsidization can have an impact on dumping margin when the subsidies are granted upon exportation of products since an export subsidy will enable the exporting producer to lower its export price. Given that the amount of the dumping margin is calculated by comparing domestic and export prices, export subsidies will in effect increase the difference between both prices, and hence the amount of dumping.

In such cases, combining CVD duties (in order to offset countervailable export subsidies) and AD duties (in order to offset dumping) could result in compensating domestic industry twice for the same situation: once through the CVD duty (targeting the export subsidization directly) and once through the AD duty (which is higher due to the export subsidy).

GATT Article VI:5 forbids WTO members from imposing both AD and CVD duties in order to compensate for the same situation caused by dumping and export subsidization. It reads as follows:

> No product of the territory of any contracting party imported into the territory of any other contracting party shall be subject to both anti-dumping and countervailing duties to compensate for the same situation of dumping or export subsidization.

In otherwords, GATT Article VI:5 was adopted in order to avoid the double compensation that could result from the combined imposition of CVD and AD duties. This provision, however, has never been applied by the GATT or WTO panels, although major trading partners, such as the EU, the US and Canada, frequently conduct combined CVD and AD investigations against imports.

Moreover, Article VI:5 did not mention whether an importing country can impose combined AD and CVD duties to offset dumping and domestic subsidies. Given the absence of a clear prohibition in the GATT, it becomes the common practice of the EU and the US not to adjust domestic subsidy CVDs in the dumping margin calculation.

The US DOC explained its methodology in *Cold-Rolled Corrosion Resistant Carbon Steel Flat Products from Korea* as follows:[97]

> Domestic subsidies presumably lower the price of the subject merchandise both in the home and the U.S. markets, and therefore have no effect on the measurement of any dumping that might also occur. Export subsidies, by contrast, benefit only exported merchandise. Accordingly, an export subsidy brings about a lower U.S. price, which could be ascribed to either dumping or export subsidization, as well as the potential for double remedies. Imposing both an export-subsidy CVD and an AD duty, calculated with no adjustment for that CVD, would impose a double remedy specifically prohibited by Article VI.5 of the GATT. Thus, the only reasonable explanation for Congress' decision to provide for the addition to U.S. price of export-subsidy CVDs is protection against double remedies.

97. US DOC 'Certain Cold-Rolled and Corrosion-Resistant Carbon Steel Flat Products From Korea: Final Results of Antidumping Duty Administrative Reviews', 62 Federal Register, 18422 (15 Apr. 1997).

The US DOC also stated its different approach towards export and domestic subsidies in *Low Enriched Uranium from France*:[98]

> With respect to CVDs to offset export subsidies, the 1979 amendments to the statute provide a straightforward response to the argument that they should be deducted from initial U.S. prices in calculating dumping margins – they require that CVDs to offset export subsidies be added to initial U.S. prices. *We do not interpret the statute to require CVDs to offset export subsidies first to be added to initial U.S. prices and then to permit this addition to be negated by their subsequent subtraction.*
>
> Domestic subsidies present a closer question, as the statute does not speak directly to them. The fact that the statute addresses CVDs to offset export subsidies directly, however, and then remains silent about the plainly related issue of CVDs to offset domestic subsidies, is not complete silence . . . *implies that no adjustment is appropriate.* There is no reason why Congress would have provided for the addition of export subsidy CVDs, but not considered the plainly related issue of domestic subsidy CVDs. (emphasis added)

This means that in the dumping margin calculation, when the export price is compared to the normal value that contains any AD and CVD duty paid upon importation of the product into the US, these duties are not deducted.[99] However, in cases where CVD duties are paid to offset export subsidies, the US DOC can increase the export price and in turn reduces the dumping margin.[100]

This practice of the US has neither been denied nor upheld by a WTO panel or the AB. In fact, in WTO jurisprudence, Article VI:5 was only examined, indirectly, in *Indonesia – Autos*, in order to support the panel's argument that the ASCM was not intended to be the exclusive mechanism for challenging subsidy

98. US DOC, 'Notice of Final Results of Antidumping Duty Administrative Review: Low Enriched Uranium From France', 69 Federal Register, 46505 (3 Aug. 2004).

99. This is the case for instance if the goods are sold 'duty paid', and the price agreed therefore includes duties paid by the exporter. It would also be the case if the export price is constructed, in which case the price to a purchaser in the US not affiliated with the producer or exporter (which will include any duties paid) is used as the starting point for calculating the export price.

100. This is a significant difference with the EU practice, where countervailing and anti-dumping duties are always deducted from the export price when calculating the dumping margin, and therefore have no impact on the margin.

There is one exception in the EU practice, under Art. 11(10) of the EU Basic Regulation. This provision specifies in the relevant part that: 'In any investigation carried out pursuant to this Article [reviews], the Commission shall examine the reliability of export prices in accordance with Article 2. However, where it is decided to construct the export price in accordance with Article 2(9), it shall calculate it with no deduction for the amount of anti-dumping duties paid when conclusive evidence is provided that the duty is duly reflected in resale prices and the subsequent selling prices in the Community.' However, Art. 11(10) only applies to anti-dumping duties, and not to countervailing duties.

measures.[101] No guidance can therefore be found in either the panel or the AB decisions concerning the interpretation of GATT Article VI:5.

Yet, when the NME concept enters into the picture, the interplay between subsidization and dumping becomes much more complicated as is suggested in the analysis of the US's arguments in *US – AD and CVD on Chinese Products* below.

3.3.2.2 The US's Arguments on Double Remedy

In *US – AD and CVD on Chinese Products*, the US summarized China's main argument on double remedy as 'imposing CVDs results in a 'double remedy' when a WTO member is also imposing AD duties that have been calculated using normal value derived from a methodology based on surrogate, third-country values rather than actual Chinese prices or costs'.[102] The US elaborated upon China's 'theory' on the 'overlapping rationales' for the NME methodology and the imposition of CVDs in its Second Written Submission as follows:[103]

> China's theory as to the existence of a so-called double remedy is premised on its view of the 'overlapping rationales' of an NME methodology and the imposition of CVDs. According to China, the rationale for an NME methodology is to place the producer in the position of having 'market-determined' costs and prices when calculating normal value, which necessarily includes ensuring that the effects of subsidies are removed from those costs. The rationale for imposing CVDs, in China's understanding, is to offset the 'competitive advantage' or 'correct distortions' that result from the granting of subsidies to a particular firm. In China's words, '[t]hese are two different approaches to remedying the fact that a producer's costs and prices were not determined by market forces'.
>
> China argues that a double remedy is created because the NME normal value 'necessarily captures any trade-distorting effects of alleged subsidies'. According to China, the NME methodology not only produces market-economy normal values (i.e., the normal values that would be found if China were a market economy country) but also embodies some sort of built-in 'correction' for all of the subsidies provided to Chinese respondents. Thus, in China's view, it is precisely the NME methodology itself – that is, the use of market-determined costs and prices outside China – that creates the higher normal value, which also remedies the effects of the subsidy. (Footnote omitted)

---

101. WTO *Indonesia – Certain Measures Affecting the Automobile Industry*, Report of the Panel, WT/DS54/R, WT/DS55/R, WT/DS59/R, WT/DS64/R and Corr.1, 2, 3, and 4, adopted 23 Jul. 1998, DSR 1998:VI, 2201, para. 5.324.

102. *United States – (WT/DS379)*, the First Written Submission of the United States, para. 384.

103. *United States – Definitive Anti-dumping and Countervailing Duties on Certain Products from China (WT/DS379)*, the Second Written Submission of the United States, 27 Aug. 2009, available at: <www.ustr.gov/trade-topics/enforcement/dispute-settlement-proceedings/wto-dosîte-settlement/definitive-anti-dump-2>, paras 180–181.

The US rebutted this argument by first legitimizing its concurrent application of CVD and NME methodology in the combined investigations and then argued that it did not act inconsistently with either the ASCM or Article 1 of the GATT 1994.[104]

To legitimize its concurrent application, the US argues that China rests its claims 'on a direct challenge to the right of WTO members' because it 'fundamentally challenges the right of Members to apply AD and CVD measures concurrently to imports from China where those imports have been found to be both dumped and subsidized and the importing Member treats China as a non-market economy'.[105] It first excludes the application of Article VI:5 in this dispute on the ground that 'GATT Article VI:5 does not permit imports to be subject to AD and CVD measures for the "same situation" of dumping and export subsidization, but this restriction does not apply to domestic subsidies'.[106] The US also argues that, according to section 15 of the Protocol, 'Members, including China, contemplated the concurrent application of CVD and AD measures calculated on the basis of a surrogate value methodology without any limitation on the use of CVDs'.[107] In the US's view, 'GATT and WTO rules have generally placed no limitation on a member's ability to impose AD duties and CVDs to the fullest extent permitted under the covered agreements'.[108] Hence, China's claim is without legal basis in the text of the covered agreements. This is to say, 'the failure to explicitly restrict Members' resort to AD and CVD remedies concurrently in the current rules, including China's Accession Protocol, can mean only that Members retain such right'.[109]

The second part of US's rebuttal concerns China's claims under Articles 19.3 and 19.4 of the ASCM and Article I:1 of the GATT. With respect to Articles 19.3 and 19.4, the US argues that:

> The AD duties calculated on the basis of Commerce's non-market methodology are levied to offset dumping of imported products that have caused injury. As a result, these duties do not fall within the definition of 'countervailing duty' under the SCM Agreement and Article19.4 does not apply.
>
> . . . Again, as in the case of Article 19.4, the basis for China's claim under Article 19.3 of the SCM Agreement appears to be that the AD duties imposed in the four AD investigations are actually CVDs in disguise, and that the sum of these duties exceeds the 'appropriate amounts' in the CVD investigations . . . . In arguing otherwise, China essentially seeks to deny the United States its right to levy AD duties up to the margin of dumping under the AD Agreement and CVDs up to the amount of the subsidy under the SCM Agreement.

104. *Ibid.*, 133–149.
105. *Ibid.*, para. 177.
106. *United States – (WT/DS379)*, the First Written Submission of the United States, para. 396.
107. *Ibid.*, para. 410.
108. *Ibid.*, para. 470.
109. *Ibid.*, para. 417.

Finally, the US claims that the US DOC equally takes actions to avoid a double remedy for market economies and non-market economies, and thus it did not act inconsistently with Article I:1 of the GATT.[110] Most importantly, 'China's complaint centers on the application of the NME methodology, and that because such application is expressly authorized by paragraph 15(a) of China's Protocol, it does not contravene Article I:1.'[111]

A close reading of the US's two Written Submissions suggests that the US takes the 'textual' approach to the extreme in addressing this 'double remedy' issue. It isolates the obligations imposed by each covered agreement, including the Protocol, and rebuts China's claims under each agreement separately. Following this approach, it asserts that it fully complies with WTO rules by exercising three rights that have not been explicitly prohibited by the covered agreements and the Protocol: first, the right to apply the NME methodology in the AD investigations against China; second, the right to conduct combined AD and CVD investigations; and finally, the right to levy AD duties up to the margin of dumping under the AD Agreement and CVDs up to the amount of the subsidy under the SCM Agreement.

When China attempts to argue the underlying 'overlapping rationale' for the NME methodology and the imposition of CVDs, the US's response is straightforward – '[T]he basis for the asserted prohibition on such concurrent application is not in the text of the covered agreements'.[112]

Theoretically, the panel can have sympathy to the theory advanced by China, which explains why the concurrent application of the NME methodology and the subsidy rules could be 'overlapping'. The panel can also consider that the application of NME methodology may change the situation in such a way that the fundamental rationale for not prohibiting the imposition of combined AD and domestic subsidy CVD is no longer valid.

In a market economy situation, AD and CVD could indeed be considered to be 'distinct remedies targeting distinct practices', as the US observed.[113] The only connection in the covered agreements between the ADA and the ASCM is that under circumstances where export subsidy CVD duties and AD duties are imposed to compensate the same situation, the concurrent application of CVD and AD is prohibited, according to Article VI:5 of the GATT. The rationale behind it is that domestic subsidies will result in an even drop of domestic and export prices, that is, these subsidies will have no impact on the dumping margin calculation, whereas export subsidies will have an impact on the export prices only and thus affect dumping margin calculation.

In an NME scenario, the situation is different. The panel may find China's theory to be appealing if it acknowledges the underlying purpose of the application of NME methodology is to ensure that the costs and prices used in the dumping margin calculation are not distorted by the Chinese government. Subsidies from the Chinese government, if any, could already have been offset by the dumping

110. *United States – (WT/DS379)*, the Second Written Submission of the United States, para. 210.
111. *Ibid.*
112. *Ibid.*, para. 175.
113. *Ibid.*, para. 183.

margin calculated under the NME methodology. That is, 'from a standpoint of the potential double remedy, Commerce's NME methodology has the same effects as adding subsidies to a producer's cost of production in a market economy investigation'.[114]

Unfortunately, this theory, as pointed out by the US, has no 'textual' basis in the covered agreements and the Protocol. Even if the panel supports China's theory, it is difficult for it to conclude that the US breached its obligations under a particular covered agreement or the Protocol based on the arguments presented by parties by far.

This is a perfect example of how the low level of legalization in the covered agreements (including the Protocol) on a particular issue presents a considerable challenge to WTO members when making use of the DSM to 'litigate' the matter. In this dispute, the low level of legalization is caused, not only by the silence of the covered agreements and the Protocol on the 'double remedy' issue, but also by the disconnection between them. In particular, the Protocol, which brings in a methodology that could shake the foundation of the existing rules on the concurrent application of AD and CVD rules, failed to establish new rules to form a bridge between the NME methodology and the imposition of CVD duties. This is exactly the reason for which the US can isolate China's claims in each covered agreements and the Protocol and rebut them individually.

However, is it true that none of the provision in the existing covered agreement can help China to challenge the US's practice, if arguably China's theory is economically sound? The next subsection explores whether the potential arguments in relation to 'fair comparison' under Article 2.4 of the ADA could enable China to present its case with a better 'textual' basis.

3.3.2.3 Unanswered Question under the ADA: Fair Comparison?

Although the US argued that 'China's assertion that a double remedy exists whenever CVD measures are imposed concurrently with AD measures calculated under an NME methodology' cannot be supported by any text of the covered agreements, it has not addressed the question of whether the concurrent application of AD and CVD measures to imports from China could result in 'unfair comparison' between the export price and the normal value, which is prohibited by Article 2.4 of the ADA.[115] It is possible that since China did not further elaborate this argument in its Written Submissions due to the particular factual situation of the case (although it was listed as one of the claims in the Request for Consultation), the US does not need to address it.

However, hypothetically, if, in the original investigations, Chinese producers' requests to adjust the NV and/or the export price under Article 2.4 of the ADA to

114. China First Written Submission, paragraph 412, as cited by the US in the US First Submission fn 597.
115. *Ibid.*, para. 176.

factor in the domestic subsidization of China are denied by the US DOC and China pursues this claim in the penal proceeding, could a panel support this argument?

The US has correctly pointed out that 'the use of an NME methodology is meant to replace unreliable costs and prices in the NME with surrogate value from a market economy at a comparable stage of economic development, in order to calculate normal value to assess whether international price discrimination exists'.[116] Thus, '[A] fter the derivation of this special normal value, the export price is then subtracted from normal value, just as in any other anti-dumping proceeding'.[117]

However, it must be borne in mind that in a 'normal' AD investigation, the comparison between the export price and the normal value should be 'fair' in accordance with Article 2.4 of the ADA. To ensure fairness, Article 2.4 emphasized that apart from the allowances for costs listed in the second sentence of this provision, 'any other differences which are also demonstrated to affect price comparability' should be taken into account in the comparison between the export price and the normal value and finally reflected in the dumping margin calculation.

In investigations where an investigating authority determines that the Chinese government provides countervailable domestic subsidies to the exporting producers, as the US authorities did in the contested investigations, those countervailable subsidies reduce both domestic prices and export prices of the product under investigation. In other words, the export prices used by the US authorities in the dumping margin calculation are influenced by the domestic subsidies provided by the Chinese government.

The normal value, as calculated under the NME methodology, does not, however, reflect the subsidies provided by the Chinese government, as they are constructed based on non-China prices and costs. Even if the US argued that it cannot ensure that 'the NME constructed normal value is a "subsidy-free" price, and is under no obligation to do so under U.S. law (or the covered agreements) precisely because the NME methodology is neither intended nor designed to "counteract" subsidization', it is impossible to argue that the producers in the surrogate country received the same Chinese subsidies as the Chinese producers did. The focus of the argument is therefore not whether an NME constructed NV is 'subsidy-free', possibly to be interpreted as free from subsidies from the governments of surrogate countries, but whether the producers in the surrogate countries have been affected by the subsides provided by the Chinese government in the same way as the Chinese exporters.

Under this logic, the comparison between the Chinese subsidy-affected export price and the Chinese subsidy-free normal value can hardly be considered as 'fair' if no adjustment is made in the calculation of dumping margin. It is arguable that an investigating authority would violate Article 2.4 since it fails to make a 'fair comparison' and adjusts a major factor which are 'demonstrated to affect price comparability', if appropriate adjustments are not made to eliminate the effects of Chinese subsidies.

116. *Ibid.*, para. 186.
117. *Ibid.*

As mentioned above, the rationale behind the endorsement of the concurrent application of CVD and AD in cases where no export subsidies are involved is that if the effects of domestic subsidization cause an even drop in both domestic and export prices, the domestic subsidy will have no effect on the dumping margin, since dumping is the difference between the domestic price (NV) and the export price. In the investigations against Chinese products, however, one side of the dumping equation, namely the export prices, has been affected by the domestic subsidies provided by the Chinese government. Conversely, the other side of the dumping equation, namely the NVs constructed on the basis of the NME methodology, cannot by definition be affected by the Chinese subsidies exactly at the level that the Chinese export prices are affected.

To a large extent, the basic rationale behind this argument is the same as that China which argued in its submission, namely '[I]t is a question of whether it is permissible under the covered agreements to offset the same subsidies twice.'[118] However, instead of arguing that 'the normal value calculated under an NME methodology necessarily captures the entire effects of subsidization in every instance, as a result of which the imposition of any level of CVDs would constitute a "double remedy" ', the argument under Article 2.4 of the ADA focuses more on the explicit obligation of the investigating authority to compare the export price and the normal value fairly.

Nevertheless, the US can argue that subsidies are not a factor explicitly mentioned in Article 2.4 that can possibly affect price comparability, and thus they are not under any obligation to adjust them in the dumping margin calculation. Although the AB confirmed in *US – Zeroing (EC)* that 'the "fair comparison" language in the first sentence of Article 2.4 creates an independent obligation, and, secondly, that the scope of this obligation is not exhausted by the general subject matter expressly addressed by paragraph 4 (i.e., to say, the price comparability)',[119] there is no exact wording in the ADA that prohibits the US to refuse this kind of adjustment. On the contrary, the obligation imposed on the US authorities is very general: to 'act as an unbiased and objective investigating authority' when assessing the requested adjustments to ensure 'fair comparison'. A panel's interpretation of 'fair comparison' under Article 2.4 will determine whether an investigating authority needs to take the domestic subsidization of the Chinese government as a factor for adjustments or not.

However, even if the panel rules in favor of the US in the ongoing panel proceeding, it is unlikely that the US DOC can completely ignore the argument of "fair comparison" under Article 2.4.2 of the ADA. As the US Court of International Trade (ITC) stated in a recent judgement, '[I]f Commerce has a

118. 'China Answers to First Panel Questions', para. 217, as cited in *United States – (WT/DS379)*, the Second Written Submission of the United States, para. 177.

119. WTO, *United States – Laws, Regulations and Methodology for Calculating Dumping Margins ('Zeroing')*, Report of the Appellate Body, 18 Apr. 2006, WT/DS294/AB/R, paras 136–147.

way of fine-tuning adjustments so that it is more likely no double counting will occur, this may be acceptable, but Commerce must make such a decision'.[120]

4 CONCLUSION

This chapter discusses how WTO members make efforts to more effectively utilize the DSM in order to respond to the rise of legalization in the GATT/WTO system. The response of WTO members can be demonstrated by two aspects: first, to build up capacity to utilize the DSM by forming public-private networks, and second to pursue matters in the DSM that traditionally are considered as unlitigatable in the WTO.

China's efforts to engage private sectors and to litigate NME issues in the WTO illustrates that WTO members are making efforts to deprive benefits from the higher level of legalization in the WTO as a whole. In the meanwhile, the discussion of arguments in *US – AD and CVD on certain Chinese Products* demonstrates that the low level of legalization of covered agreements on a particular issue can present a huge challenge for WTO members when litigating that matter in the DSM. The uneven and imbalanced expansion of legalization hence can significantly affect the utilization of DSM by WTO members.

120. GPX International Tire Corp. Vo. United States, Consolidated Court No. 08-00285 (Slip Op. 09-103), 18 Sep. 2009, page 24.

Chapter 7

Conclusion

From the outset, this monograph centres upon three inter-related themes: the proliferation of legalization in the trade regime, the unevenness of the ongoing process and the complicated consequences of the process.

Separately, the rule-orientation trend in the trade regime, the uneven expansion of judicialization in the GATT/WTO and the effects of the multilateral system on domestic systems have attracted considerable scholarly attention. However, many assume that the rise of legalization is a single-faceted phenomenon and has a straightforward policy path. Based on this assumption, few have attempted to break down the legalization process into different dimensions and evaluate its complicated consequences.

This monograph takes a different approach. It assumes that the rise of legalization in the trade regime is a multifaceted phenomenon with a pragmatic policy path, which has both intended and unintended effects on domestic systems. Therefore, although this increasingly 'legalized' GATT/WTO system has often been used to advance the free trade agenda, the function of the 'legal' system does not always support the policy goal of trade liberalization. The analysis in this monograph, hence, not only confirms the positive effects of the rise of legalization in the trade regime, as has been widely observed, but also identifies in which dimension legalization has increased, explores why the ongoing process is imbalanced and what are the complicated consequences of the legalization process.

To precisely analyze the phenomenon of legalization in the GATT/WTO, as one of the most cited examples of a successfully 'legalized' international institution, a definition of legalization must be offered in the first place. Drawing upon the international relations theory, this monograph bases its theoretical foundation on this definition of legalization. Legalization is a particular form of institutionalization characterized along three dimensions: obligation, precision and delegation. In the context of the GATT/WTO system, obligation refers to norms set out in all

WTO agreements, Understandings and other binding documents. Precision measures not only the clarity of the wording of related WTO agreements, but also the extent to which these substantive WTO obligations require (or prohibit) specific action by WTO members. Delegation reflects the willingness of the WTO members to relinquish their sovereignty in terms of both the DSM and the other activities of WTO institutions.

Based on this three-pronged definition, this monograph evaluated the dynamic process of legalization in the GATT/WTO by further breaking down the system into three different parts: a decision-making mechanism, a surveillance mechanism and the DSM. By reviewing both the current status of legalization in each part and the historical developments, this monograph concludes that as a general pattern, all three parts of the GATT/WTO have been significantly legalized and there are certain degrees of correlation between the processes. However, the 'legalizing' process of each of these parts did not always take place at the same pace and the expansion of legalization in the system is uneven and unbalanced.

The dynamic process of legalization cannot therefore be understood as an isolated development happening in a particular part of the GATT/WTO. Instead, the rise of legalization in different parts of the GATT/WTO is interrelated. The entire 'legalized' system becomes unbalanced when the expansion of legalization is uneven in each part of the GATT/WTO. Therefore, the rise of legalization in the trade regime has taken, and will always take, a pragmatic path. The 'legalized' GATT/WTO has always operated under the constraints generated by the imbalance of the system.

The empirical study of international AD regimes provides an illustrative example of the significant contribution that legalization made to decades of successful trade liberalization as well as the apparent unbalance of the legalization process.

On the one hand, multiple rounds of trade negotiations generate tighter and more precise obligations in the AD regime. From GATT Article VI to the ADA, it is undeniable that international AD rules have improved significantly in terms of obligation, precision and delegation.

On the other hand, a closer analysis of the ADA indicates that the uneven expansion of legalization in the AD regime restricts further developments of legalization. Although fairly detailed, a fairly large number of obligations, in particular substantive obligation, in the ADA, are unspecific or contingent in nature. WTO members can therefore interpret them in the way they prefer since most substantive provisions in the ADA do not explicitly instruct an investigating authority to act (or not to act) in a particular manner in an AD investigation. This feature of the ADA also influences the level of precision, namely the reasonable interpretations of the ADA obligations cannot be narrowed down. Even if the Doha Round rules negotiations move ahead, it is still not feasible to change all of the general obligations of the ADA to specific obligations and make the ADA cover every single detail of an AD investigation. Nevertheless, given the fact that the delegation to the DSM is limited and there is no parallel delegation to political organs, the gaps and discontinuities of the ADA can hardly be filled under the current system. It is therefore difficult for the AD regime to move to a higher level of legalization without addressing the imbalance of the current system.

This monograph then explores the consequences of legalization at the domestic level, both from a formal, institutional perspective and an informal perspective. The discussion on the EU anti-dumping regime attempts to exemplify the mixed effects of multilateral legalization on formal legal institutions of a domestic regime: on the one hand, increased obligations, frequently joined by greater precision and stronger delegation, largely changed the landscape of domestic trade policy-making. On the other hand, WTO-plus features have been developed to counterbalance the impact of increased legalization at the international level on domestic systems. This is exactly the reason for which although the EU anti-dumping instruments essentially repeat the basic principles of international rules, a close analysis of the instruments and the administration of them suggests a compromise between different interests.

The discussion of China's AD-related activities demonstrates the mixed effects of legalization on the utilization of the DSM by WTO members. On the one hand, the development of legalization provides incentives for China to effectively utilize the DSM and changes the strategic behaviour of China: Instead of addressing trading partners in bilateral negotiations as it preferred in the past, China now actively selects matters to be litigated in the DSM. On the other hand, the fact that China's efforts can largely be undermined by the low degree of legalization of NME provisions, in another way, illustrates that the uneven expansion of legalization in the GATT/WTO can present considerable obstacles to WTO members when utilizing the DSM. This also reinforces the assumption underlying this monograph: The function of a 'legalized' system is significantly impaired by the unbalance of the system. Even if the DSM has a relatively high level of legalization, China cannot take full advantage of this due to the low level of legalization of the covered agreements and the Protocol. As demonstrated in the discussion of the 'double remedy' issue in Chapter VI, when the US took the 'textual' approach to the extreme, there was little that China could do under the unbalanced system.

In conclusion, the phenomenal rise of legalization is one of the most important institutional developments which has taken place over the past half century in the trade regime. While it is important to acknowledge its significance, it is even more important to fully understand the unevenness of the ongoing process and its complicated consequences. This monograph, by using three identifiable variables adopted from international relations, presents one angle to analyze this complicated institutional development and its consequences.

Bibliography

Aamantopoulos, K. & D. Notaris, 'The Future of the WTO & the Reform of the Anti-Dumping Agreement: A Legal Perspective'. *Fordham International Law Journal* 24 (2000): 30.

Abbott, F. 'NAFTA and the Legalization of World Politics: A Case Study'. *International Organization* 54 (2000): 519.

Abbott, K. et al. 'The Concept of Legalization'. *International Organization* 54 (2000); 401.

Abbott, K. 'The Many Faces of International Legalization'. *American Society of International Law Proceedings* 92 (1998): 57.

Abbott K. & D. Snidal, 'Hard and Soft Law in International Governance'. *International Organization* 54 (2000): 421.

Acharya, R. & M. Daly, 'Selected Issues Concerning the Multilateral Trading System'. (2004) WTO Discussion Paper No. 7, available at: <www.wto.int/english/res_e/booksp_e/discussion_papers7_e.pdf>, 5 January 2006, 20.

Adamantopoulos, K. & D. Notaris. 'The Future of the WTO and the Reform of the Anti-dumping Agreement: A Legal Perspective'. *Fordham International Law Journal* 24 (2000): 30.

Ahn, D. 'Korea on the GATT/WTO Dispute Settlement. System: Legal Battles for Economic Development'. *Journal of International Economic Law* 6 (2003): 598.

Ahn, D. 'WTO Dispute Settlements in East Asia'. National Bureau of Economic Research Working Paper 10178, (2003), available at: <www.nber.org/papers/w10178>, last visited 10 March 2006.

Alter, K. 'The European Union's Legal System and Domestic Policy: Spillover or Backlash?'. *International Organization* 54 (2000): 489.

Anderson, A. 'Peculiarities of Retaliation in WTO Dispute Settlement'. *World Trade Review* 1 (2002): 123.

Barnard, C. & J. Scott. (eds). *The Law of the Single European Market – Unpacking the Premises.* (Oxford: Hart Publishing, 2002).

Bartels, L. 'Applicable Law in WTO Dispute Settlement Proceedings'. *Journal of World Trade* 35 (2001): 499.

Bartels, L. 'The Separation of Powers in the WTO: How to Avoid Judicial Activism'. *International and Comparative Law Quarterly* 53 (2004): 861.

Belderbos, R. *Japanese Electronics Multinationals and Strategic Trade Policies.* Oxford: Oxford University Press, 1997.

Bierwagen, R. *GATT Article VI and the Protectionist Bias in Anti-dumping Laws* (Deventer and Boston: Kluwer Law and Taxation Publishers, 1990).

Bhala, R. 'New WTO Anti-dumping Precedents (Part One: The Dumping Margin Determination)'. *Singapore Journal of International and Comparative Law* 6 (2002): 335.

Bhala, R. 'New WTO Anti-dumping Precedents (Part Two: Causation, Injury, Determination, and Penalties)'. *Singapore Journal of International and Comparative Law* 6 (2002): 980.

Bhala, R. 'Rethinking Anti-dumping Law'. *George Washington Journal of International Law and Economics* 29 (1995): 1.

Bhala, R. & D. Gantz. 'WTO Case Review 2003'. *Arizona Journal of International and Comparative Law* 21 (2004): 317.

Bhuiyan, S. *National Law in WTO Law, Effectiveness and Good Governance in the World Trading System.* (Cambridge: Cambridge University Press, 2007).

Biernat, E. 'The Locus Standi of Private Applicants under Article 230 (4) EC and the Principle of Judicial Protection in the European Community'. Jean Monnet Working Paper 12/03, (2003), available at: <http://ideas.repec.org/p/erp/jeanmo/p0151.html>.

Bierwagen, R. *GATT Article VI and the Protectionist Bias in Anti-dumping Laws.* (Deventer: Kluwer Law and Taxation Publishers, 1990).

Blackmore, D. 'Eradicating the Long Standing Existence of a No-precedent Rule in International Trade Law – Looking Towards Stare Decisis in WTO Dispute Settlement'. *North Carolina Journal of International and Comparative Law* 29 (2004): 487.

BNA International Trade Reporter. 'WTO Members Discuss Services Conference; Doha Rules Chair Promises New Revised Text'. 20 March 2008, <http://pubs.bna.com/NWSSTND/IP/BNA/itr.nsf/SearchAllView/259E1C65883BD6B1852574110071B0E8?Open&highlight=ZEROING>, accessed 5 May 2008.

BNA International Trade Reporter. 'WTO Rules Chairman Under Fire for Zeroing Provisions in Draft Text'. 20 December 2007, available at: <http://pubs.bna.com/NWSSTND/IP/BNA/itr.nsf/SearchAllView/AE69821877658FC3852573B5007CED0A?Open&highlight=ZEROING>, 5 May 2008.

Bown, C. 'Trade Remedies and World Trade Organization Dispute Settlement: Why are So Few Challenged?' *The Journal of Legal Studies* 34, no. 2 (2005): 515.

Bown, C. & B. Hoekman, 'WTO Dispute Settlement and the Missing Developing Country Cases: Engaging the Private Sector'. *Journal of International Economic Law* 8 (2005): 861.

Bown, C., B. Hoekman & C. Ozden. 'The Pattern of US Antidumping: The Path from Initial Filing to WTO Dispute Settlement'. *World Trade Review* 2 (2003): 349.

Broek, N. 'Legal Persuasion, Political Realism, and Legitimacy: The European Court's Recent Treatment of the Effect of WTO Agreements in the EC Legal Order'. *Journal of International Economic Law* (2001): 411.

Bronckers, M. & R. Quick (eds). *New Directions in International Economic Law – Essays in Honour of John. H. Jackson.* (The Hague: Kluwer Law International, 2002).

Broude, T. 'An Anti-dumping "To Be or Not To Be" in Five Accuse New Agenda for Research and Reform'. *Journal of World Trade* 37 (2003): 305, 308–312.

Bulletin Quotidien Europe No. 9548, 'Peter Mandelson Gives Himself Extra-time before Submitting His New Revision Proposals'. 22 November 2007.

Burea, E. & J. Scott (eds). *The EU and the WTO – Legal and Constitutional Issues.* (Oxford: Hart Publishing, 2001).

Bureau of Foreign Trade and Economic Cooperation of Guangzhou Municipality. 'An Association Established in Guangzhou in Response to the EU's Footwear Anti-dumping Investigation'. news release, at <www.gzboftec.gov.cn/articles/2006-2/17214.htm>.

Busch, M. & E. Reinhardt, 'Bargaining in the Shadow of the Law: Early Settlement in GATT/WTO Disputes'. *Fordham Journal of International Law* 24 (2000): 158.

Carl, M. P. 'From Common Market to European Union: The New Europe's Place in the Trading World'. *Fordham Int Law Journal* 26 (2002): 36.

Carman, H. 'A Critical Analysis of the Standard of Review Applied by the Court of Appeals for the Federal Circuit in Antidumping and Countervailing Duty Cases'. *St. John's Journal of Legal Commentary* 17 (2003): 177.

Carmody, C. 'Remedies and Conformity under the WTO Agreement'. *Journal of International Economic Law* 5 (2002): 307.

Carmody, C. 'WTO Obligations as Collective'. *European Journal of International Law* 17 (2006): 419.

Cass, D. 'The "Constitutionalization" of International Trade Law: Judicial Norm-Generation as the Engine of Constitutional Development in International Trade'. *European Journal of International Law* 39 (2001): 31.

Cass, D. *The Constitutionalization of the World Trade Organization: Legitimacy, Democracy, and Community in the International Trading System* (Oxford: Oxford University Press, 2005).

Cass, D., B. Williams & G. Barker. *China and the World Trading System – Entering the New Millennium.* (Cambridge: Cambridge University Press, 2003).

Cetlan, M. 'WTO Dispute Settlement: Issues in Anti-dumping and Countervailing Duty Law'. *Practising Law Institute/Corporate Law and Practice Course Handbook Series* 1075 (1998): 799.

Chathain, C. 'The European Community and the Member States in the Dispute Settlement Understanding of the WTO: United or Divided?'. *European Law Journal* 5 (1999): 461.

Cini, M. (ed.). *European Union Politics.* Oxford: Oxford University Press, 2003.

Clark, W., E. Duchesne & W. Reed. 'Strategic Interaction and Trade Policymaking: Formal Analysis and Simulation'. *The World Economy* 29 (2006): 507.

Competition Law360. 'Disgruntled with US Duties, China Goes to WTO'. 14 September 2007, available at: <http://competition.law360.com/>. See also, MOFCOM, 'China Seeks WTO Resolution over Paper Disputes with US'. 17 September 2007, available at: <http://melbourne2.mofcom.gov.cn/aarticle/chinanews/200709/20070905127303.html>.

Cornelis, J. 'China's Quest for Market Economy Status and its Impact on the Use of Trade Remedies by the European Communities and the United States'. *Global Trade and Customs Journal* 2 (2007): 105.

Cottier, T. & M. Oesch. *International Trade Regulation: Law and Policy in the WTO, the European Union and Switzerland – Case, Materials and Comments.* London: Cameron May, 2005.

Cunningham, R. 'Commentary on the First Five Years of the WTO Antidumping Agreement and Agreement on Subsidies and Countervailing Measures'. *Law and Policy in Intl Business* 31 (2000): 897.

Czako, J., J. Human & J. Miranda. *A Handbook on Anti-dumping Investigation.* Cambridge: Cambridge University Press, 2003.

Damme, I. 'Seventh Annual WTO Conference: An Overview'. *Journal of International Economic Law* 11 (2008): 155.

Davey, W. 'Has the WTO Dispute Settlement System Exceeded its Authority? – A Consideration of Deference Shown by the System to Member Government Decisions and Its Use of Issue-avoidance Techniques'. *Journal of International Economic Law* 4 (2001), 79.

Detlof, H. & H. Fridh. 'The EU Treatment of Non-Market Economy Countries in Anti-dumping Proceedings'. *Global Trade and Customs Journal* 2 (2007): 265.

Didier, P. 'The WTO Anti-dumping Code and EC Practice – Issues for Review in Trade Negotiations'. *Journal of World Trade* 35 (2001): 33.

Diehl, P., C. Ku & D. Zamora. 'The Dynamics of International Law: The Interaction of Normative and Operating Systems'. *International Organization* 57 (2003): 43.

DiSalvo, N. 'Let's Dump the 1916 Antidumping Act: Why the 1944 GATT Provides Better Price Protecion for US Industries'.*Vanderbilt Journal of Transnational Law* 37 (2004): 791.

Drope, J. & W. Hansen. 'Anti-dumping's Happy Birthday?'. *The World Economy* 29 (2006): 459.

Dunoff, J. & J. Trachtman. 'Economic Analysis of International Law'. *The Yale Journal of International Law* 24 (1999): 1.

Dunoff, J. 'Rethinking International Trade'. *University of Pennsylvania Journal of International Economic Law* 19 (1998): 347.

Durling, J. 'Deference, But Only When Due: WTO Review of Anti-dumping Measures'. *Journal of International Economic Law* 6 (2003): 125.

Eeckhot, P. *External Relations of the European Union – Legal and Constitutional Foundations.* (Oxford: Oxford University Press, 2004).

Ehlermann, C. 'Reflections on the Appellate Body of the WTO'. *Journal of International Economic Law* 6 (2003): 695.

Ehlermann, C. 'Six Years on the Bench of the "World Trade Court" – Some personal Experiences as Member of the Appellate Body of the World Trade Organization'. *Journal of World Trade* 36 (2002): 605.

Ehlermann, C. 'Tensions Between the Dispute Settlement Process and the Diplomatic and Treaty-making Activities of the WTO'. *World Trade Review* 1 (2002): 301.

Ehlermann, C. & L. Ehring. 'Decision-making in the– Is the Consensus Practice of the World Trade Organization Adequate for Making, Revising and Implementing Rules on International Trade?'. *Journal of International Economic Law* 8 (2005): 51.

Ehlermann, C. & L. Ehring. 'The Authoritative Interpretation under Article IX:2 of the Agreement Establishing the World Trade Organization: Current Law, Practice and Possible Improvements'. *Journal of International Economic Law* 8 (2005): 803.

Ehlermann, C. & N. Lockhart. 'Standard of Review in WTO Law'. *Journal of International Economic Law* 7 (2004): 491.

Emiliou, N. & D. O'Keeffe (eds). *The European Union and World Trade Law – After the GATT Uruguay Round.* Chichester: John Wiley & Sons, 1996.

Esty, D. 'Good Governance at the World Trade Organization: Building a Foundation of Administrative Law'. *Journal of International Economic Law* 10 (2007): 509.

European Commission, Information Note on the Community's Anti-Dumping Instrument and Practice (January 1998), Appendices 7A–7C.

European Commission, Communication from the European Commission. *Global Europe: Europe's trade defence instruments in a changing global economy – A Green Paper for public consultation*, COM (2006) 763 final, Brussels 6 Dec. 2006.

Evans, G. *Lawmaking Under the Trade Constitution – A Study in Legislating by the World Trade Organization*. (The Hague: Kluwer Law International, 2000).

Finnemore, M. & S. Toope. 'Alternatives to "Legalization": Richer Views of Law and Politics'. *International Organization* 55 (2001): 743.

Gao, H. 'Aggressive Legalism: The East Asian Experience and Lesson for China' In *China's Participation in the WTO*, edited by H. Gao & D. Lewis. London: Cameron May, 2006.

Garret, G. 'Global Market and National Politics: Collision Course or Virtuous Circle?'. *International Organization* 52 (1998): 787.

Gathii, J.T. 'Insulating Domestic Policy Through International Legal Minimalism: A Re-characterization of the Foreign Affairs Trade Doctrine'. *University of Pennsylvania Journal of International Economic Law* 25 (2004): 105.

GATT, *Anti-dumping and Countervailing Duties, Report of Group of Experts*, GATT Sales No. GATT/1961–2.

GATT, *Agreement on Implementation of Article VI of the General Agreement on Tariffs and Trade*, (1980) reprinted in GATT, BISD 26th Supp., 171.

GATT, *Contracting Parties – Ninth Session – Report of Review Working Party III on Barriers to Trade Other than Restrictions or Tariffs*, L/334, 1 March 1955, Annex 1, paragraph 10.

GATT, *European Community-Anti-dumping Duties on Audio Tapes in Cassettes Originating in Japan*, Report of the Panel (28 Apr. 1995) ADP/136 (unadopted).

GATT, *European Economic Community – Regulation on Imports of Parts and Components*, Report of the Panel, adopted 16 May 1990, BISD 37S/132, 152.

GATT, *Understanding Regarding Notification, Consultation, Dispute Settlement and Surveillance*, BISD 26th Supp. 210 (1980).

George, S. & I. Bache. *Politics in the European Union.* (Oxford: Oxford University Press, 2001).

Goh, G. & A. Ziegler. 'Retrospective Remedies in the WTO after Automotive Leather'. *Journal of International Economic Law* 6 (2003): 1.

Goldstein, J. & L. Martin. 'Legalization, Trade Liberalization, and Domestic Politics: A Cautionary Note'. *International Organization* 54 (2000): 603.

Goldstein, J., M. Kahler, R. Keohane & A. Slaughter. 'Introduction: Legalization and World Politics'. *International Organization* 54 (2000): 385.

Gong, B., 'Shanghai's WTO Affairs Consultation Centre: Working Together to Take Advantage of WTO Membership'. in *WTO Managing the Challenges of WTO Participation: Case Studies* – Case study 2: An Early-warning System for Anti-dumping Disputes in China, at <www.wto.org/english/res_e/booxksp_e/casestudies_e/case11_e.htm>.

Graafsma, F. & J. Comelis. 'The EC's Green Paper on Trade Defence Instruments: Guillotine on Anti-dumping or Smokescreen for More Basic Predicaments?'. *Global Trade and Customs Journal* 2 (2007): 255.

Grane, P. 'Remedies under WTO Law'. *Journal of International Economic Law* 4 (2001): 756.

Greenwald, J. 'WTO Dispute Settlement: An Exercise in Trade Law Legalization?'. *Journal of International Economic Law* 6 (2003): 113.

Greenwald, J. & G. Horlick. 'Dumping Margin Calculation Problems in the United States'. *Global Trade and Custom Journal* 2 (2007): 67.

Griller, S. 'Judicial Enforceability of WTO Law in the European Union – Annotation to Case C-149/96'. *Portugal v. Council*'. *Journal of International Economic Law 2* (2000): 441.

Guzman, A. & B. Simmons. 'To Settle or Empanel? An Empirical Analysis of Litigation and Settlement at the World Trade Organization'. *Journal of Legal Study* 31 (2002).

Hamilton, L. 'US Antidumping Decisions and the WTO Standard of Review: Deference or Disregard?'. *Chicago Journal of International Law* 4 (2003): 265.

Harlow, C. 'Codification of EC Administrative Procedures? Fitting the Foot to the Shoe or the Shoe to the Foot' Jean Monnet Chair Papers 27, The Robert Schuman Centre at the European University Institute, 1995.

Harpaz, G. '"Dumping" the Anti-dumping Instruments in the Trade Relations Between the European Union and the State of Israel? – The European Union's Perspective'. *Journal of World Trade* 39 (2005): 445.

Hawkins, A. 'Anti-dumping Beyond the GATT 1994: Supporting International Enactment of Legislation Providing Supplemental Remedies'. *Indiana International & Comparitive Law Review* 10 (1999): 149.

Hehl, H. *Principles of Administrative Procedure in EC Law.* (Oxford: Hart Publishing, 1999).

Herrmann, C. 'Common Commercial Policy After Nice: Sisyphus Would Have Done a Better Job'. *Common Market Law Review* (2002): 7.

Hilf, M. & E. Petersmann (eds). *National Constitutions and International Economic Law.* Deventer: Kluwer Law and Taxation Publishers, 1993.

Hix, S. *The Political System of the European Union* (Basingstoke: Macmillan, 1999).

Hoekman, B. & M. Kostechi. *The Political Economy of the World Trading System – The WTO and Beyond.* 2nd edn. Oxford: Oxford University Press, 2001.

Hoogmartens, J. *EC Trade Law Following China's Accession to the WTO.* (The Hague: Kluwer Law International, 2004).

Horlick, G. & E. Vermulst. 'The 10 Major Problems With the Anti-dumping Instruments: An Attempt at Synthesis'. *Journal of World Trade* 39 (2005): 67.

Horlick, G. 'The 10 Major Problems with the Anti-dumping Instrument in the United States'. *Journal of World Trade* 39 (2005): 169.

Howse, R. 'From Politics to Technocracy – And Back Again: The Fate of the Multilateral Trading Regime'. *The American Journal of International Law* 96 (2002): 94.

Hudec, R. *Essays on the Nature of International Trade Law.* (London: Cameron May, 1999).

Hudec, R. 'New WTO Dispute Settlement Procedure: An Overview of the First Three Years'. *Minnesota Journal of Global Trade* 8 (1999): 1.

Hutton, S. & M. Trebilcock, 'An Empirical Study of the Application of Canadian Anti-dumping Laws: A Search for Normative Rationales'. *Journal of World Trade* 24 (1999): 123, 135.

Ibanez, A. *The Administrative Supervision and Enforcement of EC Law: Powers, Procedures and Limits.* Oxford: Hart Publishing, 1999.

Iwasava, Y. 'WTO Dispute Settlement as Judicial Supervision'. *Journal of International Economic Law* 5 (2002): 287.

Jackson, J. 'The Varied Policies of International Judicial Bodies – Reflection on Theory and Practice'. *Michigan Journal of International Law.* 25 (2004): 869–871.

Jackson, J. *Sovereignty, the WTO and Changing Fundamentals of International Law.* Cambridge: Cambridge University Press, 2006.

Jackson, J. *World Trade and the Law of GATT.* New York: Bobbs-Merrill, 1999.

Jackson, J. *The World Trading System – Law and Policy of International Economic Relations.* 2nd edn. Massachusetts: The MIT Press, 1997.

Jackson, J., E. Vermulst & A. Arbor (eds). *Anti-dumping Law and Practice: A Comparative Study*. Michigan: The University of Michigan Press, 1989.

Jackson, J., W. Davey & A. Sykes. *Legal Problems of International Economic Relations – Cases, Materials and Texts*. 4th edn. St. Paul: West Group, 2002.

Kahler, M. 'Conclusion: The Causes and Consequences of Legalization'. *International Organization* 54 (2000): 661.

Kahler, M. 'Legalization as Strategy: The Asia-Pacific Case'. *International Organization* 54 (2000): 549.

Kearns, J. & S. Chornovitz, 'Adjudicating Compliance in the WTO: A Review of DSU Art 21.5'. *Journal of International Economic Law* 5 (2002): 331.

Keesing, D. *Improving Trade Policy Reviews in the World Trade Organization.* Washington DC: Institute for International Economic, 1998.

Kelly, B. 'The Law and Economics of Simultaneous Countervailing Duty and Anti-dumping Duty Proceedings'. *Global Trade and Customs Journal* 3 (2008): 41.

Kelsey, J. (ed.). *International Economic Regulation.* England: Dartmouth/Ashgate, 2002.

Kempton, J. & C. Stevenson. 'Agreement on the Implement of Article VI of the GATT 1994: Practical Problems and Possible Solutions'. *International Trade Law and Regulations* 6 (2000): 6.

Kempton, J., P. Holmes & C. Stevenson. 'Globalization of Anti-dumping and the EU' (1999) SEI Working Paper No. 32, Centre on European Political Economy Working Paper No. 6, Sussex European Institute, available at: <www.sussex.ac.uk/sei/documents/wp32.pdf>, last visited 25 February 2006).

Kennedy, D. & J. Southwick. (eds). *The Political Economy of International Trade Law – Essays in Honour of Robert E. Hudec.* Cambridge: Cambridge University Press, 2002.

Keohane, R., A. Moravcsik & A. Slaughter, 'Legalized Dispute Resolution: Interstate and Transnational'. *International Organization* 54 (2000): 457.

Kerr, W. & L. Loppacher. 'Anti-dumping in the Doha Negotiations – Fairy Tales at the WTO'. *Journal of World Trade* 38 (2004): 211–215.

Kim, J. 'Fair Price Comparison in the WTO Anti-dumping Agreement – Recent WTO Panel Decisions against the "Zeroing" Method'. *Journal of World Trade* 36, no. 1 (2002): 39.

King, J. 'In Need of Enlightenment: The International Trade Commission's Misguided Analysis in Sunset Review'. *William and Mary Law Rev* 43 (2002): 2151.

Komuro, N. 'EC Anti-dumping Measures vis-à-vis Japan'. Paper presented for the Third ECSA-WORLD Conference, Brussels, on 12/13 September 1996, available at: <www.ecsanet.org/conferences/ecsaworld3/komuro.htm>, last visited 25 February 2006.

Kong, Q. *China and the WTO – A Legal Perspective.* New Jersey: World Scientific, 2002.

Krajewski, M. 'External Trade Law and the Constitution Treaty: Towards a Federal and more Democratic Common Commercial Policy'. *Common Market Law Review* 30 (2005): 91.

Krenzler, H. & C. Pitschas. 'Progress or Stagnation?: The Common Commercial Policy After Nice'. *European Foreign Affairs Review* 6 (2001): 291.

Krikorian, J. 'Planes, Trains and Automobiles: the Impact of the WTO "Court" on Canada in Its First Ten Years'. *Journal of International Economic Law* (2005): 921.

Kritzer, H. (ed.). *Legal Systems of the World – A Political, Social, and Culture Encyclopaedia.* Santa Barbara: ABC-CLIO, 2002, 353.

Kuijper, P. & M. Bronckers. 'WTO Law in the European Court of Justice'. *Common Market Law Review* 42 (2005): 1313.

Kumaran, V. 'The 10 Major Problems with the Anti-dumping Instrument in India'. *Journal of World Trade* 39 (2005): 115.

Lacarte-Muró, J. & P. Gappah. 'Developing Countries and the WTO Legal and Dispute Settlement System: A View from the Bench'. *Journal of International Economic Law* 5 (2000): 395.

Lamy, P. 'The Place and Role of the WTO (WTO Law) in the International Legal Order' (Address before the European Society of International Law, 19 May 2006, Sorbonne, Paris) <www.wto.org/english/news_e/sppl_e/sppl26_e.htm>, accessed on 14 June 2006.

Lang, A. 'Reconstructing Embedded Liberalism: John Gerard Ruggie and Constructivist Approaches to the Study of the International Trade Regime'. *Journal of International Economic Law* 9 (2006): 81.

Layton, D. & J. Miranda. 'Advocacy Before World Trade Organization Dispute Settlement Panels in Trade Remedy Cases'. *Journal of World Trade* 37 (2003): 69.

Leal-Arcas, R. 'Exclusive or Shared Competence in the Common Commercial Policy: From Amsterdam to Nice'. *Legal Issue of Economic Integration* (2003): 3.

Leclerc, J. 'Reforming Anti-dumping Law: Balancing the Interests of Consumers and Domestic Industries'. *McGill Law Journal* 44 (1999): 111.

Lee, S. & S. Jun. 'On the Investigation Effects of United States Anti-dumping Petitions'. *Journal of World Trade* 38 (2004): 425.

Lindsey, B. 'The US Antidumping Law – Rhetoric versus Reality'. *Journal of World Trade* 34 (2000): 1.

Liu, X. & H. Vandenbussche. 'European Union Anti-dumping Cases Against China – An Overview and Future Prospects With Respect to China's World Trade Organization Membership'. *Journal of World Trade* 36 (2002): 1125–1132.

Lowenfeld, A. *International Economic Law.* Oxford: Oxford University Press, 2002.

Luo, Y. 'Engaging the Private Sector: EU–China trade Disputes Under the Shadow of WTO Law?'. *European Law Journal* 13, no.6 (November 2007): 800.

Lutz, E. & K. Sikkink, 'International Human Rights Law and Practice in Latin America'. *International Organization* 54 (2000): 633.

Maloney, J. & G. Horlick, 'Market Economy Status for Ukraine in Anti-dumping Cases in the United States and European Union'. *Global Trade and Customs Journal* 1 (2006): 49.

Matsushita M., T. Schoenbaum & P. Mavroidis, *The World Trade Organization: Law, Practice and Policy*. (Oxford: Oxford University Press, 2003).

Mathijsen, P. *A Guide to European Union Law*. 8th edn. London: Sweet & Maxwell, 2004.

Matsushita, M. & D. Ahn (eds). *WTO and East Asia: New Perspectives*. London: Cameron May, 2004.

Matsushita, M. 'A Japanese View of United States Trade Laws'. *Northwest Journal of International Law and Business* 29 (1987): 29.

McNelis, N. 'What Obligations Are Created by World Trade Organization Dispute Settlement Reports?'. *Journal of World Trade* 37 (2003): 647.

Mendez, M. 'The Impact of WTO Rulings in the Community Legal Order'. *European Law Review* 29 (2004): 517.

Messerlin, P. 'China in the WTO: Anti-dumping and Safeguards'. In *China in the WTO: Accession, Policy Reform, and Poverty Reduction Strategies*, edited by D. Bhattasali, S. Li & W. Martin (eds). Oxford: World Bank and Oxford University Press, 2003.

Meunier, S & K. Nicolaidis. 'Who Speaks for Europe? The Delegation of Trade Authority in the EU'. *Journal of Common Market Studies* 37, no. 3 (1999): 477.

Ministry of Commerce of People's Republic of China (MOFCOM). 'Foreign Market Access Report 2009'. 12 Apr. 2008, available at: <http://henan.mofcom.gov.cn/accessory/200804/1176368802629.pdf>.

Ministry of Commerce of People's Republic of China (MOFCOM). 'Decree No. 12, 2006 of the Ministry of Commerce of the People's Republic of China, Promulgating the Regulations on Responding to Anti-dumping Cases of Export Products'. 29 August 2006, at <http://english.mofcom.gov.cn/aarticle/policyrelease/gazettee/200608/20060803009941.html>.

Mitchell, A. 'The Legal Basis for Using Legal Principles in WTO Disputes'. *Journal of International Economic Law* (2007): 795.

Molyneux, C. *Domestic Structures and International Trade – The Unfair Trade Instruments of the US and the EU*. Oxford: Hart Publishing, 2001.

Müller, W., N. Khan & H. Neumann. *EC Anti-dumping Law – A Commentary on Regulation 384/96*. Chichester: John Wiley & Sons, 1998.

Neill, M. 'On the Boundary Clash between EC Commercial Law and WTO Law'. *Legal Issue of Economic Integration* 32 (2005): 65.

Nordström, H. 'The World Trade Organization Secretariat in a Changing World'. *Journal of World Trade* 39 (2005): 819.

Nordström, H. & G. Shaffer. 'Access to Justice in the World Trade Organization: The Case for a Small Claims Procedure – A Preliminary Analysis' ICTSD Issue paper No. 2, June 2007.

O'Conner, B. 'Remedies in the WTO Dispute Settlement System – The Bananas and Hormones Cases'. *Journal of World Trade* 38 (2004): 245–249.

O'Keeffe, D & A. Bavasso (eds). *Judicial Review in European Union Law.* (The Hague: Kluwer Law International, 2000).

Oesch, M. *Standards of Review in the WTO Dispute Resolution.* (Oxford: Oxford University Press, 2003).

Ortino, F & E. Pertersmann. *The WTO Dispute Settlement System 1995–2003.* (The Hague: Kluwer Law International, 2004).

Palmeter, D. 'The WTO as a Legal System'. *Fordham Journal of International Law* 24 (2000): 444.

Palmeter, D & P. Mavroidis. *Dispute Settlement in the WTO: Practice and Procedure.* 2nd edn. Cambridge: Cambridge University Press, 2004.

Pekkanen, S. 'Aggressive Legalism: The Rules of the WTO and Japan's Emerging Trade Strategy'. *The World Economy* 24 (2001): 707.

Perez, O. 'Ecological Sensitivity and Global Legal Pluralism: Rethinking the Trade and Environment Debate'. PhD Thesis, London School of Economics and Political Science (2001).

Pescatore, P. 'Opinion 1/94 on "Conclusion" of the WTO Agreement: Is There an Escape from a Programmed Disaster?'. *Common Market Law Review* 36 (1999): 387.

Petersmann, E. 'Multilevel Judicial Governance of International Trade Requires a Common Conception of Rule of Law and Justice'. *Journal of International Economic Law* 10 (2007): 529.

Petersmann, E. *The GATT/WTO Dispute Settlement System – International Law, International Organization and Dispute Settlement.* The Hague: Kluwer Law International, 1997.

Philip, R., M. Iain & G. Carol (eds). *The WTO and International Trade Regulation.* London: Cameron May, 1998.

Philip, R., M. Iain & M. Ahmad (eds). *Liberalization and Protectionism in the World Trading System.* London: Cameron May, 1999.

Picciotto, S. 'The WTO as a Node of Global Governance: Economic Regulations and Human Rights Discourses'. *Law, Social Justice & Global Development Journal (LGD)* 1 (2007), <http://go.warwick.ac.uk/lgd/2007_1/picciotto>.

Pierre, D. *WTO Trade Instruments in EU Law.* London: Cameron May, 1999.

Polouektov, A. 'Non-market Economy Issues in the WTO Anti-dumping Law and Accession Negotiations Revival of a Two-tier Membership'. *Journal of World Trade* 36 (2002): 1.

Posenthal, P & R.Vermylen. 'The WTO Antidumping and Subsidies Agreements: Did the United States Achieve its Objectives During the Uruguay Round?'. *Law and Policy in International Business* 31 (2000): 871.

Price, V. 'New Institutional Developments in GATT'. *Minnesota Journal of Global Trade* 1 (1992): 87.

Princen, S. 'EC Complaince with WTO Law – The Interplay of Law and Politics'. *European Journal of International Law* 3 (2004): 555.

Prusa, T. 'Anti-dumping: A Growing Problem in International Trade'. *The World Economy* 28 (2005): 683.
Prusa, T. 'East Asia's Anti-dumping Problem'. *The World Economy* 29 (2006): 743.
Ragosta, J. 'Unmasking the WTO – Access to the DSB System: Can the WTO DSB Live Up to the Moniker "World Trade Court"?'. *Law and Policy of International Business* 31 (2000), 739.
Ragosta, J., N. Joneja & M. Zeldovich. 'WTO Dispute Settlement: The System Is Flawed and Must be Fixed'. *International Lawyer* 37 (2003): 697.
Raisch, M. 'Book Survey 2007'. *Journal of International Economic Law* 11 (2008): 217.
Roessler, F. *The Legal Structure, Function and Limits of the World Trade Order.* London: Cameron May, 2000.
Sarooshi, D. 'Sovereignty, Economic Autonomy, the United States, and the International Trading System: Representations of a Relationship'. *European Journal of International Law* 15 (2004): 651.
Schneider, A. 'Getting Along: The Evolution of Dispute Resolution Regimes in International Trade Organizations'. *Michigan Journal of International Law* 20 (1999): 697.
Schutzman, M. 'Antidumping and the Continued Dumping and Subsidy Offset Act of 2000: A Renewed Debate'. *Cardozo Journal of International and Comparative Law* 11 (2004): 1069.
Schwartz, W & A. Sykes. 'The Economic Structure of Renegotiation and Dispute Resolution in the World Trade Organization'. *Journal of Legal Study* 31 (2002): S179.
Seastrum, E. 'Chevron Deference and the Charming Betsy: is there a Place for the Schooner in the Standard of Review of Commerce Antidumping and Countervailing Duty Determinations?'. *Federal Circuit Bar J* 13 (2003): 229.
Shaffer, G. 'The Challenges of WTO Law: Strategies for Developing Country Adaptation'. *World Trade Review* (2006): 177.
Shaffer, G. 'What's New in EU Trade Dispute Settlement? Judicialisation, Public-private Networks and the WTO Legal Order'. *Journal of European Public Policy* 13 (2006): 832.
Shell, R. 'Trade Legalism and International Relations Theory: An Analysis of the World Trade Organization'. *Duke Law Journal* 44 (1995): 829.
Simmons, B. 'The Legalization of International Monetary Affairs'. *International Organization* 54 (2000): 573.
Sinnaeve, A. 'The "Community Interest Test" in Anti-dumping Investigations: Time for Reform?'. *Global Trade and Customs Journal* 2 (2007): 157.
Sliberston, A. 'Anti-dumping Rules – Time for Change?'. *Journal of World Trade* 37 (2003): 1063.
Snyder, F. 'Governing Economic Globalisation: Global Legal Pluralism and European Law'. *European Law Journal* 4 (1999): 334.
Snyder, F. 'The Gatekeepers: The European Courts and WTO Law'. *Common Market Law Review* 40 (2003): 313.

Snyder, F. 'The Origins of the "Nonmarket Economy": Ideas, Pluralism and Power in EC Anti-dumping Law about China'. *European Law Journal* 7 (2001): 369.

Stanbrook, C. & P. Bentley. *Dumping and Subsides: The Law and Procedures Governing the Imposition of Anti-dumping and Countervailing Duties in the European Community*, 3rd edn. The Hague: Kluwer Law International, 1996.

Steele, K (ed.). *Anti-dumping Under the WTO: A Comparative Review*. The Hague: Kluwer Law International and International Bar Association, 1996.

Steger, D. 'Appellate Body Jurisprudence Relating to Trade Remedies'. *Journal of World Trade* 35 (2001): 799.

Steinberg, R. 'In the Shadow of Law or Power? Consensus-Based Bargaining and Outcomes in the GATT/WTO'. *International Organization* 56 (2002): 339.

Steinberg, R. 'Judicial Lawmaking at the WTO: Discursive, Constitutional, and Political Constraints'. *American Journal of International Law* 98 (2004): 247.

Stewart, T. (ed.). *The GATT Uruguay Round: A Negotiation History 1986–1992, Volume II: Commentary*. Deventer and Boston: Kluwer Law and Taxation Publisher, 1992.

Sutherland, P., et al. 'The Future of the WTO – Addressing Institutional Challenges in the New Millennium'. Report by the Consultative Board to the former Director-General Supachai Panitchpakdi, 2005. <www.wto.org/english/thewto_e/10anniv_e/future_wto_e.htm>, 31 July 2006, 10.

Swaine, E. 'The Constitutionality of International Delegations'. *Columbia Law Review* 104 (2004): 1492.

Sykes, A. 'Protectionism as a "Safeguard": A Positive Analysis of the GATT "Escape Clause" with Normative Speculations'. *University of Chicago Law Review* 58 (1991): 255.

Tarullo, D. 'The Hidden Costs of International Dispute Settlement: WTO Review of Domestic Anti-dumping Decisions'. *Law and Policy of International Business* 34 (2002): 109.

Tarullo, D. 'Paved With Good Intentions: The Dynamic Effects of WTO Review of Anti-dumping Action'. *World Trade Review* 2 (2003): 373.

Tracey, K. 'Non-market Economy Methodology Under US Anti-dumping Laws: A Protectionist Shield from Chinese Competition'. *Current: International Trade Law Journal* 15 (2006): 81.

Trachtman, J. 'Regulatory Jurisdiction and the WTO'. *Journal of International Economic Law* 10 (2007): 631.

Trachtman, J. 'The World Trading System, the International Legal System and Multilevel Choice'. *European Law Journal* 12 (2006): 469.

Tridimas, T & P. Nebbia (eds). *European Union law for the Twenty-first Century – Rethinking the New Legal Order*. vol. 1. Oxford and Portland Oregon: Hart Publishing, 2004.

United States International Trade Commission (ITC). 'Coated Free Sheet Paper from China, Indonesia, and Korea Does Not Injure US Industry, says ITC'. <www.usitc.gov/ext_relations/news_release/2007/er1120ee1.htm>.

United States – Definitive Anti-dumping and Countervailing Duties on Certain Products from China (WT/DS379), the First Written Submission of the United States, 27 May 2009, available at: <www.ustr.gov/trade-topics/enforcement/dispute-settlement-proceedings/wto-dosîte-settlement/definitive-anti-dump-1>, paras 21–22.

United States Department of Commerce, *Import Administration Antidumping Manual*, 1997 edition, available at: <http://ia.ita.doc.gov/admanual/index.html>.

United States General Accounting Office (GAO). 'World Trade Organization Standard of Review and Impact of Trade Remedy Rules – Report to the Ranking Minority Member, Committee on Finance, US Senate' GAO-03-824, July 2003 <www.gao.gov/cgi-bin/getrpt?GAT-03-824>, last visited 20 October 2005.

US Department of State, *The Language of International Trade*, available at: <http://usinfo.state.gov/products/pubs/trade/glossjr.htm#nonmarkeco>, last accessed 15 July 2008.

'U.S. Import Penalties New Problem for WTO Pact'. *Reuters*, 12 Dec. 2007, available at: <http://in.reuters.com/article/businessNews/idINIndia-30957720071212?pageNumber=1&virtualBrandChannel=0>, accessed 5 May 2008.

Van Bael, I. & J. Bellis. *Anti-dumping and Other Trade Protection Laws of the EC*. 4th edn. The Hague: Kluwer Law International, 2004.

Van den Bossche, P. 'From Afterthought to Centrepiece: The WTO Appellate Body and its Rise to Prominence in the World Trading System' Maastricht Faculty of Law Working Paper 2005/1, 5.

Vandenbussche, H. & M. Zanardi. 'What Explains the Proliferation of Antidumping Laws?'. *Economic Policy* 23 (2008): 93.

Vermulst, E. 'The 10 Major Problems with the Anti-dumping Instrument in the European Community'. *Journal of World Trade* 39 (2005): 105–108.

Vermulst E. & F. Graafsma, 'EC Dumping and Injury Margin Calculation Methods: The Major Problem'. *Global Trade and Custom Journal* 2 (2007): 27–30.

Vermulst E. & F. Graafsma. 'Recent EC Anti-dumping Practice towards China and Vietnam: The Great Leap Backward?'. *International Trade Law Review* 5 (2006): 124–128.

Vermulst, E. & F. Graafsma. 'WTO Dispute Settlement with Respect to Trade Contingency Measures'. *Journal of World Trade* 35(2001): 209.

Vermulst, E. & P. Waer. *EC Anti-dumping Law and Practice.* London: Sweet & Maxwell, 1996.

Viner, J. *Dumping: A Problem in International Law.* Chicago: University of Chicago Press, 1923.

Vito, A. & A. Lima-Campos. 'Abuse and Discretion – The Impact of Anti-dumping and Countervailing Duty Proceedings on Brazilian Exports to the US'. *Journal of World Trade* 38 (2004): 37.

Vyboldina, E. 'The Green Paper on Trade Defence Instruments: Anti-dumping'. *Global Trade and Customs Journal* 2 (2007): 411.

Waer, P. & E. Vermulst. 'The GATT Panel Report on the EC Anti-dumping Proceeding Concerning Audio Tapes in Cassettes – Back to Basics in the Concept of Dumping'. *Journal of World Trade* 29 (1995): 31.

Wallace, H. & W. Wallace (eds). *Policy-making in the European Union.* Oxford: Oxford University Press, 2002.

Walsh, T. 'Dispute Settlement at the World Trade Organization: Do Municipal Laws Promoting Private Party Identification of Trade Disputes Affect State Participation?'. *Journal of World Trade* 40 (2006): 889.

Ward, A. *Judicial Review and the Rights of Private Parties in EC Law.* Oxford: Oxford University Press, 2000.

Weiler, J (ed.). *The EU, The WTO and the NAFTA – Towards a Common Law of International Trade.* Oxford: Oxford University Press, 2000.

Weiss, F. 'WTO Decision-making: Is It Reformable?'. In *The Political Economy of International Trade Law*, edited by D. Kennedy & J. Southwick – Essays in Honour of Robert E. Hudec. Cambridge: Cambridge University Press, 2002.

Wenig, H. 'The European Community's Anti-dumping System: Salient Features'. *Journal of World Trade* 39 (2005): 787–794.

The White House Office of Public Liaison, 'Summary of US-China Bilateral WTO Agreement'. 17 November 1999, available at: <www.uschina.org/public/991115a.html>, last accessed 15 July 2008.

Wilson, S. 'Can the WTO Dispute Settlement Body be a Judicial Tribunal Rather than a Diplomatic Club?'. *Law and Policy of International Business* 31 (2000): 779.

Wolfe, R. 'See You in Geneva? Legal (Mis)Representations of the Trading System'. *European Journal of International Relations* 11 (2005): 339.

WTO, Communication for the United States, Proposal for Improvements to the Anti-Dumping Code, MTN.GNG/NG8/W59 of 20 Dec. 1989.

WTO. Anti-dumping: Notifications Under the Agreement on Implementation of Art. VI of GATT 1994, available at: <www.wto.org/english/tratop_e/adp_e/antidum3_e.htm>, last visited 4 January 2005.

WTO. *A Handbook on the WTO Dispute Settlement System.* Cambridge: Cambridge University Press, 2004.

WTO. *WTO Analytical Index: Guide to WTO Law and Practice.* 1st edn. Geneva: WTO and Bernan, 2003.

WTO. 'Negotiations, Implementation and Development: The Doha Agenda'. available at: <www.wto.org/english/tratop_e/dda_e/dda_e.htm>, 25 October 2005.

WTO. 'WTO Secretariat Reports Increase in New Anti-dumping Investigations'. 7 May 2009, available at: <www.wto.org/english/news_e/pres09_e/pr556_e.htm>, 10 July 2009.

WTO Appellate Body Secretariat. *WTO Appellate Body Repertory of Reports and Awards 1995–2004.* Cambridge: Cambridge University Press, 2005.

Yerxa, R & B. Wilson. *Key Issues in WTO Dispute Settlement – the First Ten Years.* Cambridge: Cambridge University Press, 2005.

Yu, T. 'The 10 Major Problems with the Anti-dumping Instrument in China'. *Journal of World Trade* 39 (2005): 97.

Yu, Y. 'Circumvention and Anti-circumvention in Anti-dumping Practice: A New Problem in China's Outbound Trade'. *Journal of World Trade* 41 (2007): 1015–1023.

Zanardi, M. 'Anti-dumping: What Are the Numbers to Discuss at Doha'. *The World Economy* 27 (2004): 403.

Zeitler, H. '"Good Faith" in the WTO Jurisprudence – Necessary Balancing Element or an Open Door to Judicial Activism?'. *Journal of International Economic Law* 8 (2005): 721.

Zonnekeyn, G. 'The Latest on Indirect Effect of WTO Law in the EC Legal Order The Nakajima Case Law Misjudged?'. *Journal of International Economic Law* 2 (2001): 597.

Zonnekeyn, G. 'The Status of Adopted Panel and Appellate Body Reports in the European Court of Justice and the European Court of First Instance'. *Journal of World Trade* 34 (2000): 93.

Cases and Regulations

Case 113/77, *NTN Toyo Bearing Company Ltd and Others v. Council of European Communities* [1979] ECR 1185.
Case 191/82 *EEC Seed Crushers' and Oil Processors' Federation (FEDIOL) v. Commission of the European Communities* [1983] ECR 2913.
Case 239, 275/82, *Allied Corporation and others v. Commission of the European Communities* [1984] ECR 1005.
Case 264/82, *Timex Corporation v. Council and Commission of the European Communities* [1985] ECR 849.
Case C-358/89, *Extramet Industrie SA v. Council of the European Communities* [1991] ECR I-2501.
Joint Case T-163, 165/94, *NTN Corporation and Koyo Seiko Co. Ltd v. Council* [1995] ECR II-01381.
Case T-210/95, *European Fertilizer Manufacturer's Association (EFMA) v. Council of the European Union* [1999] ECR II-3291.
Case T-232/95, *Committee of European Copier Manufactures (Cecom) v. Council of the European Union* [1998] ECR II-2679.
Case T-256/97, *Bureau European des Unions de Consommateurs (BEUC) v. Commission of the European Communities*[2000] ECR II-101.
Case T-132/01, *Euroalliages and Others v. Commission of the European Communities* [2003] ECR II-2359.
Case C-50/00, *Union de Pequenos Agricultores v. Council of the European Union* [2002] ECR I-6677.
Case C-76/00 P, *Petrotub and Republica v. Council of the European Union* [2003] ECR I-89.
Case T-498/04, *Zhejiang Xinan Chemical Industrial Group Co. Ltd v. Council of the European Union*, ECR II-0000 (Appeal C-337/09 P *Council of the*

European Union v. Zhejiang Xinan Chemical Industrial Group and Others, pending case).

Case T-459/07, *Hangzhou Duralamp Electronics v. Council of the European Union*, pending case.

Case T-466/07 *Osram v. Council of the European Union*, Removed from the register on 05/09/2008.

Case T-469/07 *Philips Lighting Poland and Philips Lighting v. Council of the European Union*, pending case.

Commission Decision of 28 May 1999, OJ L 135, 95.

Commission Decision of 19 Jun. 2007, OJ L 160/30, 21.

Council Decision (EC) of 22 Dec. 1994, OJ L 336, 23.12.1994, 1–2.

Council Regulation (EC) No. 384/96 of 22 Dec. 1995, OJ L 56/1, as amended by Council Regulation (EC) No. 2331/96 of 2 Dec. 1996, OJ L 317/1.

Council Regulation (EC) No. 905/98 of 27 Apr. 1998, OJ L 128/18, 30.

Commission Regulation (EC) No. 617/1999 of 23 Mar. 1999, OJ L 79, 13.

Council Regulation (EC) No. 348/2000 of 14 Feb. 2000, OJ L 45, 1.

Council Regulation (EC) No. 969/2000 of 8 May 2000, OJ L 112, 4..

Council Regulation (EC) No. 2238/2000 of 9 Oct. 2000, OJ L 257/2;

Council Regulation (EC) No. 1972/2002 of 5 Nov. 2002, OJ L 305/1.

Council Regulation (EC) No. 461/2004 of 8 Mar. 2004, OJ L 77/12.

Council Regulation (EC) No. 2117/2005 of 21 Dec. 2005, OJ L 340/17.

Council Regulation (EC) No. 1472/2006 of 5 Oct. 2006, OJ L 275, 1.

Council Regulation (EEC) No. 1761/87 of 22 Jun. 1987 amending Regulation (EEC) No. 2176/84, OJ L 167, 9.

Council Regulation 459/68 [1968] OJ L 93/1, Eng Spec. Ed. Series I-68 (1), 80.

Council Regulation 2011/73 [1973] OJ L 206/3.

Council Regulation 1411/77 [1977] OJ L 160/ 4.

Council Regulation 905/79 [1979] OJ L 277/10.

Council Regulation 2176/84 [1984] OJ L 201/1, corrected at [1984] OJ L227/35.

Council Regulation 3283/94 [1994] OJ L 349/1, as amended by Council Regulation 355/95 [1995] OJ L 41/2.

Council Regulation 2513/97 [1997] OJ L 346/1.

Council Regulation 984/97 [1997] OJ L 141/57.

Council Regulation 763/2000 [2000] OJ L 94/1.

Council Regulation 1208/2004 [2004] OJ L 232/1.

Council Regulation 1975/2004 [2004] OJ L 342/1.

Council Regulation 2272/2004 [2004] OJ L 396/18.

Council Regulation 866/2005 [2005] OJ L 145/1.

Council Regulation 465/2006 [2006] OJ L 83/6

Council Regulation 260/2007 [2007] OJ L 72/1.

GATT. *Record of Work Performed*, UN Econ. Social Council, GATT Doc. No. E/PC/T/103 (19 Jun. 1947).

GATT. *Swedish Anti-dumping Duties: Statement by the Government of Italy*, GATT Doc. No. L.215 (29 Jul. 1954).

GATT. *Agreement on Implementation of Article VI of the General Agreement on Tariffs and Trade* (1968), reprinted in GATT, BISD.

GATT. *Anti-dumping and Countervailing Duties*, GATT Sales No. GATT/1958–2, 1958.

GATT. *Anti-dumping and Countervailing Duties, Report of Group of Experts*, GATT Sales No. GATT/1961–2, 1961.

GATT. *Draft Final Act Embodying the Results of the Uruguay Round of Multilateral Trade Negotiations, Agreement on Implementation of Article VI of the General Agreement on Tariff and Trade*, GATT Document MTN. TNC/W/FA, December 1991, Art. 2.4.2.

GATT. *European Community-Anti-dumping Duties on Audio Tapes in Cassettes Originating in Japan*, Report of the Panel (28 Apr. 1995) ADP/136 (unadopted).

GATT. Report of the Acting Chairman of the Informal Group on Anti-dumping, MTN. GNG/NG8/W/83/Add5 (Jul. 1990), 7.

GATT. *United States – Imposition of Anti-dumping Duties on Imports of Fresh and Chilled Atlantic Salmon from Norway*, Report of the Panel adopted by the Committee on Anti-dumping Practices on 27 Apr. 1994, GATT Document ADP87, November 1992, paragraph 474.

GATT Secretariat, *Draft Final Act Embodying the Results of the Uruguay Round of Multilateral Trade Negotiations*, MTN.TNC/W/FA/F-21 (20 Dec. 1991).

Uruguay Round Agreements Act, H.R. 5110, 103rd Congress, 2nd session, 807.

WTO. *Annex 3: Trade Policy Review Mechanism*, LT/UR/A-3/TPR/1, 15 Apr. 1994.

WTO. *Agreement on Implementation of Article VI of the General Agreement on Tariffs and Trade 1994* (15 Apr. 1994) LT/UR/A-1A/3.

WTO. 'Anti-dumping: Illustrative Major Issues', Paper from Friends of Anti-dumping – Brazil, Chile, Colombia, Costa Rica, Hong Kong, China, Israel, Japan, Korea, Mexico, Norway, Singapore, Switzerland, Thailand and Turkey, 26 Apr. 2002, TN/RL/W/6.

WTO. *Canada – Measures Affecting the Export of Civilian Aircraft*, Report of the Panel (20 Aug. 1999) WT/DS70/R.

WTO. 'Basic Concepts and Principles of the Trade Remedy Rules', Communication from the United States, 22 Oct. 2002, TN/RL/W/27.

WTO. *Doha WTO Ministerial Declaration 2001*, WT/MIN (01)/DEC/1, 20 Nov. 2001.

WTO. *EC – Measures Concerning Meat and Meat Products (Hormones)* – Report of Appellate Body, (13 Feb. 1998) WT/DS26/AB/R, WT/DS48/AB/R.

WTO. *European Communities – Anti-Dumping Duties on Imports of Cotton-Type Bed Linen from India*, AB-2000-13 – Report of the Appellate Body (1 Mar. 2001) WT/DS141/AB/R.

Cases and Regulations

WTO. 'Further Issues Identified Under the Anti-dumping and Subsidies Agreements for Discussion by the Negotiating Group on Rules' Communication from the United States (20 Jun. 2003) TN/RL/W/130.

WTO. *Guatemala – Anti-Dumping Investigation Regarding Portland Cement from Mexico*, AB-1998-6 – Report of the Appellate Body (2 Nov. 1998) WT/DS60/AB/R.

WTO. *Guatemala – Anti-Dumping Investigation Regarding Portland Cement from Mexico*, Report of the Panel (19 Jun. 1998) WT/DS60/R.

WTO. *Final Act Embodying the Results of the Uruguay Round of Multilateral Trade Negotiations* LT/UR/A/1 (15 Apr. 1994).

WTO. 'Identification of Additional Issues Under the Anti-dumping and Subsidies Agreements', Paper submitted by the United States (6 May 2003) TN/RL/W/98.

WTO *India – Anti-Dumping Measure on Batteries from Bangladesh*, Request for Consultations by Bangladesh, WT/DS306/1 (2 Feb. 2004).

WTO. *India – Patent Protection for Pharmaceutical and Agricultural Chemical Products*, Report of the Appellate Body (adopted 16 Jan. 1998) WT/DS50/AB/R.

WTO. *Indonesia – Certain Measures Affecting the Automobile Industry*, Report of the Panel (adopted 23 Jul. 1998) WT/DS54/R, WT/DS55/R, WT/DS59/R, WT/DS64/R and Corr.1, 2, 3, and 4.

WTO. *Japan – Taxes on Alcoholic Beverages*, AB-1996-2 – Report of the Appellate Body (4 Oct. 1996) WT/DS10/AB/R, WT/DS11/AB/R, WT/DS8/AB/R.

WTO. *Japan – Taxes on Alcoholic Beverages*, WT/DS8/R, WT/DS10/R, WT/DS11/R, as modified by the AB report, WT/DS8/AB/R, WT/DS10/AB/R, WT/DS11/AB/R.

WTO *Korea – Anti-dumping Duties on Imports of Certain Paper from Indonesia*, Report of the Panel (28 Oct. 2005) WT/DS312/R.

WTO. *Korea – Definitive Safeguard Measure on Imports of Certain Dairy Products* – Report of Appellate Body (12 Jan. 2000) WT/DS98/AB/R.

WTO. *Marrakesh Agreement Establishing the World Trade Organization*, LT/UR/A/2, 15 Apr. 1994.

WTO. 'Proposals on Cost Saving in Anti-Dumping Proceedings', Paper from the European Communities and Japan WTO TN/RL/W/138 (17 Jul. 2003) available at: <http://docsonline.wto.org/GEN_searchResult.asp>, (21 Jul. 2004).

WTO. 'Proposal on Determination of Normal Value', Paper from the Friends of Anti-dumping – Chile, Colombia, Costa Rica, Hong Kong, China, Japan, Korea, Norway, Singapore, Switzerland, the Separate Customs Territory of Taiwan, Penghu, Kinmen and Matsu, and Thailand (16 Apr. 2004) TN/RL/W/150, at 8–9.

WTO. 'Proposal on Sunset', Paper from the Friends of Anti-dumping: Brazil, Chile, Colombia, Costa Rica, Hong Kong, China, Israel, Japan, Korea, Mexico, Norway, Singapore, Switzerland, Thailand and Turkey (19 Mar. 2003) TN/RL/W/76.

WTO. *Report (2007) of the Committee on Anti-Dumping Practices*, G/L/830 (26 Oct. 2007).

WTO. *Report of TPRB to the Third Ministerial Conference*, WT/MIN (99) 2 (8 Oct. 1999).
WTO. *Thailand – Anti-Dumping Duties on Angles, Shapes and Sections of Iron or Non-Alloy Steel and H-Beams from Poland*, AB-2000-12 – Report of the Appellate Body (12 Mar. 2001)WT/DS122/AB/R.
WTO. *Understanding on Rules and Procedures Governing the Settlement of Disputes*, (15 Apr. 1994) LT/UR/A-2/DS/U/1.
WTO. *United States – Anti-Dumping Act of 1916*, Report of the Apellate Body (28 Aug. 2000) WT/DS162/AB/R.
WTO. *United States – Anti-Dumping Act of 1916 – Complaint by the European Communities*, – Report of the Panel (31 Mar. 2000), WT/DS136/R.
WTO. *United States – Anti-Dumping Act of 1916, Complaint by the European Communities*, Report of the Panel, WT/DS136/R and Corr.1 (adopted 26 Sep. 2000), upheld by Appellate Body Report, WT/DS136/AB/R, WT/DS162/AB/R.
WTO. *United States – Anti-Dumping Act of 1916 – Complaint by Japan*, Report of the Panel (Part 1 and Part 2) (29 May 2000) WT/DS162/R.
WTO. *United States – Definitive Anti-dumping and Countervailing Duties on Certain Products from China, Request for Consultation by China*, WT/DS379/1, G/L/845, G/SCM/D78/1, G/ADP/D74/1, 22 (Sep. 2008).
WTO, *United States – Anti-Dumping and Countervailing Measures on Steel Plate from India*, Report of the Panel WT/DS206/R and Corr.1 (29 Jul. 2002) DSR 2002:VI, 2073.
WTO. *United States – Anti-Dumping Measures on Certain Hot-Rolled Steel Products from Japan-* Report of Appellate Body (23 Aug. 2001) WT/DS184/AB/R.
WTO. *United States – Anti-dumping Measures on Stainless Steel Plate in Coils and Stainless Steel Sheet and Strip from Korea* – Report of the Panel (Part 1 and Part 2) (22 Dec. 2000)WT/DS179/R.
WTO. *United States – Continued Dumping and Subsidy Offset Act of 2000* – Report of Panel (16 Sep. 2002) WT/DS217/R, WT/DS234/R.
WTO, *United States – Final Dumping Determination on Softwood Lumber from Canada*, Report of the Panel, 13 Apr. 2004, WT/DS264/R.
WTO, *United States – Laws, Regulations and Methodology for Calculating Dumping Margins ('Zeroing')*, Report of the Appellate Body (18 Apr. 2006) WT/DS294/AB/R.
WTO. *United States – Preliminary Anti-dumping and Countervailing Duty Determinations on Coated Free Sheet Paper from China, Request for Consultation by China*, WT/DS368/1, G/L/826, G/SCM/D77/1, G/ADP/D72/1 (18 Sep. 2007).
WTO. *United States – Transitional Safeguard Measure on Combed Cotton Yarn from Pakistan* – Report of Appellate Body (5 Nov. 2001) WT/DS192/AB/R.
WTO General Council. 'Request for an Authoritative Interpretation Pursuant to Article IX:2 of the Marrakech Agreement Establishing the World Trade Organization – Communication from the European Communities', WT/GC/W/133 (25 Jan. 1999).

Index

EUROPEAN MONOGRAPH SERIES

1. Lamm Betten (ed.), *The Future of European Social Policy*, 1991 (ISBN 90-654-4585-4).
2. Annemarie Loman, Kamiel Mortelmans, Harry H.G. Post & Stewart Watson, *Culture and Common Law: Before and After Maastricht*, 1992 (ISBN 90-654-4638-9).
3. John A.E. Vervaele, *Fraud against the Community: The Need for European Fraud Legislation*, 1994 (ISBN 90-654-4634-6).
4. Philip Raworth, *The Legislative Process in the European Community*, 1993 (ISBN 90-654-4690-7).
5. Jules Stuyck, *Financial and Monetary Integration in the European Economic Community*, 1993 (ISBN 90-654-4718-0).
6. Jules Stuyck & A.J. Vossestein (eds), *State Entrepreneurship, National Monopolies and European Community Law*, 1993 (ISBN 90-654-4773-3).
7. Jules Stuyck & A. Looijestijn-Clearie (eds), *The European Economic Area EC-EFTA*, 1994 (ISBN 90-654-4815-2).
8. Rosita B. Bouterse, *Competition and Integration: What Goals Count?*, 1995 (ISBN 90-654-4816-0).
9. René Barents, *The Agricultural Law of the EC: An Inquiry into the Administrative Law*, 1994 (ISBN 90-654-4867-5).
10. Nicholas Emiliou, *Principles of Proportionality in European Law: A Comparative Study*, 1996 (ISBN 90-411-0866-1).
11. Eivind Smith, *National Parliaments as Cornerstones of European Integration*, 1996 (ISBN 90-411-0898-X).
12. Jan H. Jans, *European Environmental Law*, 1996 (ISBN 90-411-0877-7).
13. Síofra O'Leary, *The Evolving Concept of Community Citizenship: From the Free Movement of Persons to Union Citizenship*, 1997 (ISBN 90-411-0878-5).
14. Laurence W. Gormley (ed.), *Current and Future Perspectives on EC Competition Law*, 1983 (ISBN 90-411-0691-X).
15. Simone White, *Protection of the Financial Interests of the European Communities: The Fight against Fraud and Corruption*, 1998 (ISBN 90-411-9647-1).
16. Morten P. Broberg, *The European Commission's Jurisdiction to Scrutinize Mergers*, 3rd Edition, 2006 (ISBN 978-90-411-2474-6).
17. Doris Hildebrand, *The Role of Economic Analysis in the EC Competition Rules: The European School*, 2nd Edition, 2002 (ISBN 90-411-1706-7).
18. Christof R.A. Swaak, *European Community Law and the Automobile Industry*, 1999 (ISBN 90-411-1140-9).
19. Dorthe Dahlgaard Dingel, *Public Procurement: A Harmonization of the National Judicial Review of the Application of European Community Law*, 1999 (ISBN 90-411-1161-1).
20. John A.E. Vervaele (ed.), *Compliance and Enforcement of European Community Law*, 1999 (ISBN 90-411-1151-4).

21. Martin Trybus, *European Defence Procurement Law: International and National Procurement Systems as Models for a Liberalized Defence Procurement Market in Europe*, 1999 (ISBN 90-411-1167-0).
22. Helen Staples, *The Legal Status of Third Country Nationals Resident in the European Union*, 1999 (ISBN 90-411-1277-4).
23. Damien Geradin (ed.), *The Liberalization of State Monopolies in the European Union and Beyond*, 1999 (ISBN 90-411-1264-2).
24. Katja Heede, *European Ombudsman: Redress and Control at Union Level*, 2000 (ISBN 90-411-1413-0).
25. Ulf Bernitz & Joakim Nergelius (eds), *General Principles of European Community Law*, 2000 (ISBN 90-411-1402-5).
26. Michaela Drahos, *Convergence of Competition Laws and Policies in the European Community*, 2002 (ISBN 90-411-1562-5).
27. Damien Geradin (ed.), *The Liberalization of Electricity and Natural Gas in the European Union*, 2001 (ISBN 90-411-1560-9).
28. Gisella Gori, *Towards an EU Right to Education*, 2001 (ISBN 90-411-1670-2).
29. Brendan P.G. Smith, *Constitution Building in the European Union*, 2001 (ISBN 90-411-1695-8).
30. Friedl Weiss & Frank Wooldridge, *Free Movement of Persons within the European Community*, 2nd Edition, 2007 (ISBN 978-90-411-2545-3).
31. Ingrid Boccardi, *Europe and Refugees: Towards an EU Asylum Policy*, 2002 (ISBN 90-411-1709-1).
32. John A.E. Vervaele & André Klip (eds), *European Cooperation Between Tax, Customs and Judicial Authorities*, 2001 (ISBN 90-411-1747-4).
33. Wouter P.J. Wils, *The Optimal Enforcement of EC Antitrust Law: Essays in Law and Economics*, 2002 (ISBN 90-411-1757-1).
34. Damien Geradin (ed.), *The Liberalization of Postal Services in the European Union*, 2002 (ISBN 90-411-1780-6).
35. Nick Bernard, *Multilevel Governance in the European Union*, 2002 (ISBN 90-411-1812-8).
36. Jill Wakefield, *Judicial Protection through the Use of Article 288(2) EC*, 2002 (ISBN 90-411-1823-3).
37. Sebastiaan Princen, *EU Regulation and Transatlantic Trade*, 2002 (ISBN 90-411-1871-3).
38. Amaryllis Verhoeven, *The European Union in Search of a Democratic and Constitutional Theory*, 2002 (ISBN 90-411-1872-1).
39. Paul L.C. Torremans, *Cross Border Insolvencies in EU, English and Belgian Law*, 2002 (ISBN 90-411-1888-8).
40. Malcolm Anderson & Joanna Apap (eds), *Police and Justice Cooperation and the New European Borders*, 2002 (ISBN 90-411-1893-4).
41. Christin M. Forstinger, *Takeover Law in EU and USA: A Comparative Analysis*, 2002 (ISBN 90-411-1919-1).

42. Antonio Bavasso, *Communications in EU Antitrust Law: Market Power and Public Interest*, 2003 (ISBN 90-411-1974-4).
43. Fiona G. Wishlade, *Regional State Aid and Competition Policy in the European Union*, 2003 (ISBN 90-411-1975-2).
44. Gareth Davies, *Nationality Discrimination in the European Internal Market*, 2003 (ISBN 90-411-1998-1).
45. René Barents, *The Autonomy of Community Law*, 2003 (ISBN 90-411-2251-6).
46. Gerhard Dannecker & Oswald Jansen (eds), *Competition Law Sanctioning in the European Union*, 2004 (ISBN 90-411-2100-5).
47. Nauta Dutilh (ed.), *Dealing with Dominance: The Experience of National Competition Authorities*, 2004 (ISBN 90-411-2211-7).
48. Stefaan van den Bogaert, *Practical Regulation of the Mobility of Sportsmen in the EU Post Bosman*, 2005 (ISBN 90-411-2327-X).
49. Katalin Judit Cseres, *Competition Law and Consumer Protection*, 2005 (ISBN 90-411-2380-6).
50. Philipp Kiiver, *The National Parliaments in the European Union: A Critical View on EU Constitution Building*, 2006 (ISBN 978-90-411-2452-4).
51. Alexander Turk, *The Concept of Legislation in European Community Law*, 2006 (ISBN 978-90-411-2472-2).
52. Dimitrios Sinaniotis, *The Interim Protection of Individuals before the European and National Courts*, 2006 (ISBN 978-90-411-2498-2).
53. M. Holoubek & D. Damjanovic, M. Traimer (eds), *Regulating Content: The European Regulatory Framework for the Media and Related Creative Sectors*, 2006 (ISBN 978-90-411-2597-2).
54. Anneli Albi & Jacques Ziller (eds), *The European Constitution and National Constitutions: Ratification and Beyond*, 2006 (ISBN 978-90-411-2524-8).
55. Gustavo E. Luengo, *Regulation of Subsidies and State Aids in WTO and EC Law: Conflicts in International Trade Law*, 2007 (ISBN 978-90-411-2547-7).
56. Eniko Horvath, *Mandating Identity: Citizenship, Kinship Laws and Plural Nationality in the European Union*, 2007 (ISBN 978-90-411-2662-7).
57. Rass Holdgaard, *External Relations Law of the European Community: Legal Reasoning and Legal Discourses*, 2007 (ISBN 978-90-411-2604-7).
58. Jill Wakefield, *The Right to Good Administration*, 2007 (ISBN 978-90-411-2697-9).
59. Dimitry Kochenov, *EU Enlargement and the Failure of Conditionality: Pre-accession Conditionality in the Fields of Democracy and the Rule of Law*, 2008 (ISBN 978-90-411-2696-2).
60. Despina Mavromati, *The Law of Payment Services in the EU: The EC Directive on Payment Services in the Internal Market*, 2008 (ISBN 978-90-411-2700-6).
61. Anne Meuwese, *Impact Assessment in EU Lawmaking*, 2008 (ISBN 978-90-411-2720-4).

62. Ulf Bernitz, Joakim Nergelius & Cecilia Cardner (eds.), *General Principles of EC Law in a Process of Development*, 2008 (ISBN 978-90-411-2705-1).
63. Johan van de Gronden (ed.), *The EU and WTO Law on Services: Limits to the Realisation of General Interest Policies within the Services Markets?*, 2008 (ISBN 978-90-411-2809-6).
64. Alina Tryfonidou, *Reverse Discrimination in EC Law*, 2009 (ISBN 978-90-411-2751-8).
65. Mikael Berglund, *Cross-Border Enforcement of Claims in the EU: History Present Time and Future*, 2009 (ISBN 978-90-411-2861-4).
66. Theodore Konstadinides, *Division of Powers in European Union Law: The Delimitation of Internal Competence between the EU and the Member States*, 2009 (ISBN 978-90-411-2615-3).
67. Mattias Derlén, *Multilingual Interpretation of European Union Law*, 2009 (ISBN 978-90-411-2853-9).
68. René Barents, *Directory of EU Case Law on the Preliminary Ruling Procedure*, 2009 (ISBN 978-90-411-3150-8).
69. Yan Luo, *Anti-dumping in the WTO, the EU and China: The Rise of Legalization in the Trade Regime and its Consequences*, 2010 (ISBN 978-90-411-3207-9).